OCR GCSE (9–1)

GEOGRAPHY A

Geographical Themes

OCR GCSE (9–1)

GEOGRAPHY A
Geographical Themes

Jo **Debens**
Alan **Parkinson**
Jo **Payne**
Simon **Ross**
Editor: David **Rogers**

This resource is endorsed by OCR for use with specification **J383 OCR GCSE (9–1) Geography A (Geographical Themes)**. In order to gain OCR endorsement, this resource has undergone an independent quality check. Any references to assessment and/or assessment preparation are the publisher's interpretation of the specification requirements and are not endorsed by OCR. OCR recommends that a range of teaching and learning resources are used in preparing learners for assessment. OCR has not paid for the production of this resource, nor does OCR receive any royalties from its sale. For more information about the endorsement process, please visit the OCR website, **www.ocr.org.uk.**

The Publishers would like to thank the following for permission to reproduce copyright material.

Acknowledgements

p.29 *Sidmouth Herald*, 5 August 2014, Beachgoers warned after huge Sidmouth cliff fall, www.sidmouthherald.co.uk/news/beachgoers_warned_after_huge_sidmouth_cliff_fall_1_3709172; **p.34** © North Norfolk District Council; **p.57** Office for National Statistics, a population pyramid from the ONS website, www.ons.gov.uk/ons/rel/census/2011-census/population-andhousehold-estimates-for-the-united-kingdom/stb-2011-census-populationestimates-for-the-united-kingdom.html#tab-The-structure-of-the-population-ofthe-United-Kingdom; **p.61** Cool Geography, www.coolgeography.co.uk/GCSE/AQA/Population/Demographic%20Transition/Demographic_Transition_Model.jpg; **p.62** © Philip's; **p.74** Lymperopoulou, K (2015) Geographies of deprivation and diversity in the Leeds City Region. Local Dynamics of Diversity: Evidence from the 2011 Census, Centre on Dynamics of Ethnicity, The University of Manchester, UK; **p.156** © Philip's; **p.171** © Philip,'s; **p.180** *The Economist*, www.economist.com/node/21642053?fsrc=scn/tw/te/dc/brightlightsbigcities; **p.181** United Nations, Department of Economic and Social Affairs, Population Division (2014). World Urbanization Prospects: The 2014 Revision, Highlights (ST/ ESA/SER.A/352) http://esa.un.org/unpd/wup/highlights/wup2014-highlights.pdf, © 2014 United Nations. Reprinted with the permission of the United Nations; **p.187** UN World Urbanisation Prospects 2014/LSE Cities © 2014 United Nations. Reprinted with the permission of the United Nations; **p. 217** The Met Office, www.metoffice.gov.uk; **p.234** The Met Office, www. metoffice.gov.uk; **p.255** *t* Environment Agency showing flood risks of various areas, https://flood-warninginformation. service.gov.uk; *b* Google Earth Pro Maps on **p.33** and **p.55** reproduced from Ordnance Survey mapping with the permission of the Controller of HMSO. © Crown copyright and/or database right. All rights reserved. Licence number 100036470.

Every effort has been made to trace all copyright holders, but if any have been inadvertently overlooked, the Publishers will be pleased to make the necessary arrangements at the first opportunity.

Although every effort has been made to ensure that website addresses are correct at time of going to press, Hodder Education cannot be held responsible for the content of any website mentioned in this book. It is sometimes possible to find a relocated web page by typing in the address of the home page for a website in the URL window of your browser.

Hachette UK's policy is to use papers that are natural, renewable and recyclable products and made from wood grown in sustainable forests. The logging and manufacturing processes are expected to conform to the environmental regulations of the country of origin.

Orders: please contact Bookpoint Ltd, 130 Park Drive, Milton Park, Abingdon, Oxon OX14 4SE. Telephone: +44 (0)1235 827720. Fax: +44 (0)1235 400454. Email education@bookpoint.co.uk Lines are open from 9 a.m. to 5 p.m., Monday to Saturday, with a 24-hour message answering service. You can also order through our website: www.hoddereducation.co.uk

ISBN: 978 1 4718 53081

© Jo Debens, Alan Parkinson, Jo Payne, Simon Ross 2016

First published in 2016 by

Hodder Education

An Hachette UK Company

Carmelite House

50 Victoria Embankment

London EC4Y 0DZ

www.hoddereducation.co.uk

Impression number   10 9 8 7 6 5 4 3 2

Year   2020 2019 2018 2017 2016

Cover photo © Jim Zuckerman/Corbis

Illustrations by Aptara and Oxford Designers & Illustrators Ltd.

Typeset by Aptara, Inc.

Printed in Italy

A catalogue record for this title is available from the British Library.

Contents

Part 1: Living in the UK Today

Theme 1 Landscapes of the UK

Theme 2 People of the UK

Theme 3 UK Environmental Challenges

Part 2: The World Around Us

Theme 1 Ecosystems of the Planet

Theme 2 People of the Planet

Theme 3 Environmental Threats to Our Planet

Part 3: Geographical Skills and Fieldwork

Introduction

This book has been written specifically for the OCR GCSE Geography A: Geographical Themes specification to be first examined in September 2018. The writers are all experienced teachers and subject specialists who provide comprehensive and up-to-date information that is both accessible and informative.

This book includes a range of features designed to give you confidence and make the most of your course in a clear and accessible way, as well as supporting you in your revision and exam preparation.

→ Learning objectives:

At the start of each chapter is a list of what you will cover to help you track your learning. At the end of each chapter, you can return to this feature and check whether you feel confident that you have covered everything required.

Activities

Throughout each chapter you will find activities designed to help you think about the content on the pages. These are made up of different question types:

- activities that help you analyse and understand the information and illustrations contained within the pages, including individual, paired and group work
- activities that help you prepare notes and summaries to help you with your revision
- questions that are similar to those you will find in your exams
- questions that help you to develop and practise your geographical skills.

→ Take it further

Take it further questions are included for students aiming for the higher grades, and may ask questions that require you to go beyond the information found in this student's book.

Fieldwork ideas

Possible ideas for fieldwork projects appear in boxes throughout the book. Chapter 30 will help you to pull all these ideas together and plan for fieldwork, including how it will be assessed in your exam.

Key term:

Key terms relating to the specification are highlighted in red throughout the book. You will find definitions of these key terms in the glossary on pages 250–53. You should learn these key terms and definitions so that you can use them effectively in your exams.

Geographical skills

Geographers need certain skills in order to be able to process information from maps, graphs or text extracts. These skills include being able to read an Ordnance Survey map, or describe the trend on a graph. The Geographical skills boxes in this book will help you to develop these important skills and will help you tackle the activities on each page.

Practice questions

At the end of each theme is a dedicated page with practice questions to help you prepare for assessment. This includes information on how many marks each question is worth. You can use these as an end-of-theme test to check that you can understand and remember what you need to know for this theme in the exams.

Case study

Case studies of real-life places will help you to put the geographical concepts that you learn into context. For your exams, you need a detailed and thorough knowledge of some places to help you answer some of the case study questions. The UK map on page viii and the world map on page ix show you the location of the case studies found in this book.

Tips

Throughout the book and alongside the practice questions you will find tips to help you relate the content to the assessment questions.

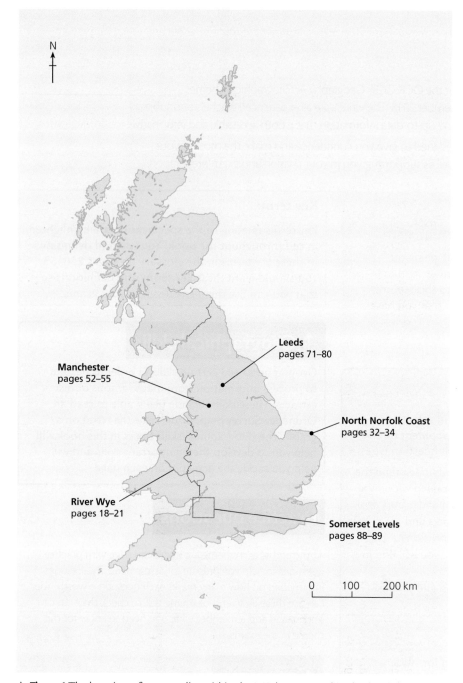

Manchester
pages 52–55

Leeds
pages 71–80

North Norfolk Coast
pages 32–34

River Wye
pages 18–21

Somerset Levels
pages 88–89

N

0   100   200 km

▲ **Figure 1** The location of case studies within the UK that are used in this book

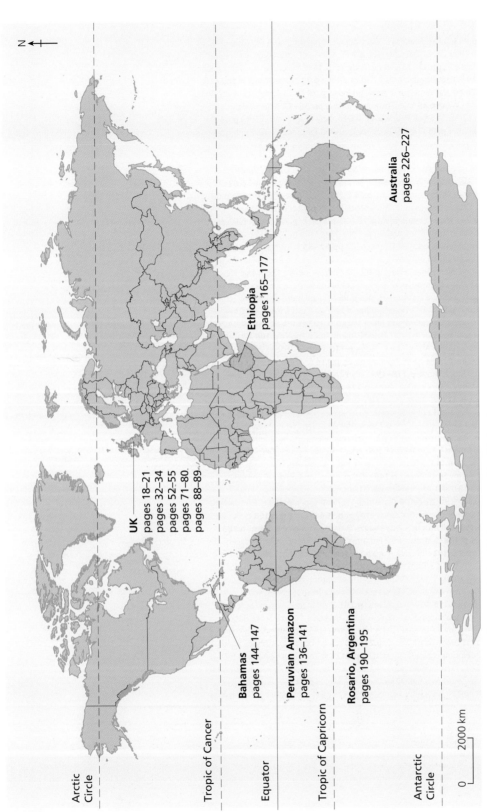

N

UK
pages 18–21
pages 32–34
pages 52–55
pages 71–80.
pages 88–89

Ethiopia
pages 165–177

Australia
pages 226–227

Bahamas
pages 144–147

Peruvian Amazon
pages 136–141

Rosario, Argentina
pages 190–195

Arctic Circle

Tropic of Cancer

Equator

Tropic of Capricorn

Antarctic Circle

0   2000 km

▲ **Figure 2** The location of case studies outside the UK that are used in this book

Photo credits

PART

1

Living in the UK Today

THEME 1

Landscapes of the UK

The UK has a very distinct natural landscape. This has been shaped over millions of years by geomorphic processes. This theme explores the physical geography of the UK, its key landscapes and the geomorphic processes which changed UK landscapes.

Chapter 1: The physical landscapes of the UK

Key idea: The physical landscapes of the UK have distinctive characteristics.

In this chapter you will study:

➜ the distribution of areas of upland, lowland and glaciated landscapes

➜ the distinctive characteristics of these landscapes including their geology, climate and human activity.

Chapter 2: Geomorphic processes

Key idea: There are a number of geomorphic processes which create distinctive landscapes.

In this chapter you will study:

➜ the definitions of the main geomorphic processes including: types of weathering – mechanical, chemical, biological; mass movement – sliding, slumping; erosion – abrasion, hydraulic action, attrition, solution; transport – traction, saltation, suspension, solution; deposition.

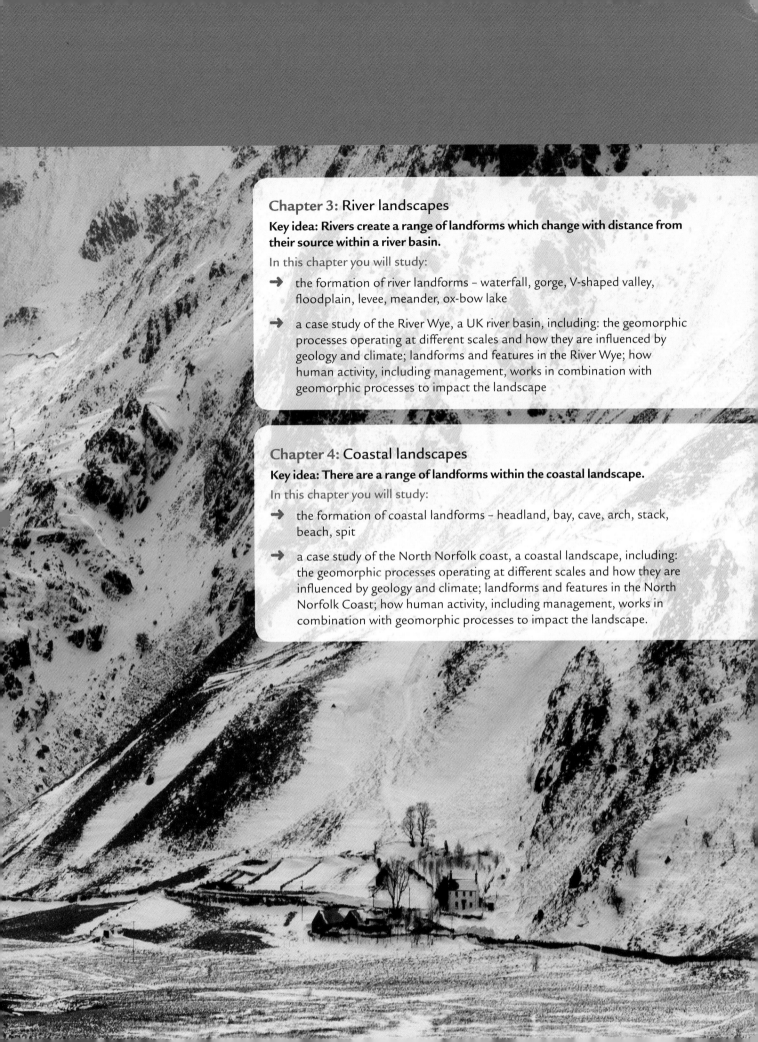

Chapter 3: River landscapes

Key idea: Rivers create a range of landforms which change with distance from their source within a river basin.

In this chapter you will study:

→ the formation of river landforms – waterfall, gorge, V-shaped valley, floodplain, levee, meander, ox-bow lake

→ a case study of the River Wye, a UK river basin, including: the geomorphic processes operating at different scales and how they are influenced by geology and climate; landforms and features in the River Wye; how human activity, including management, works in combination with geomorphic processes to impact the landscape

Chapter 4: Coastal landscapes

Key idea: There are a range of landforms within the coastal landscape.

In this chapter you will study:

→ the formation of coastal landforms – headland, bay, cave, arch, stack, beach, spit

→ a case study of the North Norfolk coast, a coastal landscape, including: the geomorphic processes operating at different scales and how they are influenced by geology and climate; landforms and features in the North Norfolk Coast; how human activity, including management, works in combination with geomorphic processes to impact the landscape.

CHAPTER 1

The physical landscapes of the UK

Key idea: The physical landscapes of the UK have distinctive characteristics.

➜ In this chapter you will study:

➜ the distribution of areas of upland, lowland and glaciated landscapes

➜ the distinctive characteristics of these landscapes including their geology, climate and human activity.

The distribution of areas of upland, lowland and glaciated landscapes

Upland, lowland and glaciated landscapes

A mountain is often defined as being an area of land that rises considerably above the surrounding land, with 600 m (2000 feet) sometimes used as the height that separates mountains from hills. Upland areas can include dramatic peaks and ridges with weathered rock, or moorland with heather. They include some of our most interesting landscapes.

Higher land experiences colder weather (temperature drops by 1 °C for every 100 m of altitude) and more mist, cloud and snow, which can increase the rate of physical **weathering** because of the presence of water and greater changes in temperature either side of freezing point.

Lowland areas are closer to sea level and lie below 200 m. The UK's lowlands are found in central and southern England with the most extensive areas of lowland found in East Anglia (see Figure 3).

Naming mountains

Mountains over 3000 feet (914 m) high are called 'Munros' in the UK, after Hugh Munro who compiled a list. Most of the 282 Munros are in Scotland. The name 'Corbetts' is given to those peaks between 2500 and 3000 feet (762 and 914 m) high. Can you find out what a 'Marilyn' is?

Activities

1. Study Figure 1.
   a. Describe the location of glaciated upland areas.
   b. Is the place where you live classed as lowland or upland?
   c. What evidence did you use to help you make your decision?

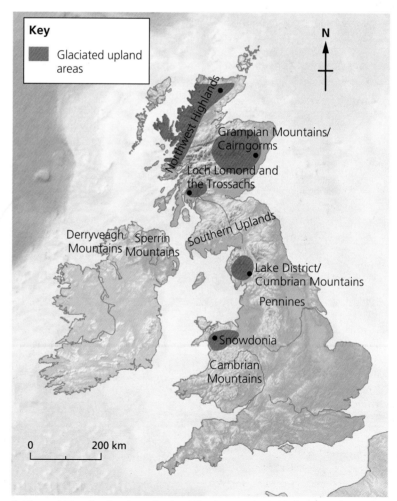

▲ Figure 1 The distribution of upland, lowland and glaciated areas in the UK

How the landscape of the UK was formed

In the UK, our most spectacular mountain ranges, such as the Cairngorms in Scotland and Snowdonia in North Wales (see Figure 1), were sculpted by the action of ice. **Ice Ages** are periods of time when the surface temperatures in temperate latitudes were lower than average, which allowed ice sheets to grow in size in northern latitudes and to move to cover new areas further south, including the UK. Ice Ages have occurred numerous times over the last 2 million years. As temperatures warmed again, the ice melted and the land was revealed.

For the last ten thousand years, the UK has been in a geological time called the **Holocene**. The lighter area shown in Figure 2 is that covered by the most recent ice advance, around 10 000 years ago.

Ice has great strength, and has eroded and weathered landscapes to create dramatic mountain scenery. Glacial processes may not be happening now, but many landscapes – such as Glencoe in the Grampians (see Figure 4) – bear the scars of the ice that previously scoured out deep valleys. Ice has also moved into lowland areas, scraping away the soil of the Yorkshire Dales, bulldozing clay and boulders into large ridges, such as the Cromer Ridge on the Norfolk Coast, or leaving piles of rocks that differ from the local geology.

Large sections of the south coast which were not covered by ice were instead covered by a mixture of boulders and sediment called **drift**. While less spectacular, this has also sometimes influenced the present-day landscape.

Activities

1. Was the place where you live covered by ice during the last period of advance, according to Figure 2?

2. Describe the evidence that ice shaped the land that you can still see in your local landscape.

Mapping mountains

Use Ordnance Survey maps or digital mapping to 'visit' some of the places the ice covered, and identify the characteristic features shown in upland glaciated areas. Look out for the steepness of the land, the absence of soil or vegetation, piles of stone, and place names such as corrie, tarn or cwm, depending on which area you visit.

▲ **Figure 2** Area covered by the last major ice advance over the UK

▲ **Figure 3** The Fens, East Anglia

▲ **Figure 4** Glencoe in the Grampian Mountains

👣 Fieldwork idea

You can often see what the local geology is by looking at nearby buildings, particularly churches or other buildings with older walls. These tend to have been built with local stone, unlike modern buildings which use bricks and concrete. Older buildings may also use local vegetation such as reeds for roofing, as in traditional thatched cottages. Survey the buildings in your local area, find the oldest buildings and look at their design and materials.

The distinctive characteristics of upland, lowland and glaciated landscapes

How geology affects landscapes

The **geology** of the rocks that lie beneath the ground influences the nature of the landscape seen on the surface. The rocks beneath your feet vary depending on where you live in the UK (see Figure 5), because they were created at different times, in different environments and by different processes.

Rocks are placed into three groups according to their origin: **igneous**, **sedimentary** and **metamorphic** (see Figure 6). The shape and height of the land is partly a result of the relative hardness of the underlying rock. Relatively harder rocks – such as igneous granite and gabbro – often make up the high mountains, whereas chalk and clays lie under many low-lying areas.

In mountain areas, the rock may also be easier to see as it is exposed at the surface. This may be because moving ice removed the surface covering during an ice advance (see page 5). The same ice then covered the geology in the south of England with layers of clay, producing a more subdued landscape there.

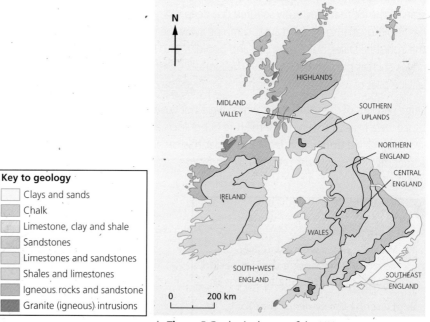

Key to geology
- Clays and sands
- Chalk
- Limestone, clay and shale
- Sandstones
- Limestones and sandstones
- Shales and limestones
- Igneous rocks and sandstone
- Granite (igneous) intrusions

▲ **Figure 5** Geological map of the UK

Rock type	Method of formation	Examples in the UK
Igneous	Produced when magma (molten rock) cools, either beneath the ground (intrusive) or above the surface (extrusive). These rocks were formed when the UK had active volcanoes. There are now extinct volcanoes in Scotland.	• Granite (intrusive) – Dartmoor • Gabbro (intrusive) – Cuillin Hills • Basalt (extrusive) – Island of Arran, Scotland
Sedimentary	Made from the skeletons of marine organisms (coccoliths) and other sediments, laid down and compacted at the bottom of the ocean.	• Chalk – White Cliffs of Dover; North Downs • Limestone – Yorkshire Dales; Cheddar Gorge • Gritstone – Peak District
Metamorphic	The action of heat and pressure on an existing igneous or sedimentary rock changes its structure to form a new type of metamorphic rock.	• Slate – North Wales • Gneiss – Lewis, Outer Hebrides

▲ **Figure 6** Rock types

Soils and the landscape

Soils are created from the weathering of rocks (with the addition of organic material and water). The rocks are the parent material and they influence the type of soil that develops on top of them and therefore the type of vegetation that grows in an area. This will also determine whether farming is likely to happen at all, and if it is, whether crops will be grown or animals will be kept. Areas of deep soil are often found in low-lying areas, and steep ground tends to have thin soil.

The most productive soils in the UK are found in the East Anglian Fens (see Figure 3, page 5), where the dark silty soil is the result of the land being reclaimed from beneath the sea and then drained. These are deep soils with no stones, and with a texture that drains well and warms up quickly.

Geology determines whether there is water draining over the surface, the density of streams and rivers, and the direction in which these flow over the ground. Water that stays on the surface speeds up the production of peat soils, which are found on upland moors and in heathland.

Deep soils can also form beneath woodland, because of the organic material that falls from the trees over time. This is less true in **coniferous** woodland and plantations.

If an area of the UK were left untouched by people, the 'natural' vegetation that would develop over the years would be **deciduous** woodland. Much of the UK was once covered with trees, but people cleared them for settlement, resources and fuel, and to make way for farmland. The importance of wood is shown by the formation in 1919 of the Forestry Commission (see Figure 7) to guarantee future supplies after the depletion of many woodlands during the First World War. Large parts of the country have a landscape cloaked in woodland as a result.

Activities

1. Explain how the geology beneath an area influences the landscape that sits above it, with reference to a named location.

2. Research the age, hardness and permeability of ten rocks and make a 'Top Trumps' card game.

3. Research other national or regional organisations or charities that are concerned with the protection of landscapes. You could start by exploring the work of the RSPB, the largest wildlife conservation charity in the UK, or areas designated as Sites of Special Scientific Interest (SSSIs).

▲ **Figure 7** The Forestry Commission logo

Granite and the landscape of Dartmoor

Some rocks are connected to particular landscapes, an example of which is the granite that lies beneath Dartmoor in Devon, in the south-west of England. This is **impermeable** and encourages water to stay on the surface, which produces areas of boggy land called mires.

The weathering of the rock by slightly acidic rainwater causes the slow chemical decomposition of some of the minerals within the granite when they are exposed to it. The result is that the most resistant areas of rock stand out on the tops of hills as distinctive rounded features: the famous **tors** (see Figure 8). The stone is also used to build the dry-stone walls that fence in the sheep that graze the moor, along with the Dartmoor ponies. The moor is used by the military as a suitably challenging place to test their skills of navigation and survival. There is also an annual Ten Tors challenge, which is open to teams of young people.

▲ **Figure 8** Tor on Dartmoor

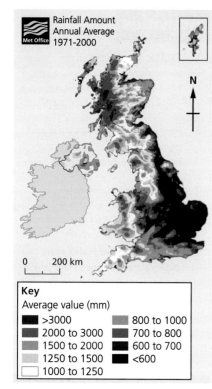

Key
Average value (mm)

■	>3000	■	800 to 1000
■	2000 to 3000	■	700 to 800
■	1500 to 2000	■	600 to 700
■	1250 to 1500	■	<600
■	1000 to 1250		

▲ **Figure 9** UK rainfall averages, 1971–2000

Activity

1. Explain the pattern of the distribution of rainfall shown in Figure 9.

Think of how human activity affects the landscape around your school grounds: the fields are mowed, flowers are planted, trees are pruned for safety reasons and fallen leaves picked up in the autumn. This is not a natural landscape. How has the natural landscape been changed by human activity?

How climate affects landscapes

Climate is the long-term average of the temperature and rainfall experienced at a location. Climate has an obvious influence on the development of all landscapes because they are exposed to it, and may have been for millions of years. Rain, frost and wind are features of the climate of an area. The UK has a maritime climate, meaning its climate is heavily influenced by the seas that surround it. Onshore winds bring moist air, and the UK's location means it is influenced by different air masses. Temperatures drop quickly with increased altitude, which results in increased cloud over higher ground to the west. The prevailing (most common) wind direction also carries air up over mountains, and produces drier regions in the 'rain shadow' to the east. The climate influences the rate at which geomorphic processes occur in these areas. Upland areas have much higher rainfall totals than lowland areas, and are also windier.

One main factor in how climate affects the landscape is the number of times that a rock experiences a **freeze-thaw cycle**: a change in temperature either side of freezing, which happens on a daily (diurnal) basis (see Figure 10). This increases stress on rocks and speeds up weathering. Windy, exposed places may also weather faster than sheltered locations.

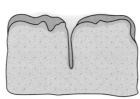 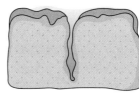 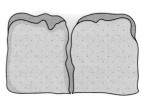

Water seeps into cracks and fractures in the rock.

When the water freezes, it expands about 9% in volume, which wedges apart the rock.

With repeated freeze/thaw cycles, the rock breaks into pieces.

▲ **Figure 10** The freeze-thaw cycle

How human activity affects landscapes

There are very few areas of a densely populated country like the UK that have not been affected by human activity, even those which remain relatively sparsely populated. Centuries of farming and human settlement have changed the surface in many ways, including the type of vegetation that grows, the depth and health of the soil, the drainage pattern, the ability to travel through an area and the nature of the surface itself.

Many low-lying areas have been drained to improve the usability of farmland – creating the fertile soils of the Fens, for instance, a landscape that lies below sea level in places.

Plantations in many upland areas of the UK, or lowland areas such as the Brecklands in East Anglia, may be no more than a few decades old, but even ancient-looking woodlands were originally planted by people. Coastal marshes and windswept moorlands are also managed by people for various purposes. Many upland areas were settled in the past, when defence from attack was considered an important factor in settlement location.

It can be hard to escape the influence of people even in remote rural areas, whether it's a stone wall, a distant electricity pylon, the rising column of clouds above a power station, or the remnants of an old settlement on a Scottish hillside.

Rural or urban?

An important distinction needs to be made between **built (urban)** and natural **(rural)** landscapes. The Office for National Statistics (ONS), which collects census data, classifies areas according to the types of houses and their density. Suburban landscapes on the edge of a town can have elements of both rural and urban landscapes in them. Housing is one indicator that an area might be urban but there are others too. Some indicators of a built landscape are shown in Figure 11. Given the choice, different people prefer to live in particular types of area, and this may result in population change or migration.

In January 2015 Boris Johnson, then Mayor of London, said that the city had reached its highest ever population of 8.6 million, after years of people leaving the city. Where there are people there is a need for housing, which results in the loss of open space, woodland and habitat for wildlife.

Will the future mean more built landscapes and fewer natural ones? Some argue the opposite and hope to 'rewild' landscapes by re-introducing animal species that had previously disappeared.

Indicator	Impact on landscape
Traffic infrastructure	Roads – including dual carriageways and motorways – create noise and act as a barrier to the movement of people and wildlife.
Street lighting	Light pollution can often be seen close to urban areas. Lighting improves safety and is thought to reduce crime, but hides the night sky.
Construction activity	Usually a sign that areas are becoming more of a built landscape, perhaps with cranes on the skyline and scaffolding being erected.
High-rise development	Usually indicating higher land values, which are a function of better accessibility.
Services that require a high population to support	Signs indicating 'land acquired for redevelopment', housing developments, retail parks, and warehousing and distribution centres. These remove open fields, but trees are sometimes planted to screen the buildings.
Solar farms	Many of these have appeared in the last decade. While less obvious than wind turbines, they result in the loss of wildlife and change the nature of surface drainage.
Golf courses	Although they may look green and open, chemicals are used to keep the greens free of weeds, drainage is altered and there may be restrictions on access to the public.
Pedestrianisation	As traffic increases, there is pressure to remove traffic from areas with high numbers of pedestrians in order to reduce accidents and improve the area. There may also be changes to the high street design to increase planting and urban trees.

▲ **Figure 11** Selected indicators that an area has a built landscape

Weblinks

→ Enter your school's postcode into this site and see whether your area is classed as urban or rural: www.neighbourhood.statistics.gov.uk/HTMLDocs/urbanrural.html. How far do you have to travel before the type of area changes?

→ Do a place check on www.placecheck.info to identify what could be changed in your local area.

Activities

1. Look at the signs of a built landscape shown in Figure 11. Can you suggest some other examples that you might be able to spot in your local area? Think of the range of human activities that might influence the landscape.

2. a. Over the course of a weekend, take note of the landscapes that are featured in the TV programmes or films you watch, or in the games you play. What landscapes can you identify? Are certain types of programmes set in particular landscapes?

   b. Some programmes are associated with particular types of landscapes, e.g. the urban landscape of London is shown in *Eastenders*. This may even lead to an increase in tourists visiting the locations connected with them; for instance Northern Ireland and Iceland have both benefited from their association with the filming of *Games of Thrones*. Which other landscapes or locations have an association with a particular TV programme or film?

3. Look at the landscape words below.

Soils	Apple trees
Sky	Wind
Weathering	Sand dunes
Flowing water	Coniferous trees
Clouds	Wave action
Mountains	Salt marshes
Farmland (arable)	Downs
Frost	Beaches
Farm smells	Reservoirs

Categorise these terms into:

a. processes that shape the landscape
b. landforms (features found in the landscape)
c. landscape elements (the different ingredients that combine to make landscapes).

2

Geomorphic processes

Key idea: There are a number of geomorphic processes which create distinctive landscapes.

→ **In this chapter you will study:**

the definitions of the main geomorphic processes including:

→ types of weathering – mechanical, chemical, biological

→ mass movement – sliding, slumping

→ erosion – abrasion, hydraulic action, attrition, solution

→ transport – traction, saltation, suspension, solution

→ deposition.

What are geomorphic processes?

Geomorphic processes change the shape of the Earth. 'Geo' means 'earth' and 'morph' refers to the way that the shape of the Earth's surface is changed over time. Geomorphology involves physical, chemical and biological processes. These act on, and alter, the Earth's surface.

Geomorphic processes act over different timescales. Some happen very quickly, while others take place much more slowly. For example:

● waves hit the coastline every few seconds
● stones might be washed down a river over a period of hours
● a cliff might stand for centuries before a section of it is weakened enough to collapse.

As we live our lives on a human timescale, some of the geological changes that made the landscape we stand in today happen so slowly that we can never really 'see' the happening, but we do see the result of them.

As described in Chapter 1, the UK has so many different landscapes because of its **geodiversity**, which can be defined as 'the natural range (diversity) of geological features (rocks, minerals, fossils, structures) geomorphological features (landforms and processes) soil and water features that compose and shape the physical landscape'.

Geomorphic processes are the result of the weather, chemical reactions, moving water and ice, and the force of gravity. Each of these has the effect of wearing away the surface in some places, moving small pieces of the surface that have broken off to other locations, and building them up in new landforms. On these pages you will see a range of geomorphic processes that have affected the UK. Each process is looked at in more detail later in this book as it relates to rivers (Chapter 3) and coasts (Chapter 4).

Weathering

Weathering is the breakdown of material in the place they were found (without being transported) by mechanical (physical), chemical and biological processes.

→ **Mechanical weathering** – the physical actions of rain, frost and wind that create weaknesses in rocks.

→ **Chemical weathering** – minerals can react chemically in different ways, which weakens them. For example, water can reach with some rocks to break them down, and air can weaken minerals through a process called **oxidation**.

→ **Biological weathering** – rocks and land can be broken down by the actions of living organisms such as plants and animals, for example, rabbits burrowing into river banks.

Mass movement

Mass movement is when material moves downhill; due to the pull of gravity. Gravity is an important force, as any steep slope or cliff will be constantly put under stress by processes which try to make it fall down. Other forces help to keep the feature standing, but given enough time, gravity usually wins.

➡ Sliding – where a section of land falls down a slope and dislodges other material on its way down.

➡ Slumping – where material at the bottom of a slope moves outward.

Erosion

Erosion is the wearing away of materials by a moving force, such as a river, waves, ice or wind, which take the material away.

➡ **Abrasion** (also called corrasion) – when sediment is thrown against a surface by water and rubs the material to smooth the landform.

➡ **Hydraulic action** – where water forces its way into cracks, which creates weaknesses in rocks, splitting them apart.

➡ **Attrition** – where pebbles hit each other or landforms, making rocks break and get smaller and rounder.

➡ **Solution** (also called corrosion) – where rocks are dissolved in water.

Transport

Transportation is the movement of material along the coast by waves, or along a river bed by the river.

➡ Traction – the movement of larger sediment rolling the bottom of the sea or a river.

➡ Saltation – small pieces of sediment picked up temporarily in the water.

➡ Suspension – smaller particles can be suspended in water.

➡ Solution – when minerals dissolve in water.

Deposition

Deposition is the laying down of materials that have been transported, and can create new landforms such as beaches.

Tip

Be careful not to confuse the terms 'weathering' and 'erosion'. They are often placed at the start of exam questions. You should remember the names of the key processes involved and be able to define them.

CHAPTER

3

River landscapes

Key idea: Rivers create a range of landforms which change with distance from their source within a river basin.

➜ In this section you will study:

➜ the formation of river landforms – waterfall, gorge, V-shaped valley, floodplain, levee, meander, ox-bow lake

➜ a case study of the River Wye, a UK river basin, including: the geomorphic processes operating at diff erent scales and how they are infl uenced by geology and climate; landforms and features in the River Wye; how human activity, including management, works in combination with geomorphic processes to impact the landscape

e 1 Glen Fyne, Scotland

Activities

1. Take a look at the photograph on these pages.
   a. What landscape features can you already recognise?
   b. What processes do you think are active in this area?
   c. What other sources of information would be useful to add to your knowledge about this place?
   d. How will this area change in the short or long term in terms of its physical geography?
   e. How do people use areas like this, and what impact does this have on the landscape?

What physical processes shape river landscapes?

Weathering

The following processes are involved in the weathering of river landscapes.

Mechanical weathering

- **Rain:** water washes away loose material and also enters cracks in the rocks. If it soaks into softer rocks such as sandstone it adds weight to the river banks, increasing the risk of collapse.
- **Frost:** when water gets into cracks in rocks and freezes, it expands in volume. This puts pressure on the rock and results in the break-up of rocks on river banks.
- **Wind:** strong winds remove fine sediment which may then be used to abrade the river banks.

Chemical weathering

- Rainwater reacts chemically with certain minerals which weakens them.
- Minerals are also weakened when they are exposed to the air in a process called oxidation.
- Some minerals are affected by water in a process called hydrolysis. This involves acidic rainfall reacting with minerals to produce material which is soluble and easily washed away.
- Rocks such as chalk and limestone are affected by solution, as calcium carbonate is broken down to soluble calcium bicarbonate.

Biological weathering

Rocks in river banks are broken down by the action of living organisms, which include plants and animals. Tree roots act to loosen rocks and provide crevices into which water can penetrate. Rabbits and other animals can burrow into river banks which can lead to rocks breaking up.

Mass movement

Mass movement refers to the sudden movement of material down a slope due to the pull of gravity. Heavy rain soaking into permeable rocks can add weight to them, and the water can also lubricate the boundaries where materials meet, so that flow is more likely as the material making up the river banks 'fails'. Rotational slumping occurs on the banks of rivers, where the bottom of the river bank slips into the river and other material slumps down the bank. Soft, clay river banks are particularly susceptible to slumping.

Erosion

Erosion is the wearing away of the river banks by a moving force. The main energy causing this erosive force is the river within the river channel.

- Water hitting the river banks will compress air into any cracks within it. The air in the cracks expands explosively outwards as the pressure is released by the receding water. This process, called **hydraulic action**, removes fine material and enlarges cracks which speeds up the erosion process.
- Water moves sand or pebbles which are then thrown or rubbed against the river banks, where the land is worn away by abrasion.
- Water can slowly dissolve certain rock types such as limestone by solution.
- Larger rocks in the river are broken down into small, more rounded sediment through **attrition** as the different rocks within the river hit each other.

◀ **Figure 2** Biological weathering from Chinese mitten crabs, an invasive species, on the banks of the Thames

▲ **Figure 3** The upper course of a river

Transportation

Water flowing downhill has the ability to carry sediment. The River Wye (see page 18) drops by around 600 m during the first 80 km of its course, providing a fast-flowing upper course which moves sediment in four main ways (see Figure 4):

- **Traction:** large boulders and rocks are rolled along the river bed, scraping against it as they do so.
- **Saltation:** small pebbles and stones are bounced along the river bed in a series of short jumps.
- **Suspension:** very fine, light material is carried along in the water; clays tend to stick together but silts and fine sand are carried in this way and make the river 'murky'.
- **Solution:** some types of sediment, such as minerals, are dissolved in the water and carried along in solution.

Traction is only likely after heavy rainfall, when the river's discharge is at its highest. In the upper course of a river, the bedload tends to be larger, as can be seen in Figure 3.

Deposition

When the river slows down and loses energy, sediment, such as sand and pebbles, are deposited on the shallow bank of a river.

It is the balance of the energy of the river, the movement of water and the transport of sediment that creates all the features that are found along the course of a river.

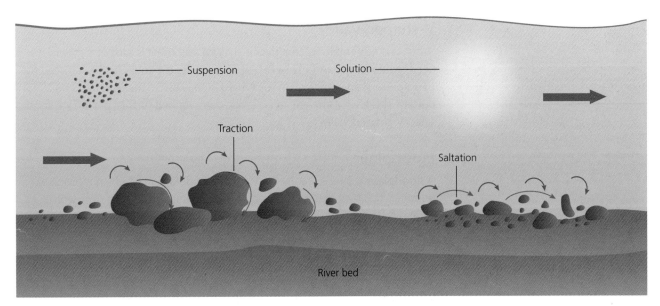

▲ **Figure 4** Forms of transportation in a river

The formation of river landforms

Waterfalls

Waterfalls occur when a river flows over bands of rock which vary in their resistance to erosion (see Figure 5). Areas of weaker rock are eroded faster, creating a steep gradient between the hard and soft rock. This means that the river can flow faster, and as it flows over the sudden drops marked by the edge of the more resistant bands of rock, it creates rapids.

With time, the softer rock is eroded more quickly and the drop becomes steeper. This creates an overhang of hard rock. A deep plunge pool is formed at the bottom of the drop and turbulence in the pool erodes the back wall of the waterfall further.

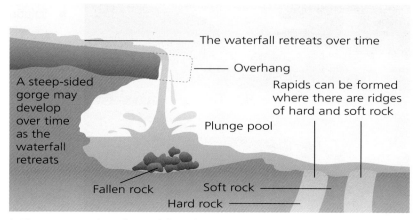

▲ **Figure 5** Formation of waterfalls and rapids

Gorges

Gorges can form when waterfalls retreat upstream over time. This happens when the softer rock is eroded and the resulting overhang of hard rock becomes too heavy and falls into the water below.

V-shaped valley

When it is nearer its source, a river is shallow and there is a lot of friction between the water and the river bed. This erodes the rocks beneath it, leading to a steeper gradient which in turn makes the water in the river descend quickly. This gives it the energy to erode the river bed further, producing a steep sided V-shaped valley.

Floodplain

A floodplain is a wide area of land on either side of a river which is prone to flooding. This is created due to centuries of lateral erosion by a river, which widens the river floor. It is also created by the deposition of fine sediment during floods.

As the river floods and flows outwards from the river channel, the flow has less energy, so it deposits the fine sediment (alluvium) being carried within it onto the surrounding area.

Levees

As the water in a floodplain retreats after a flood, the water drops the heavier material first. This means more sediment is dropped close to the river channel. After the river has been flooded several times, this can build up to form levees on either side of the river (see Figure 7).

Meander

Meanders are a natural feature of a flowing river caused by later erosion. As the river flows around the meander bend, the energy of the water and the sediment that it carries (see Figure 6) erode the outside of the bend.

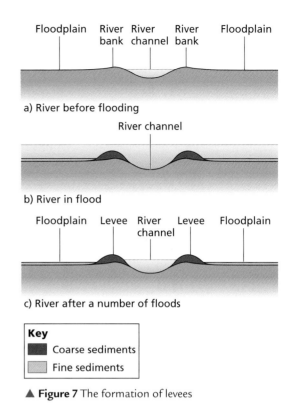

a) River before flooding

b) River in flood

c) River after a number of floods

Key
Coarse sediments
Fine sediments

▲ **Figure 7** The formation of levees

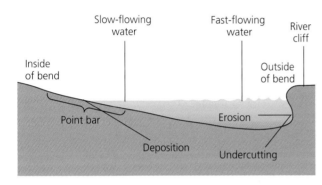

▲ **Figure 6** A cross-section of a meander bend

Ox-bow lakes

Over time, meander bends can become very large. Owing to the continual erosion, the ends of the meander bend can become closer and the neck of the meander will narrow. When the river floods, the river may then cut through the neck to take a shorter route and create a new channel. The old bend will be cut off from the main channel and eventually form a curving 'ox-bow' lake until continued deposition of sediment fills it in (see Figure 8).

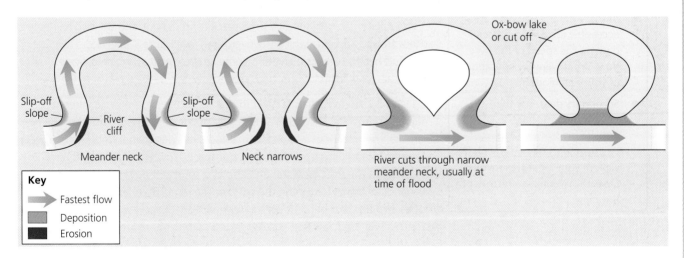

Ox-bow lake or cut off

Slip-off slope

River cliff

Meander neck

Slip-off slope

Neck narrows

River cuts through narrow meander neck, usually at time of flood

Key
Fastest flow
Deposition
Erosion

▲ **Figure 8** Ox-bow lake formation

Case study: a UK river basin

The River Wye

The River Wye is the fifth longest river in the UK, at over 150 miles (210 km) long. It has its source in the Plynlimon range in central Wales, just a few miles from the source of the River Severn, into which it flows, after descending almost 700 m during its course (see Figure 9). Plynlimon rises nearly 2500 feet high and receives one of the highest rainfall totals of any location in the UK. Rivers work to transport water and eroded sediment, taking it from higher land to the sea (or a lake) where it is deposited.

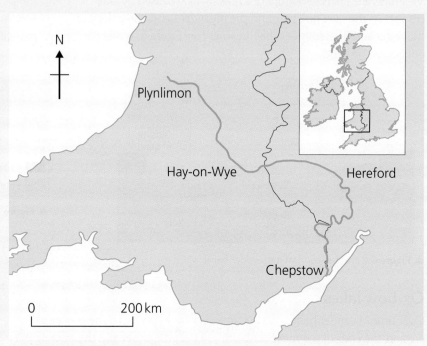

▲ **Figure 9** The course of the River Wye

Fieldwork ideas

- Primary data: if you have an accessible local river, collect data on the speed of the river flow. What were the limitations of your technique?

- Secondary data: use the Environment Agency website http://watermaps. environment-agency.gov.uk to explore your local area further. Does the river have a history of flooding?

The upper course of the River Wye runs through moorlands. Its upper valley is the result of glaciations and cuts through gritstone and shales. The river descends quickly, which gives it the energy to shape a typical steep-sided valley in places. At this stage it can only remove small pieces of sediment, and the bed has large stones around and over which the river flows (see Figure 3, page 15). There are bogs and heaths higher up and also some limestone areas, which provide a range of habitats for wildlife.

The Wye is a relatively natural river in that its course has not been altered too much by human activity, such as reservoir building (unlike its tributary the Elan). Its importance as a habitat is marked by its designation as a Site of Special Scientific Interest. It passes through a number of towns, which would have made use of the river for water and also as a source of power. Salmon swim up river and are fished for during the season. The removal of sediment from the slopes into the channel produces a steep-sided V-shaped valley.

The first town the river passes through is called Rhayader, which literally means 'waterfall on the Wye', but the waterfalls were removed when the town's bridge was built, leaving just a short stretch of rapids. This area is used by canoeists, who test themselves after heavy rainfall in the faster-flowing water. Waterfalls occur on several of the Wye's tributaries, notably at Cleddon Falls.

Below the city of Hereford, the River Wye cuts down through a broad floodplain. The fertile alluvium means that the floodplain is farmed. Traditionally, this was pasture, but it is now often cultivated. Along the river's course there is farmland and a mix of woodland, making up almost 90 per cent of the Wye Valley. This is designated as an Area of Outstanding Natural Beauty (AONB).

The River Wye floods annually and these former channels become temporary pools alongside the current meandering course, and can be picked out from the air. There are few settlements close to the river at this point, because of the flood risk.

Settlements have developed at bridging points. These include Hay-on-Wye, which hosts an annual literature festival, and marks the point where the river passes from Wales into England. One of the most visited areas is the Wye Valley (or gorge). By this point in the river's course, several other tributaries have joined the main course, providing more erosive potential. The gorge runs between Goodrich and Chepstow.

One of the viewpoints looking along the river's course at Symonds Yat is a famous place for tourists to pause. It is a limestone outcrop rising over 120 m above the river below, which winds around it, and lies down river of Goodrich Castle. Canoeists use this stretch of the river for recreation, and walkers appreciate the beautiful landscape.

The river passes the ruins of Tintern Abbey, before it widens out and flows across a flatter stretch. It then enters its tidal estuary and flows into the Bristol Estuary where it meets salt water. Salmon fishing is popular within the lower course of the river and provides employment.

▲ **Figure 10** Symonds Yat on the Wye Valley

Managing the River Wye

All rivers require management to ensure that they do not impact on the environments through which they run. All major rivers, including the Wye, have a management plan produced by the Environment Agency in consultation with other bodies.

The Wye Valley is affected by a range of processes, both human and physical, some of which are historical, and have been in place for many years (see Figure 11).

Urbanisation

Hard engineering may be required to protect settlements near to the river's channel from flooding. Over 200,000 people live in the Wye and Usk Valley, which includes large towns such as Hereford and Chepstow. These same urban environments may increase the flood risk by draining water more quickly into the channel. Around 9000 properties in the area are thought to be at particular risk of flooding. A number of strategies, including hard engineering, are used to protect these larger towns. People are also expected to be aware of methods to reduce their personal risk. Some areas of the floodplain have been zoned as being of high risk; construction is not permitted in these areas.

Agriculture

The predominant land use in the catchment is agriculture, which is a consumer of water from the river for irrigation. There are also high levels of biodiversity that need to be managed alongside the agricultural use of the land, such as controls on particular chemicals that may otherwise affect the river.

Industry

Although this is not a heavily industrialised area, the presence of the river means that some industrial activity is inevitable. Quarrying for limestone, originally to provide limestone for Llanwern Steelworks in Newport, has changed the gradient of some areas. Tintern Quarry is now a rock-climbing activity centre but quarrying still takes place at Livox Quarry for Marshalls. The rock also contains metal ores including iron ore. Woodlands were also felled for shipbuilding and to support the charcoal industry.

Today, the tourist industry employs many people in the Wye Valley, and high-profile events such as the literary festival at Hay-on-Wye draw thousands of visitors to the area. The Forest of Dean has also been used for numerous TV and film location shoots, including the 2015 film *Star Wars: The Force Awakens*.

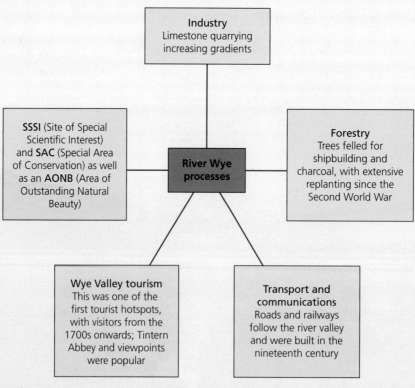

▲ **Figure 11** Processes affecting the River Wye

Geomorphic processes

The Upper Wye is steep, with mountainous impermeable landscapes, and the river responds quickly to rainfall. Some areas use the landscape to reduce the impacts of flooding, by ensuring that excess water is able to flow into areas of the floodplain that are zoned for that purpose. Further downstream, the Letton Lakes take some of the excess water during flood events to protect Hereford. Management has attempted to reduce the likelihood of flooding by slowing the rate that water enters the channel by surface runoff. Vegetation management reduces rates of runoff by increasing surface cover, and increasing interception storage. The risks of landslides or other mass movement may be reduced by planting trees which also intercept rainfall and help bind the soil surface together. There are few trees in large parts of the Wye's catchment, but other areas have seen new planting. Research conducted for the Environment Agency suggests that trees planted in the upper course of the river could reduce the height of flood water by 20 per cent by increasing interception storage. Trees also provide a local amenity for residents, as well as having an aesthetic value. Where river banks are stabilised, they can be more widely used by anglers or walkers. Otters are also returning to the upper course of the river as a result. Stabilising the channel can assist with changing the river's response to rainfall, which ultimately helps settlements further downstream. It can also reduce the rate of river erosion, which reduces the amount of sediment being transported downstream. Soil erosion will also decrease due to vegetation reducing direct raindrop impact and overland flow. Ultimately this means that depositional features such as floodplains would have less sediment available to construct them. Artificial levees would also need to be constructed. The flow of the river is in a state of dynamic equilibrium (it will adjust to any change, to bring it back to a natural flow where possible), and human attempts to manage the channel can upset this balance in the long term if care isn't taken to work with the natural processes acting along it during river management.

Activities

1. Access the Wye Valley website at http://wyevalleyaonb.org.uk and produce an illustrated set of cards describing the different ways that the Wye Valley is used by people. How will each of these potentially affect the river?
2. Investigate the way that tourism is being promoted through the use of the Wye Valley and Forest of Dean as film and TV locations: www.visitdeanwyefilm.co.uk.

⊕ Geographical skills

Rivers react to rainfall as the water enters the channel. Some rivers rise more quickly than others after rainfall and may be more prone to flooding. The Environment Agency has provided data from its network of monitoring gauges. The ones along the River Wye can be viewed on this page: http://apps.environment-agency.gov.uk/river-and-sea-levels/120764.aspx

Each gauge can also be viewed on the GaugeMap website. The one at Hereford Bridge, on the River Wye, can be seen here: www.gaugemap.co.uk/#!Detail/796/815

Each gauge can be viewed, and plotted, and even followed on Twitter.

CHAPTER 4

Coastal landscapes

Key idea: There are a range of landforms within the coastal landscape.

→ In this section you will study:

⇨ the formation of coastal landforms – headland, bay, cave, arch, stack, beach and spit

⇨ a case study of the North Norfolk coast, a coastal landscape, including: the geomorphic processes operating at different scales and how they are influenced by geology and climate; landforms and features in the North Norfolk Coast; how human activity, including management, works in combination with geomorphic processes to impact the landscape

▲ **Figure 1** Wells-next-the-Sea, North Norfolk

'All too often, chasing far-away places, we forget just what beauty we have on our doorstep'.

Michael Palin, former president of the Royal Geographical Society

▲ **Figure 2** Newquay, Cornwall

▲ **Figure 3** Groynes and surf, Tywyn, West Wales

Activities

1. Take a look at the images on these pages.
   a. What landscape features can you already recognise?
   b. What processes do you think are active in these areas?
   c. What other sources of information would be useful to add to your knowledge about these places?
   d. How will these areas change in the short or long term in terms of their physical geography?
   e. How do people use these areas, and what impact does this have on them?

Wherever you are in Great Britain, you are never more than 75 miles from the coast. The coastline is part of our history as a country, is central to our culture, and is part of our childhood as the setting for shared family experiences. In this chapter we will look closely to see what processes created (and continue to shape) this dramatic and varied landscape, which runs for over 10,000 km around England alone.

✝ Geographical skills

Interpreting photographs

● Look at a photograph and consider the features that are shown. Which are human and which natural? How do they relate to each other?
● Is the surface geology shown? Are there particular types of landscape features present?
● Look for evidence of human activity, including population, economic activity or farming. Are there any patterns to the activities shown in the photograph?
● Remember that one photo by itself can be misleading. When interpreting photographs in your exams, use them along with other resources and information, for example, an OS map extract.

How geomorphic processes shape coastal landscapes

Geomorphic processes are the processes that change the shape of the land, including: weathering, mass movement, erosion, transport and deposition. These processes cause changes that can be large or small, and that can happen very quickly or over hundreds of years.

Geomorphic processes influence and shape the land found at the coast in different ways, and across different timescales. These create coastal landforms that together make up the huge variety of coastal landscapes we can see along the coast of the UK. The daily rise and fall of the **tides** changes the shape of beaches by moving beach **sediment** around, but it is the longer-term action of waves, wind and storms that results in some of the more visible changes in coastal landforms, combined with weathering and other processes acting on the material that makes up the coast.

Much of the coastline is not wholly natural and is managed by people to reduce its susceptibility to these processes, to reduce the damage to property or the risk of loss of life. The sea is often seen as an 'enemy' to be combatted, although some recent projects have allowed the sea to reclaim areas of land in a managed realignment of the coastline.

Weathering

The processes involved in the weathering of coastal landscapes are largely the same as those which shape river landscapes (see Figure 4).

Mechanical weathering

In places including South Devon and Pembrokeshire, cliffs along the coastlines are subject to mechanical weathering.

Mechanical weathering is due to **sub-aerial processes**, which are the physical actions of rain, frost and wind.

- Rain: water washes away loose material and also enters cracks in the rocks. If it soaks into softer rocks such as sandstone it adds weight to the base of the cliff, increasing the risk of collapse.
- Frost: water gets into cracks in rocks and freezes, expanding in volume and putting pressure on the rock.
- Wind: strong winds remove fine sediment, which may then be used to abrade the cliffs.

These processes create weaknesses in the rock that are then exploited by chemical and biological processes, which speed up the weathering and disintegration of the rock.

Chemical weathering

Cliffs along the coast of Kent or the Holderness coast around Flamborough Head are composed of chalk and limestone, and are susceptible to chemical weathering.

- Water reacts chemically with certain minerals, which weakens them.
- Minerals are also weakened when they are exposed to the air in a process called **oxidation**.
- Some minerals are affected by water in a process called **hydrolysis**, which involves acidic rainfall reacting with minerals to produce material that is soluble and easily washed away.
- Rocks, such as chalk and limestone, are affected by solution, as calcium carbonate is broken down to soluble calcium bicarbonate.

Biological weathering

The rocks and land on the coast are broken down by the actions of living organisms, including plants and animals. Tree roots act to loosen rocks and provide crevices into which water can penetrate. Molluscs use their feet to cling to the rocks, but can also weaken the rock surface.

Ferriby chalk – susceptible to solution

Red chalk

Carstone – used as local building material

Hunstanton Cliffs are up to 18 m high and run for 1.3 km, northeast from the town. The three rocks form distinctive stripes. Erosion is caused by waves at the toe of the cliff, but also water saturation causes slumping. Heavy rain in 2012 caused cliff falls, which are still protecting the base of the cliff in places. Erosion rates are slow, but being monitored as there is a lighthouse, historical chapel and housing along the top.

▲ **Figure 4** Hunstanton Cliffs, North West Norfolk

Mass movement

Mass movement refers to the sudden movement of material down a slope due to the pull of gravity. Heavy rain soaking into permeable rocks can add weight to them and the water can also lubricate the boundaries where materials meet, so that flow is more likely as the cliff 'fails'. **Rotational slumping** occurs on the soft cliffs, where the base of the cliff moves; other material then slumps down the face as the bottom moves outwards and across the beach (see Figure 5). These can happen suddenly and have caused several fatalities in recent years, for example at Blackpool Sands in Devon in 2012 where a section of cliff collapsed onto sunbathers, and more recently on the same stretch of coastline in 2015. There may be crops planted at the top of the cliff which end up on the beach before they can be harvested. In some cases, livestock have even been carried down the cliff. Cliffs made of softer materials, including those along the east coast of the UK, are particularly susceptible to slumping.

On other cliffs, **rock slides** occur, where the failure occurs along a particular geological boundary within the cliff. A section falls down due to gravity and may dislodge other material on its way down. This can be caused by prolonged wet weather, or alternatively dry weather, which causes rocks such as clay to shrink. Cracks near the top of a cliff are a sign that it is an active area which may fail at any time.

Erosion

Erosion is the wearing away of the coast by a moving force. The main energy causing this erosive force at the coast is provided by **waves** (see Figure 7).

- Waves arrive every few seconds and, along with the water, they also move sand or pebbles. When this sediment is thrown or rubbed against the base of the cliff as the wave breaks, the land is worn away by abrasion. This can sometimes result in a **wave-cut notch** at the base of the cliff where there is a greater rate of erosion than higher up the cliff.
- Water hitting a rock will compress air into any cracks within it. In the pause between waves, the air in the crack expands explosively outwards as the pressure is released by the receding water. This process, called hydraulic action, removes fine material and enlarges cracks, speeding up the process.
- Seawater is slightly acidic and can slowly dissolve certain rock types such as limestone by solution. Over time, large sediment removed by the earlier processes is broken down into smaller, more rounded sediment through attrition as particles hit each other. These smaller particles may then form the ammunition for the next wave to hit the cliff. As can be seen in Figure 4 on page 25, material that has fallen from a cliff can protect the base of it for some time before it is eventually removed.

Where hard rock occurs at the coast, you will tend to see cliffed coastlines (see Figure 6). Softer rock is more likely to result in lower coastlines, with sand dunes or salt marshes. Where the two are found in close proximity, the result is often a more 'interesting' combination of **headlands** and **bays**, with the headlands being made of the more resistant rock.

▲ **Figure 5** Slumped cliffs at Alum Bay, Isle of Wight

▲ **Figure 6** Budleigh Salterton, Devon

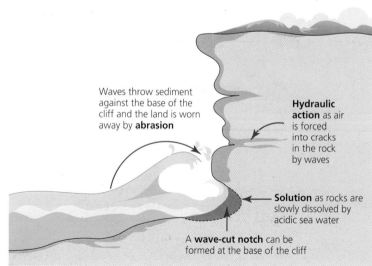

Waves throw sediment against the base of the cliff and the land is worn away by **abrasion**

Hydraulic action as air is forced into cracks in the rock by waves

Solution as rocks are slowly dissolved by acidic sea water

A **wave-cut notch** can be formed at the base of the cliff

▲ **Figure 7** Coastal erosion

Transportation

Sediment is transported along the coast in several ways. The processes are the result of wave action and may occur at different rates depending on location.

Traction refers to the movement of larger sediment. Circular wave action rolls pebbles along the sea bed, or shifts the sediment on a beach during a storm. Smaller pieces of shingle or large grains of sand may be picked up temporarily in a process called saltation before being dropped back to the sea bed. Finer clays and smaller particles may be suspended in the water, giving it a brownish colour when seen from the air, especially after storms or along easily eroded stretches of coastline. A milky colour close to chalk or limestone cliffs may also be a sign that solution has been happening: when minerals dissolve into the seawater.

Similar processes occur in a river, see page 15.

Longshore drift

Beach sediment is moved (transported) up and down the beach profile by waves in different ways:

- The **swash** is the forward movement of water up the beach as the wave breaks.
- The **backwash** is the movement of water down the beach due to gravity after a wave breaks.

The direction of the waves hitting the coastline is dependent on the wind. If the wind is blowing at an angle to the coastline, the wave swash will be at a similar angle, transporting loose sediment along the beach with it.

As the backwash is being pulled by gravity, it always returns to the sea at 90° to the coast, which is the shortest route down the beach. This means that the sediment will be moved along the beach in a zigzag manner (see Figure 8).

Although the wind may change direction from day to day on any stretch of coastline, there will be a prevailing wind direction. This will result in a net movement of sediment in one particular direction along the beach. This process of sediment being moved along the coastline is called **longshore (littoral) drift**.

Groynes are sometimes built to slow down this movement of sediment across the beach. This might be because too much sediment would be moved from vulnerable sections of coastline. They could also be built to ensure that a sandy beach remains in place for tourist or sea defence purposes.

Deposition

When waves move material along the coast, and more sediment stays on the beach than is taken away by the backwash, this is deposition. This creates landforms such as beaches and spits (see page 30).

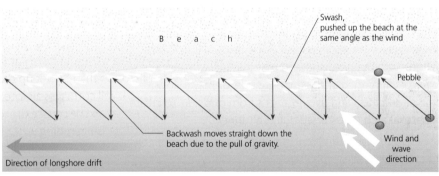

Swash, pushed up the beach at the same angle as the wind

Beach

Pebble

Backwash moves straight down the beach due to the pull of gravity.

Wind and wave direction

Direction of longshore drift

▲ **Figure 8** Longshore drift in action

Activities

1. Carry out an internet search for the term 'cliff collapse' and click the 'News' option to see where they have been happening. Read through a few of the reports and fill in an incident report containing the following information:
   - where the incident happened
   - type of rock involved
   - how much material was lost
   - any damage or casualties
   - what was done to reduce the impact.
2. Explain the processes which cause cliffs to retreat through erosion.

3. Explain the process of longshore drift, using diagrams.

→ **Take it further**

4. Identify some measures which could be taken to reduce the impact of erosion along the coastline. Research the relative advantages of each of these options. Which of these methods is likely to be the most cost-effective?

The formation of coastal landforms

Features of erosion: headlands, bays, caves, arches and stacks

A headland is a narrow piece of land that projects outwards from the coast and is surrounded by the sea on three sides. Wave energy is concentrated on these locations because the waves curve towards them as they enter shallow water. The rocks making up a headland are more resistant than the rest of that stretch of coastline. A bay is an indentation in the coastline found between two headlands. Bays are made up of a less-resistant rock type which is eroded more easily than the harder rocks of the headlands. The sea erodes the land back into a crescent shape (see Figure 9).

Weak points in headlands are exploited since the rock is not all made up of the same type. Cracks such as vertical **joints** or horizontal **bedding planes** in sedimentary rocks allow water to enter the rock. These cracks are also widened as a result of hydraulic action and abrasion. As these processes take place where waves impact the base of the cliff, there may be the creation of a wave-cut notch, resulting in a slight overhang.

Over time, small **caves** are formed at weak points as cracks are enlarged. These often form along the tide line. Caves extend into the headland, and may join up with another cave being formed at the opposite side, or may follow a line of weakness and extend across from one side, to create a **natural arch** that started out as a tunnel.

These arches start small and form close to the tide line. Water surging into these openings widens them and salt spray speeds up the process of erosion, through hydraulic action and abrasion. Rock falling from the cave walls or ceiling may form a temporary barrier that encourages water to move up and over it, increasing the height further. In time, as arches grow, the weight of the 'ceiling' may become too much, and collapse. The outer part of the arch will then become separated from the headland and form a tower called a **stack** (see Figure 10).

Stacks vary in height and stability. The Old Man of Hoy (see Figure 9), a 137 m sandstone stack in Orkney, has stood for over 200 years, but the so called Twelve Apostles along the Great Ocean Road in Victoria, Australia, are now down to just eight after the most recent collapse in 2008.

Stacks will be worn down to form a **stump**, which may eventually be covered over at high tide. The wearing down of the cliff to the level of the waves produces a **wave-cut platform**, which grows in size as the cliffs retreat ever further inland. Over time, the headland will erode back towards the rest of the coastline, where the process of headland formation will start again.

▲ **Figure 9** The Old Man of Hoy

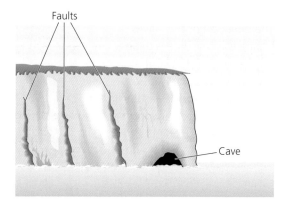

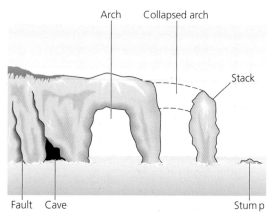

▲ **Figure 10** Formation of a headland

Beachgoers warned after huge Sidmouth cliff fall

Police say a dramatic landslide should act as a stark message to those who walk on to the pebbles on the eastern seafront. One officer spoke of how one couple told him they had been just metres from a previous rock fall. 'The couple in question were not local and had gone on to the beach, ignoring these notices and the danger of sitting under the cliffs. They stated that they were about 20 m away from the falling debris. One or both of them could have died.'

PC Jim Tyrrell wants visitors and residents to be aware of the dangers between Sidmouth and Salcombe Regis, where the rocks are prone to falls after wet weather or long spells of hot, dry weather.

'It really is becoming somewhat of an issue,' he said.

Stunned onlooker Tony Lane caught the 'spectacular' drama on camera.

'There was a huge rumble', he said. 'It started with one or two stones falling, and then it all came down in two sections. There was a massive dust cloud.'

Dry weather causes shrinkage in the Mercia mudstone which forms part of the cliff. Wet weather also caused landslides during the previous winter, threatening clifftop properties.

▲ **Figure 11** Article from *Sidmouth Herald*, 5 August 2014

Activities

1. Read the article above.
   a. What reasons are given for the cliff collapse at Sidmouth?
   b. What options do the police have for managing the risk in an area that is popular with holidaymakers?

→ **Take it further**

2. What are the options for people whose clifftop houses are threatened by coastal erosion? How can cliffs be protected?

Some GIS software allows for comparisons of maps. Where's the Path is a free tool that allows users to compare present day and historical maps side by side: http://wtp2.appspot.com/wheresthepath.htm

Figure 12 shows the small village of Kilnsea, which sits where Spurn Point meets the mainland at the mouth of the Humber estuary. There are features that can be identified on both maps, and the amount of erosion could be calculated by measuring how far the cliff has retreated, using the grids for measurement.

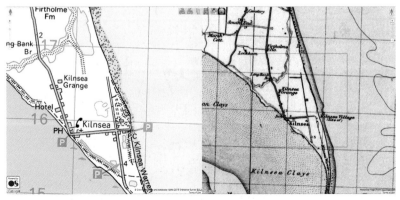

▲ **Figure 12** Screenshot from Where's the Path, showing historical and present day maps: squares are 1 km²

✢ Geographical skills

1. Draw a sketch map of Figure 14. Annotate your sketch map with the likely processes that led to its creation, including the winds that were involved and the source of sediment that helped build it.

2. Explore a stretch of coastline of around 30 km in length by looking at the area on an Ordnance Survey map. Use the map to explore the different types of landform that can be found and the way that people use your chosen stretch of the coast. If your classmates are allocated consecutive stretches of the same coastline, this could result in an interesting large-scale survey.

Features of deposition: beaches and spits

Beaches

Beaches are often found along the UK coastline. They are areas of land that lie between the storm-tide level and the low-tide level. They can be made up of sand, pebbles or a mixture of both. Some beaches are made up of mud and silt.

The charactesistics of beaches are:

● Gently sloping land; very low angle to the sea
● Stretches far inland
● Tourist resorts often have groynes to keep the beach in place
● Can be found in bays or along straight stretches of coastland

Spits

Spits are created when the coastline ends and the process of longshore drift continues, so sediment is deposited off the coast. If the conditions are right, this sediment will build up to form new land which will extend out along the existing coastline. The end of the feature will be curved by wave action and the impact of winds. Spurn Point is a spit at the mouth of the Humber.

Conditions that help the formation of spits are:

● large volumes of sediment of different sizes available
● rapid rate of movement of sediment along the coast
● shallow offshore gradient, which means that sediment is being deposited in shallow areas and can build up faster so that it comes above the surface
● sheltered from strong winds, or low wave energy
● opportunity for sediment to be vegetated which helps it become established as a permanent feature.

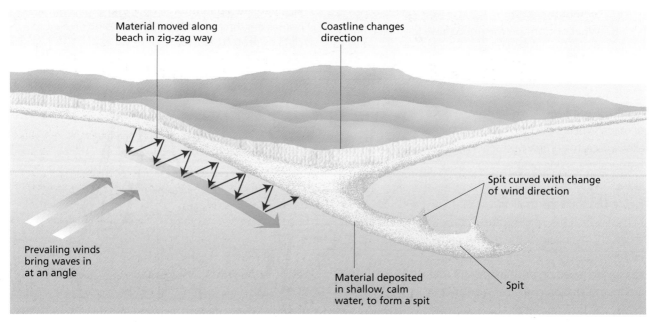

▲ **Figure 13** Formation of a spit

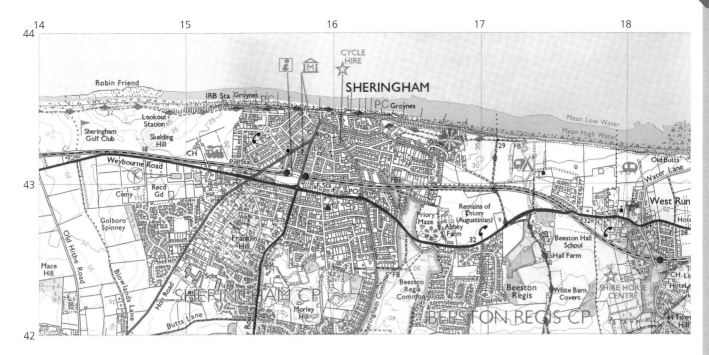

▲ **Figure 14** Ordnance Survey map of Sheringham, scale 1:25,000 © Crown copyright and/or database right. All rights reserved. Licence number 100036470

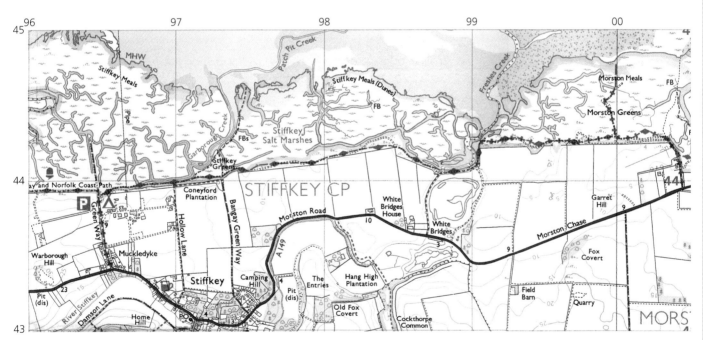

▲ **Figure 15** Ordnance Survey map of Blakeney National Nature Reserve, scale 1:25,000 © Crown copyright and/or database right. All rights reserved. Licence number 100036470

Activities

1. Compare the coastal environments shown in the two map extracts in Figures 14 and 15.
2. Comment on the reasons for the location of the main road shown in Figure 15.
3. Explain the formation of the landform found in square 9644 of Figure 15.

4. Identify the features in Figure 14 shown at the following grid references:
   a. 157432   c. 152432   e. 178423
   b. 173431   d. 159428
   Which of these is the odd one out?
5. What types of sea defence are marked on Figure 14? Explain how these work with the aid of a labelled diagram.

Case study: a UK coastal landscape

Where is Norfolk?

Norfolk is a county in the east of England, bordering Suffolk, Lincolnshire and Cambridgeshire (see Figure 16). It creates the southern border of the Wash, an inlet of the North Sea, into which several rivers including the Great Ouse flow.

The North Norfolk coast runs for almost 70 km between the towns of Wells-next-the-Sea and Cromer, and includes all the small villages that lie between.

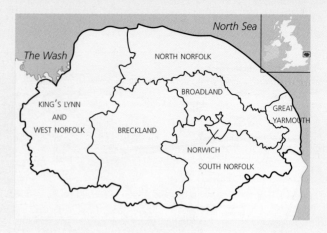

▶ **Figure 16** Location map of Norfolk

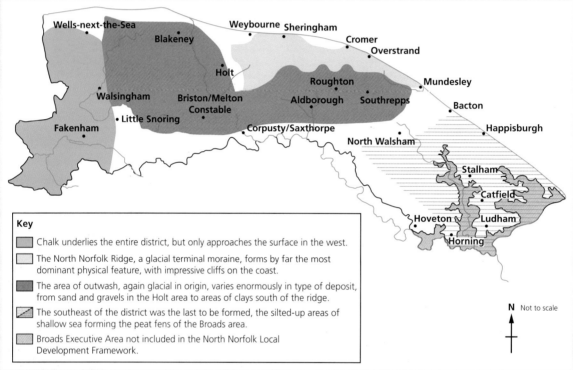

Key

▢ Chalk underlies the entire district, but only approaches the surface in the west.

▢ The North Norfolk Ridge, a glacial terminal moraine, forms by far the most dominant physical feature, with impressive cliffs on the coast.

▢ The area of outwash, again glacial in origin, varies enormously in type of deposit, from sand and gravels in the Holt area to areas of clays south of the ridge.

▨ The southeast of the district was the last to be formed, the silted-up areas of shallow sea forming the peat fens of the Broads area.

▢ Broads Executive Area not included in the North Norfolk Local Development Framework.

N Not to scale

▲ **Figure 17** Map of the landscape character of North Norfolk

What makes the Norfolk coast distinctive?

It is a low-lying coastline, with a range of habitats including salt marsh, cliffed headlands and expanses of sand dunes. The gradient of the seabed close to the coast is shallow, so the tide goes out a long way. As beach sand dries out, it is blown onshore by winds to create the sand dunes. The underlying rock is chalk. A large number of flints are found within the chalk and are used locally as a building material. At Hunstanton, the chalk appears in the famous striped cliffs seen on page 25.

The chalk is hidden by a layer of material called drift, which was laid down by an advancing ice sheet at the end of the most recent Ice Age. The ice sheet travelled from the north and also created a ridge near Cromer which provides the highest land in the whole county at just over 100 m. This produces a range of farming land and habitats including heathland and woodland (see Figure 17).

What is landscape character?

Geographers often talk about the landscape character of an area. The North Norfolk coast has a particular character which is produced by a combination of the geology, the land use and the impact of coastal processes. The subdued relief and flinty soils are part of that character. The relief also allows people to appreciate the 'big skies' in this part of the world. Dark sky tourism is a growing activity in this area. This is possible because of the low levels of light pollution as the location is far from any large cities. The coastal area is also designated as an Area of Outstanding Natural Beauty (AONB).

The coast road used by residents and tourists follows the slightly higher land and lies inland from the coastal marshes. Some of these marshes near Holkham were drained by Dutch engineers who had previously worked locally to drain the Fens. Local landowners paid for the work, so that the peat soils could be used for summer cultivation and to prevent serious winter flooding. The wide sandy beach at Holkham is regularly named as one of the world's best beaches, known for its extensive and well-developed sand dunes. It has appeared in a number of feature films.

How does human activity, including management, affect the geomorphic processes working on the coast?

The villages along this stretch of coast sit on the slightly higher land to reduce their chance of coastal flooding, although Wells-next-the-Sea and Blakeney were among those places flooded during a storm surge in January 2013, which also left homes lying on the beach further round at Hemsby.

At Blakeney Point (see Figure 18) and Scolt Head Island, spits have been produced by the transportation of sediment along the shoreline. The boat trip out to see the seals from the harbour at Morston is a popular activity for tourists and adds to the value of tourism to the local economy and for local employment. This is a coast where deposition is more important than erosion. The rapid pace at which the tide comes in and the presence of hidden hollows cause problems for those unfamiliar with the area. Local lifeboat crews have regular callouts during the summer months.

At Stiffkey, an area of salt marsh has developed where fine material has been trapped by specialist plants which can tolerate high levels of salt to create natural sea defences. Salt marshes are very low lying, but build up as sea level rises, so form a good natural defence. They are rare places and their characteristic plants are protected by the National Trust.

At Holkham, the estate has planted the dunes with pine trees to stabilise the dune system, and visitors are encouraged to use boardwalks rather than disturb the marram grass and erode the dunes, which can result in sand blowouts. The Holkham estate also manages the sea front at Wells-next-the-Sea where there are groynes to protect the famous beach huts, and gabion baskets

below the Coastwatch lookout station (see http://www.nci.org.uk/wellsnextthesea). These try to slow down the transportation of sand from in front of the resort by slowing longshore drift, but care needs to be taken as sediment held here will not be available to protect coastline further downdrift.

The coastline has been subject to erosion in the past. Entire villages such as Shipden, Keswick and Wimpwell disappeared in the last century and now lie beneath the waves. The section near Happisburgh has become quite well known as a result of news coverage of cliff retreat. This has cost people their homes, despite battles by residents for appropriate compensation for their losses. The final house in Beach Road in the village was lost following the storm surge that took place in January 2013. This event was another reminder that this is a coast that continues to be shaped and defined by the sea.

At Cley-next-the-Sea, shingle ridges were breached and large dunes were stripped of sand at Wells-next-the-Sea. The **sea walls** and **rip-rap barriers** at Sheringham, and the **gabion** boxes at Brancaster, are a reminder that no coastal settlement is safe from potential damage, despite the generally benign nature of the waves.

The management at Cley-next-the-Sea is carried out as part of the 'Living Landscape' project. This provides a home for wildlife, but also protects the shingle ridge which forms the base of the spit at Blakeney Point. A breach in the ridge could starve the spit of shingle, and threaten its future existence.

The village of Happisburgh, further south from Cromer, is a well-known example of a settlement which has seen an increased rate of erosion as a result of a decision not to repair a damaged sea defence. Villagers have fought for years for compensation for damage to their properties, which are threatened by a receding coastline, unlike the village of Sea Palling further south, which has been protected by a sea defence scheme. At Sea Palling, a sea wall has been built to reflect wave energy back into the sea which reduces erosion from waves. Offshore breakwaters have also been constructed which reduce the intensity of wave action and therefore reduce coastal erosion. This decrease in wave energy has led to a reduction of transportation of sediment which has created a wide beach.

▲ **Figure 18** Blakeney Point spit

Activities

1. Visit the Environment Agency's flood mapping page to explore flood issues along this (or any) stretch of coastline. Access a Coastal Erosion map for your chosen location.
(http://watermaps. environment-agency.gov.uk/)

→ Take it further

2. People who use an area of landscape in a specific way are often referred to as stakeholders. Some of these are landowners or manage the land for a particular purpose. Identify the range of stakeholders that would be interested in the Norfolk coast and want to have a say in its future. Some organisations to get your list started would include the Environment Agency, HM Coastguard and the RSPB.

Coastal management

For management purposes, the coastline of the UK has been split up into sections called 'littoral cells'. Each of these cells includes a stretch of coastline which lies between points that form natural boundaries. Often these represent a point where the direction of movement of sediment along the coast changes. Within each of these cells, decisions have been made by the Environment Agency and other landowners on the way that they will be managed. Coastal defence works are very costly, so need to be prioritised to areas where they are most needed.

There are four main options for any stretch of defended coastline (see Figure 19). Decisions have been made for the period up to 2030 for each section of the UK's coastline.

Strategy	What this means
No active intervention	Do nothing
Hold the existing defence line	Maintenance of the existing sea defences
Managed realignment	This includes the creation of new areas of salt marsh by deliberately breaching sea defences. This approach has been used at locations such as Wallasea Island on the Essex coast.
Advance the line	Build new defences. This became necessary after the 2013 storm surge at locations such as Clacton, which has suffered from threatened cliff collapse.

▲ **Figure 19** Management strategies to defend coastlines

The North Norfolk District Council has provided Shoreline Management Plans (SMP). These are non-statutory plans for coastal defence management planning. They look at the risks associated with the erosion processes that have shaped the coast.

Figure 20 shows the key values linked with the section from Brancaster to Brancaster Staithe and highlights the complex interactions that are needed between different groups with different interests, for example groups in the tourist industry and groups working to preserve habitats for wildlife. Shoreline management in this area consists currently of holding the existing defence lines.

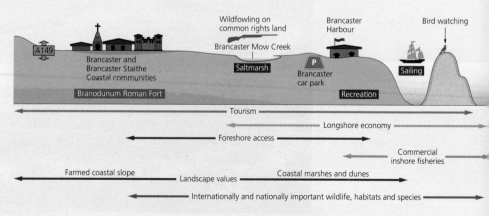

▲ **Figure 20** Cross section from Brancaster to Brancaster Staithe

Practice questions

1. Which of the following is not characteristic of a natural landscape?
   a) An area of woodland
   b) A water feature such as a river or stream
   c) A shopping centre
   d) Farmland   **[1 mark]**

2. Explain how geology can affect the landscape that forms on the surface.   **[3 marks]**

3. With the aid of an annotated diagram, explain what is likely to happen to the landform in Figure A over the next 100 years.   **[6 marks]**

▲ Figure A

> ### Tip
> When you are drawing an annotated diagram, use a sharp pencil, add a title and use a ruler to connect labels to the appropriate place on the diagram.

4. With reference to the Norfolk coast or a stretch of coastline that you have studied:
   a) Explain the processes of erosion that are affecting it.   **[3 marks]**
   b) Explain how the different groups of people who use that stretch of coastline may have conflicting views on how it should be used.   **[4 marks]**
   c) Name three different methods used to protect the coastline from erosion.   **[3 marks]**

5. Which of the following is *not* a process that results in sediment being transported by rivers?
   a) Traction
   b) Solution
   c) Convection
   d) Suspension   **[1 mark]**

> ### Tip
> Make sure that you are clear on what the main geomorphic processes are. Some of the terms are quite similar.

6. With reference to the River Wye or a river that you have studied:
   a) Describe the geomorphic processes that operate in the upper course of the river.   **[4 marks]**
   b) Explain how human activity affects the river's natural flow.   **[3 marks]**

THEME 2
People of the UK

The UK has a unique position within the world, with complex global interconnections. The history of the UK has influenced its current political and economic power on a global scale and has produced a rich culture, contributed to by a number of ethnicities. This theme explores the changes within UK society, its population and environment.

Chapter 5: The UK's major trading partners

Key idea: The UK is connected to many other countries and places.

In this chapter you will study:

→ an overview of the UK's current major trading partners, including principal exports and imports.

Chapter 6: Diversity in the UK

Key idea: The UK is a diverse and unequal society which has geographical patterns.

In this chapter you will study:

→ the UK's geographical diversity through patterns of employment, average income, life expectancy, educational attainment, ethnicity and access to broadband.

Chapter 7: Development in the UK

Key idea: There are different causes and consequences of development within the UK.

In this chapter you will study:

→ the causes of uneven development within the UK, including geographical location, economic change, infrastructure and government policy

→ a case study of Salford Quays, Manchester, to show the consequences of economic growth and/or decline in the UK.

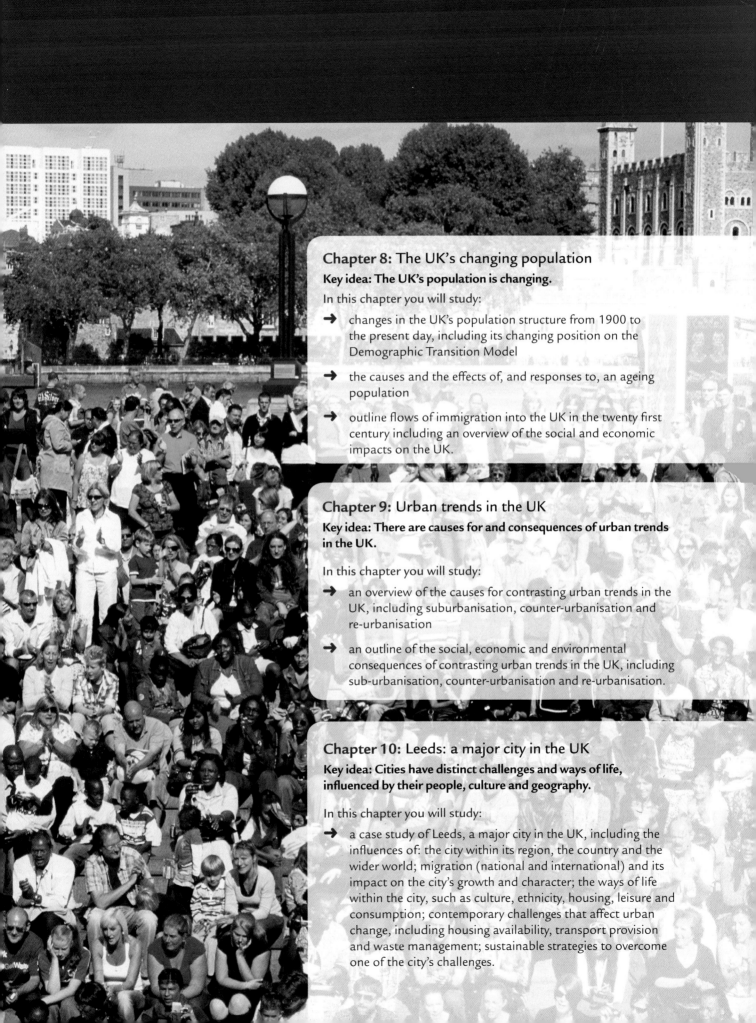

Chapter 8: The UK's changing population

Key idea: The UK's population is changing.

In this chapter you will study:

→ changes in the UK's population structure from 1900 to the present day, including its changing position on the Demographic Transition Model

→ the causes and the effects of, and responses to, an ageing population

→ outline flows of immigration into the UK in the twenty first century including an overview of the social and economic impacts on the UK.

Chapter 9: Urban trends in the UK

Key idea: There are causes for and consequences of urban trends in the UK.

In this chapter you will study:

→ an overview of the causes for contrasting urban trends in the UK, including suburbanisation, counter-urbanisation and re-urbanisation

→ an outline of the social, economic and environmental consequences of contrasting urban trends in the UK, including sub-urbanisation, counter-urbanisation and re-urbanisation.

Chapter 10: Leeds: a major city in the UK

Key idea: Cities have distinct challenges and ways of life, influenced by their people, culture and geography.

In this chapter you will study:

→ a case study of Leeds, a major city in the UK, including the influences of: the city within its region, the country and the wider world; migration (national and international) and its impact on the city's growth and character; the ways of life within the city, such as culture, ethnicity, housing, leisure and consumption; contemporary challenges that affect urban change, including housing availability, transport provision and waste management; sustainable strategies to overcome one of the city's challenges.

The UK's major trading partners

Key idea: The UK is connected to many other countries and places.

→ In this chapter you will study:

→ an overview of the UK's current major trading partners, including principal exports and imports.

With increasing globalisation the world is becoming more and more interdependent. The UK has global links through trade, culture (television, music, film), transport and electronic communications (underwater cables).

What is trade?

Trade involves the movement of goods and services across the world. While today this tends to involve transport by plane, container ships or trains, in the distant past it involved groups of people trekking vast distances over land or risking perilous sea journeys across oceans. Increasingly, modern trade involves the internet, for example in finance and the creative industries. Trade involves **imports** (products brought into a country) and **exports** (products taken out of a country).

The UK has a long tradition of trading with other countries. As an island, much of the UK's trade involved ships and many coastal settlements developed into thriving ports (see Figure 1). In the past, the UK traded a great deal with its colonies across the world, importing cotton, grain and products from the tropics such as fruit, coffee and spices. In return, the UK exported mainly manufactured products.

▲ **Figure 1** Containers being unloaded at the Port of Belfast

Who are the UK's trading partners?

To date, the UK's most important trading partners are members of the EU. As a single market, goods can be traded without tariffs between member states. The United States is an important historic trading partner and, in recent years, there has been a significant growth in trade with China. Trade is also important with former colonies, now members of the Commonwealth.

It is important to try to have a balance between exports and imports. If imports exceed exports, a country has a **trade deficit**. In the long term this can be expensive for the country. The UK has a trade deficit of about £1.4 billion. This has fallen slightly due to a reduction in imports and an increase in the export of manufacturing products.

Imports to the UK

Look at Figure 2a. It shows where imports to the UK come from. Notice the dominance of the EU but also the growth in imports from China. The bulk of the UK's imports by value are manufactured products, in particular cars, electrical items and clothing (see Figure 2b). Notice that food does not appear in the top ten!

- Most of the items imported from China – clothing and electronics – are cheaper than alternatives made in the UK so there is a ready market for them
- The UK is a relatively wealthy economy, so expensive items such as cars from Germany have a large market
- Petroleum and petroleum products are important imports, providing the UK with fuel and a versatile raw material for the chemicals industry.

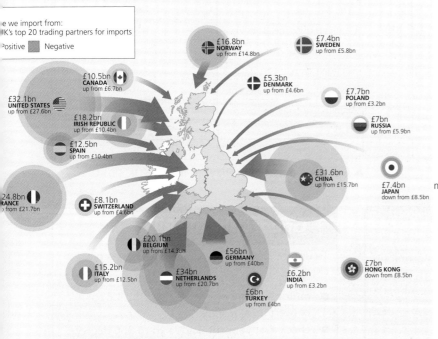

▲ **Figure 2a** Imports to the UK, 2014

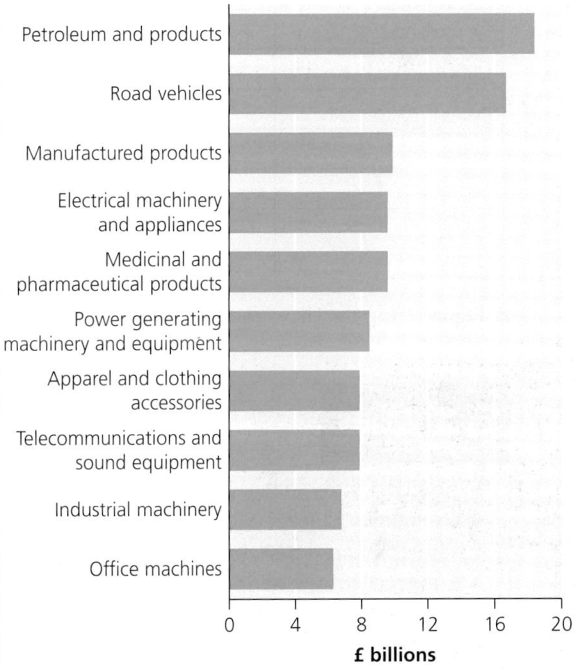

Petroleum and products
Road vehicles
Manufactured products
Electrical machinery and appliances
Medicinal and pharmaceutical products
Power generating machinery and equipment
Apparel and clothing accessories
Telecommunications and sound equipment
Industrial machinery
Office machines

0   4   8   12   16   20
£ billions

▲ **Figure 2b** What we buy

Activities

1. Define the following terms – trade, imports, exports, trade deficit.
2. Study Figure 2.
   a. Which country was the UK's top importing trading partner in 2014?
   b. Which country has seen the highest percentage growth in imports to UK?
   c. Why has China become a major importer to the UK?
   d. Germany exports high value products to the UK. Can you suggest some German imports to the UK?
   e. Why is 'petroleum and petroleum products' such an important import to the UK?

Exports from the UK

Look at Figure 3. While the USA is the main export destination, most of the UK's exports go to Europe and in particular to EU countries. Exports to China are increasing and, just outside the top ten, so are exports to the UAE.

Figure 4 shows the UK's main exports. The fastest growing exports in 2014 were gems, precious metals and coins. The UK's manufacturing sector (especially motor vehicles and aeronautical engineering) also showed a healthy increase in exports in 2014 reflecting the recent economic growth in the UK.

Country	% of total UK exports by value
United States	11.8%
Germany	9.8%
Netherlands	7.4%
Switzerland	6.6%
France	5.9%
Ireland	5.9%
China	5.1%
Belgium	4.1%
Italy	2.8%
Spain	2.8%

▲ **Figure 3** Top ten UK export countries, 2014

UK's main exports	% of overall exports from the UK
Machines, engines, pumps	14%
Oil	11.2%
Vehicles	10.6%
Gems, precious metals, coins	10.3%
Pharmaceuticals	6.6%
Electronic equipment	6.4%
Medical, technical equipment	3.9%
Aircraft, spacecraft	3.4%
Plastics	2.6%
Organic chemicals	2.4%

▲ **Figure 4** Top ten exports by value from the UK, 2014

Activities

1. Use two different diagrams to present the information in Figures 3 and 4. Consider using a bar chart, pie chart, located bar chart or a flow map. Write a brief summary of the export patterns and trends.

→ Take it further

2. Five of the leading UK export companies in 2014 are listed below. Use the internet to find out what these companies specialise in producing. Develop one of them to form a short case study.
   - Cadbury UK
   - Optivite International
   - Allied Pickfords UK
   - TIMET
   - Rothenberger UK

⸸ Geographical Skills

To use the data in Figure 3 or 4 to draw a pie chart:

- multiply each percentage figure by 3.6 to convert it to degrees
- check that your total adds up to 360 degrees
- if it doesn't add up, round the largest figure up or down
- draw a circle and mark the centre
- divide the circles into sections of the appropriate size using a protractor
- shade different sectors using different shadings or colours
- complete a key to explain what your shadings or colours indicate
- add a title.

CHAPTER 6

Diversity in the UK

Key idea: The UK is diverse and unequal society which has geographical patterns.

→ **In this chapter you will study:**

→ the UK's geographical diversity through patterns of employment, average income, life expectancy, educational attainment, ethnicity and access to broadband.

What do you think makes the UK special? One of the things that make the UK special is its cultural, social and economic diversity. The UK is a country of immigrants. Through the ages people from all over the world have arrived in the UK bringing with them a rich cultural heritage. This continues today as the UK welcomes people from war-torn parts of the world such as Syria and from other countries in the EU.

The UK is a country of physical and human contrasts. There are some significant variations across the UK at both regional and local scale.

Employment

Over the last 25 years, the patterns of employment have changed a great deal. The main trends are shown below.

Women at work – women are encouraged to work and follow careers. Employers offer flexible working hours and often help with child care. The government is also supporting child care to enable women to return to work if they wish to do so. Some work places now have crèche and child care facilities on site (see Figure 1).

Part time and self-employed – an increasing number of people now work part time or on a self-employed basis. People seek a better work–life balance or prefer to work from home. The availability of IT and broadband connections has made this possible.

Flexible hours – many people choose to operate flexible working hours, maybe combining office work with working from home. Some people work during evenings or overnight. The availability of mobile phones enable people to work on the move.

Tertiary sector – as the UK has de-industrialised, jobs in manufacturing have been replaced by employment in the services or tertiary sector, such as education and health care. A new quaternary (knowledge-based) sector has developed with jobs in research, information technology and the media.

▲ **Figure 1** Some work places have child care facilities on site

Figures 2 and 3 show the percentage of the workforce employed in the service and manufacturing industry across the UK.

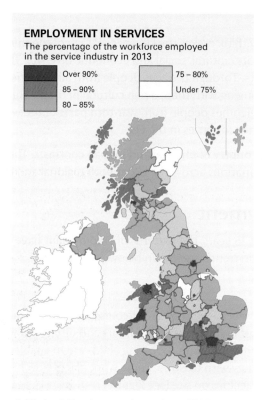

EMPLOYMENT IN SERVICES
The percentage of the workforce employed in the service industry in 2013

Over 90%		75 – 80%	
85 – 90%		Under 75%	
80 – 85%			

▲ **Figure 2** Employment in services, 2013

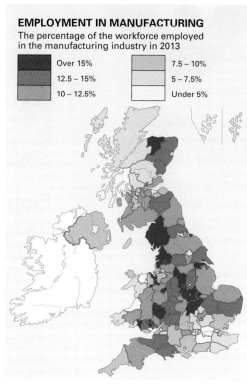

EMPLOYMENT IN MANUFACTURING
The percentage of the workforce employed in the manufacturing industry in 2013

Over 15%		7.5 – 10%	
12.5 – 15%		5 – 7.5%	
10 – 12.5%		Under 5%	

▲ **Figure 3** Employment in manufacturing, 2013

Look at Figure 4. It shows how employment patterns have changed in the UK from 1984 to 2014. Notice the growth of the tertiary and quaternary sectors and the decline of manufacturing. Over the past 25 years the patterns of employment have changed a great deal. As the UK has de-industrialised, jobs in manufacturing have been replaced by employment in the services or tertiary sector, such as education and healthcare. A new quaternary (knowledge-based) sector has developed with jobs in research, information technology and the media.

Key
- ■ Unskilled occupations
- ▪ Machine/transport
- ■ Sales/customer services
- ▫ Personal services
- ▪ Skilled trades
- ■ Administrative/clerical
- ▫ Associate professional/technical
- ■ Professional occupations
- ■ Managers/senior officials

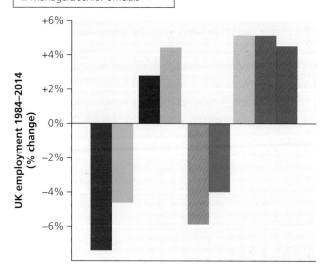

▲ **Figure 4** The changing face of UK employment, 1984–2014

Activities

1. What is the evidence that manufacturing industry has declined since 1984?
2. Describe the change that has taken place in 'personal services'.
3. What types of employment have shown the greatest increase?

Average income

Did you know that the average salary in the UK is £26,500? Averages can often be misleading and this is certainly true with UK incomes. There are huge disparities in incomes in the UK.

- Wayne Rooney earns about £300,000 a week (see Figure 5). This is 27,000 per cent more than the average income!
- The chief executives of the top 100 FTSE companies in the UK earn the average salary of the UK in just two and a half days
- At the other end of the scale, 80 per cent of new jobs have salaries of less than £16,640 for a 40-hour week
- Working on the minimum wage of £6.70 per hour brings an annual salary of just over £13,000.

Look at Figure 6. It shows variations in disposable incomes within and between regions of the UK. Disposable income is the money people have to live on once their taxes, pensions and mortgage/rent have been paid. The UK's average nearly disposable income is about £17,500. Notice how residents in Westminster have on average nearly four times the disposable income of residents in Leicester. Notice also the huge variations within regions, particularly London.

▲ **Figure 5** Wayne Rooney

Activity

1. Study Figure 6.
   a. Which two regions have disposable incomes below the UK average?
   b. Which UK region has the greatest range of disposable income?
   c. To what extent is there a north–south divide in disposable incomes?

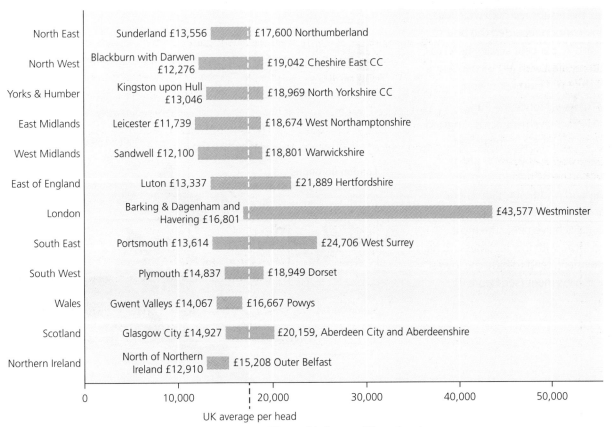

▲ **Figure 6** Disposable income in UK regions, 2013

Life expectancy

The average **life expectancy** in the UK is now 81 years. It has risen consistently in recent years as healthcare, diets and standards of living have improved. People are now living more than five years longer on average than in 1990.

However, life expectancy is not equal across the UK (see Figure 7).

- It is highest in the South East (82.4 years) and lowest in Scotland (79.1 years)
- Men living in Blackpool live an average of eight years fewer than men living in the City of London, and nine years fewer than men living in South Cambridgeshire, which has the highest life expectancy
- In England, women living in Manchester have the lowest life expectancy.

These disparities reflect variations in incomes and quality of life across the UK. Poor diets and smoking are the biggest risks leading to premature death or disability.

Region	Average life expectancy
South East England	82.4
East of England	82.2
South West England	82.0
Greater London	81.4
East Midlands	81.2
West Midlands	80.9
Yorkshire and the Humber	80.6
Wales	80.3
North East England	80.1
North West England	80.0
Northern Ireland	79.6
Scotland	79.1

▲ **Figure 7** Life expectancy by region (male and female combined) in years, 2015

Educational attainment

In 2015 across England, 68.8 per cent of GCSE entries gained an A* to C grade. This was a slight increase on the previous year. However, the results revealed wide regional variations. London recorded the best results, with 72 per cent achieving A* to C grades, compared with just 65 per cent in the Yorkshire and Humber region.

Look at Figure 8. Notice the huge variations in achievement across England. The highest values are in the richest London boroughs. The lowest are in towns in northern England such as Knowsley and Middlesbrough. There is a clear link between poverty and educational achievement. The most deprived areas, with low incomes and high unemployment, tend to have the lowest levels of achievement (see Figure 9).

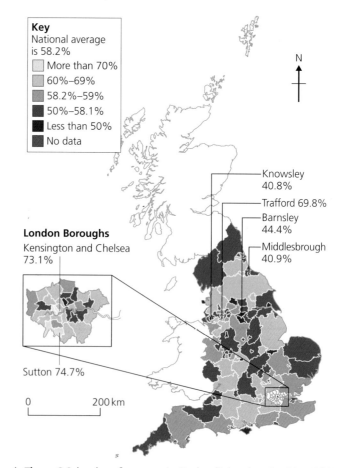

Key
National average is 58.2%
- More than 70%
- 60%–69%
- 58.2%–59%
- 50%–58.1%
- Less than 50%
- No data

Knowsley 40.8%
Trafford 69.8%
Barnsley 44.4%
Middlesbrough 40.9%

London Boroughs
Kensington and Chelsea 73.1%
Sutton 74.7%

0   200 km

▲ **Figure 8** School performance in England's local authorities, 2011

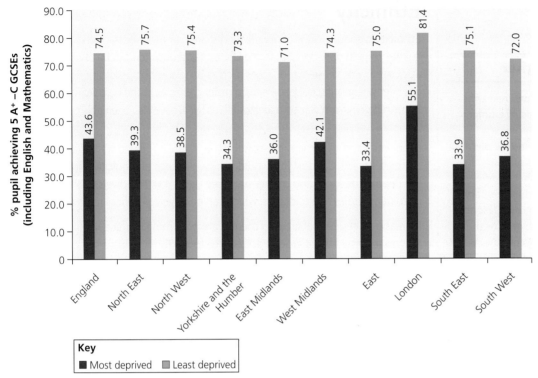

▲ **Figure 9** Percentage of students achieving more than five A* to C GCSE (or equivalent) grades including English and mathematics by deprivation, 2013–14

Activities

1. Study Figure 7. Use the data to produce a choropleth map showing life expectancy for the UK regions. You will need a blank map of the UK regions. Create four to six categories and use increasingly dark colours to represent increasing life expectancy. Describe the pattern on your completed map.

2. Study Figure 8.
   a. Describe the pattern of school achievement in England.
   b. Suggest reasons why school achievement varies so much across England.

Ethnicity

Ethnicity is about groups of people who share common roots, often based on culture, religion or nationality. In the UK, ethnic groups tend to be immigrants associated with foreign nationalities such as Bangladeshi or Pakistani. Recently, there has been a large influx of people from other countries in the European Union (EU). Some refugees from war-torn areas, such as Syria, have also been able to settle here.

While ethnic groups have settled widely across the UK there is a concentration in major cities and, in particular, in London (see Figure 10). If you walked along almost any high street in London you would see a wide range of ethnicities illustrated by the people, the shops and market stalls (see Figure 11). This diversity brings a wealth of colour, cultures and traditions, which can be hugely beneficial to an area.

Increasingly, residential areas in the UK are becoming ethnically mixed. However, some ethnic groups do tend to form distinct clusters in cities, especially Pakistanis, Bangladeshis and some black Africans. With low incomes and limited job security, ethnic groups may find themselves living in relatively deprived areas in the inner city.

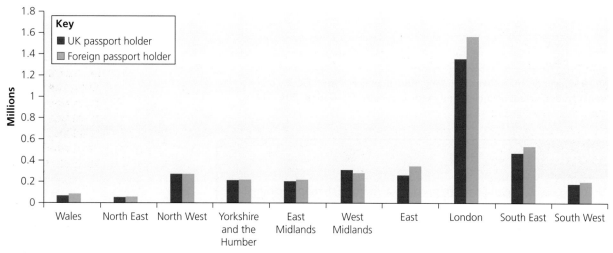

▲ **Figure 10** Foreign-born residents, 2011 Census

▼ **Figure 11** Whitechapel High Street, one of London's most multicultural areas

Access to broadband

Today almost 100 per cent of households in the UK can access the internet. Currently the government is delivering superfast (30Mbps+) broadband, which was predicted to reach 90 per cent of households in the UK by the end of 2015 (see Figure 12).

Look at Figure 13, which shows the pattern of broadband availability in Britain.

- Broadband availability reflects the pattern of the UK's population, with high availability in the population centres, particularly the large cities, but low availability in the more remote parts of the UK (e.g. Wales, Scotland and South West England)
- London and the South East together with the cities in the north of England are well served
- There are numerous small pockets of low availability across the UK, including within those areas with a generally good availability.

▲ **Figure 12** Rolling out broadband in rural areas

Activities

1. Study Figures 12 and 13.
   a. Internet availability is about 100 per cent, but internet use is closer to 90 per cent. Can you suggest why?
   b. How does broadband availability affect changes to employment?
   c. Describe the pattern of broadband availability in Figure 13. Suggest why coverage is not universal.

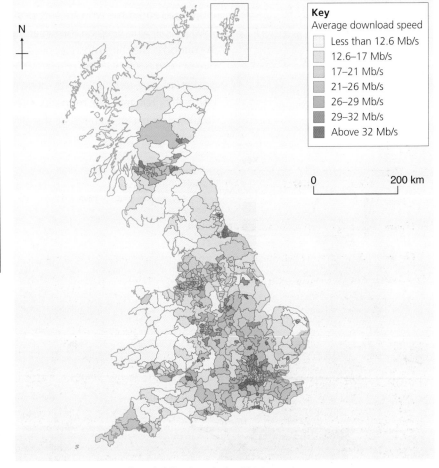

Key
Average download speed
- Less than 12.6 Mb/s
- 12.6–17 Mb/s
- 17–21 Mb/s
- 21–26 Mb/s
- 26–29 Mb/s
- 29–32 Mb/s
- Above 32 Mb/s

▲ **Figure 13** Broadband availability in Britain, 2014

CHAPTER

Development in the UK

7

Key idea: There are different causes and consequences of development within the UK.

→ **In this chapter you will study:**

→ the causes of uneven development within the UK, including:

- geographical location
- economic change
- infrastructure
- government policy.

→ a case study of Salford Quays, Manchester, to show the consequences of economic growth and/or decline in the UK.

What is the pattern of development in the UK?

Development in the UK is not even. Look at Figure 1. It shows the so-called 'north–south divide' in Britain as measured by household wealth. Notice that within the South, the South East region is much wealthier than the other regions. Over 13 per cent of households have a total wealth of close to £1 million a year. This compares with less than 7 per cent in Scotland.

Now look at Figure 2. This map showing deaths resulting from coronary heart disease also shows a clear north–south divide. High rates of coronary heart disease are most often associated with lifestyle choices including smoking, diet and exercise. Poverty and standards of living are also important factors affecting people's health.

Despite these clear regional trends, it is important to realise that regional averages do hide huge imbalances. Within all regions there will be some very wealthy individuals and some who are very poor. In London, for example, there are over 7500 people who sleep on the streets each night. The borough of Tower Hamlets in London is the third most deprived borough in England and has the highest rate of child poverty in the country (see Figure 3). Even wealthy Westminster has pockets of long-term unemployment, crime and housing issues. In the London borough of Islington, the mortality rate for coronary heart disease is 114 per 100,000. This is a lot higher that any of the regional figures in Figure 2.

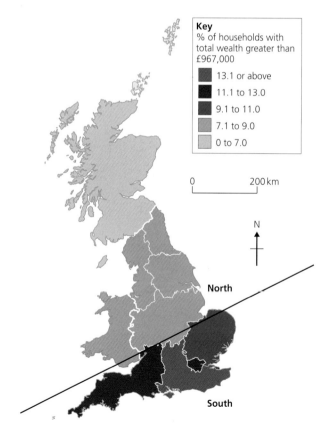

Key
% of households with total wealth greater than £967,000

- 13.1 or above
- 11.1 to 13.0
- 9.1 to 11.0
- 7.1 to 9.0
- 0 to 7.0

0   200 km

North

South

▲ **Figure 1** North–south divide

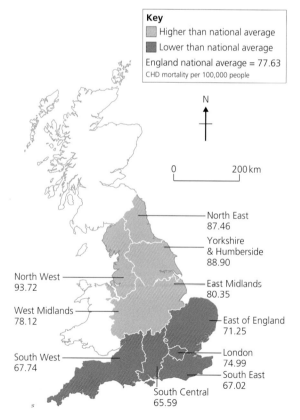

Key

- Higher than national average
- Lower than national average

England national average = 77.63
CHD mortality per 100,000 people

0   200 km

North East
87.46

Yorkshire & Humberside
88.90

North West
93.72

East Midlands
80.35

West Midlands
78.12

East of England
71.25

South West
67.74

London
74.99

South East
67.02

South Central
65.59

▲ **Figure 2** Coronary heart disease deaths, 2011

What are the causes of uneven development?

There are several reasons that help to explain the existence of a north–south divide in the UK. These include geographical location, economic change, infrastructure and government policy.

Geographical location

London is the centre of economic activity and wealth creation in the UK. This is mainly due to the city's role as capital of the UK and, in the past, as the administrative centre of a large and powerful British Empire. London has long been one of the world's major trading centres and today is a hub for business, finance and media. Many national and international companies have their headquarters in London.

As London has grown, so wealth has extended out into the rest of the South East. Many people who work in London now commute from the 'Home Counties' choosing to live in more pleasant rural surroundings. The commuter belts around London have witnessed tremendous economic growth, such as in cities like Cambridge.

In the early twenty-first century, the UK benefited from being part of the EU. Most trade, both imports and exports, is with its member states. London and the South East have excellent access to the continent. There are fast Eurostar rail services through the Channel Tunnel, several ferry routes and many air connections from London's airports, including City Airport in the centre of London (see Figure 4).

In the north and west of the UK are more distant from the European mainland. Despite good transport links with cities such as Manchester and Glasgow, many rural areas are remote and inaccessible. While some northern cities have a wealthy base, the rural districts are often much poorer, unlike the wealthy rural areas in the South East. Plans for a high speed rail link to northern cities hope to improve the links with London.

▲ **Figure 3** Poverty in the borough of Tower Hamlets, London

Activities

1. Study Figures 1 and 2.
   a. What is the evidence of a north–south divide in the UK? Use some statistics to support your answer.
   b. How can regional averages mask local variations in wealth across the UK?
   c. What are the signs of poverty shown in Figure 3?
2. In what ways has the South benefited from being close to the rest of Europe?

▲ **Figure 4** London City Airport

Economic change

Before 1900, most people in the UK worked in farming, mining or related activities – the primary sector. But the Industrial Revolution of the nineteenth century changed all that. Lots of people moved to the towns and cities for work – making steel, ships or textiles (the manufacturing sector).

During the Industrial Revolution, much of the UK's growth was centred on the northern coalfields. Heavy industries and engineering thrived in the cities and a great deal of wealth was generated. However, since de-industrialisation in the 1970s, many industries in the North have closed and people have lost their jobs. In 2015, the Teesside Steelworks in Redcar closed with the loss of some 1,700 jobs (see Figure 5). This had a huge impact on the community and the economy of the region.

In the late twentieth and early twenty-first centuries, there was a big shift to jobs in the service or tertiary sector involving jobs in healthcare, offices, financial services and retailing. Most recently, the quaternary sector has developed with jobs in research, information technology and the media. Most of these jobs have been based in London and the South East. Today London is a world centre for financial services, media, research and the creative industries, and it has benefited hugely from globalisation and the interconnectivity with the rest of the world.

▲ **Figure 5** Redcar steelworks

Infrastructure

Infrastructure involves transport, services and communications. In recent years, London and the South East has benefited from a number of developments including:

- Channel Tunnel (1994)
- Expansion of airports, such as Stansted and the construction of new terminals, such as Terminal 5 at Heathrow (2008)
- High Speed 1 Eurostar trains operating from London St Pancras (2007).

In the future, there are several planned developments in transport including Crossrail and the construction of a new airport runway, probably at Heathrow.

Crossrail, Europe's largest construction project, is due to be completed in late 2018. Costing some £15 billion, the new 100 km rail route will run from Reading and Heathrow in the west to Shenfield and Abbey Wood in the east, passing through central London in a series of tunnels (see Figure 6). Linking London's key employment, leisure and entertainment districts, it will carry some 200 million passengers a year and will add an estimated £42 billion to the economy of the UK. It will support regeneration projects and cut journey times across the capital.

▲ **Figure 6** The Crossrail project in London

Government policy

The rapid growth of the private sector and the expansion of the service sector have tended to focus on growth in London and the South East. Many companies – both UK based and international – have chosen to be in London rather than elsewhere. Government investment in infrastructure projects such as Crossrail, the regeneration of London's docklands (from the 1980s onwards) and construction of the Olympic Site for 2012 have all promoted the economic growth of the South.

In 2015, the government announced plans to create a Northern Powerhouse of modern manufacturing industries specialising in science and technology across the major cities of the North. The aim is to redress the north–south economic imbalance, and to attract investment into northern cities and towns. Several transport improvements will support this initiative:

- HS2 (High Speed 2) is a £50 billion project to build a new high-speed railway line to connect London with Birmingham and then on to Sheffield, Leeds and Manchester. It may then be extended to Newcastle and into Scotland. The scheme, which is due to start in 2017 for completion in 2033, is controversial as the route passes through several stretches of highly valued countryside and close to many people's homes.
- Electrification of the Trans-Pennine Express Railway between Manchester and York by 2020, reducing journey times by up to 15 minutes and completing the electrified link between Liverpool and Newcastle.
- Electrification of the Midland Mainline between London and Sheffield by 2023.

Case study: the consequences of economic growth and/or decline for one place or region in the UK

Economic growth and decline: the story of Salford Quays, Manchester

Where is Salford Quays?

The city of Salford is located to the west of the city of Manchester, in the heart of northern England (see Figure 7). It is an inner-city urban environment and is home to some 200,000 people. This case study focuses on Salford Quays, a heavily industrialised dockland at the head of the Manchester Ship Canal. In this area, economic growth and decline have had significant economic, social and environmental consequences.

▲ **Figure 8** The Manchester Ship Canal, 1938

Early industrial growth

During the industrial revolution Manchester became a centre for the processing of cotton, imported from the USA. It soon developed thriving manufacturing and engineering sectors, specialising in the production of machines for factories. In 1894 the Manchester Ship Canal opened, enabling large ships to journey into the heart of the city from the River Mersey and the Irish Sea. At the head of the Manchester Ship Canal a massive 90 hectare complex of inland docks (Salford Quays) were constructed during the 1890s to accommodate the thriving trade (see Figure 8). Thousands of people were employed in the docks and a large community became established with homes, factories and shops.

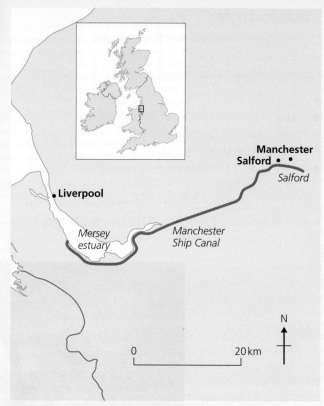
▲ **Figure 7** Location of Salford Quays and Manchester

Decline

In the 1960s and 1970s the larger container ships were unable to use the Manchester Ship Canal and rapid decline set in. Over 3,000 people lost their jobs and the docks finally closed in 1982. The land left behind was derelict and heavily contaminated. The surrounding housing areas had fallen into disrepair and there were significant social problems. There were high rates of unemployment and crime, and the whole area had become blighted and depressed (see Figure 9).

▲ **Figure 9** Derelict streets surrounding Salford Docks, 1981

Recent growth

In the mid-1980s funding from the UK's urban programme allowed reclamation of parts of the renamed Salford Quays for commercial office and residential use. While this led to some physical improvements, it provided few jobs for local people and still left large areas of land that were derelict. In 1985 the Salford Quays Development Plan was launched and since then several exciting projects have transformed the area into a thriving working and living environment.

During the past five years, massive investment has resulted in new homes, education and health facilities, new businesses and shops. There are city parks, cleansed waterways and green spaces.

One of the most ambitious and successful projects is the Lowry Building (see Figure 10). Completed in 2000 at a cost of £64 million, it is a distinctive metal and glass building that has become part of Manchester's skyline. Supported by National Lottery funding, the building houses an 1,800-seat theatre and several galleries, bars and cafés. It provides a permanent home for the paintings of local artist J.S. Lowry, after whom the building is named. A large external triangular plaza is regularly used for festivals and events. The surrounding basins have been reclaimed to create an attractive environment.

▲ **Figure 10** The Lowry Theatre, Imperial Point residential building and the Lowry footbridge

In 2007 the BBC moved five of its departments (BBC Children's, BBC Children's Learning, BBC Sport, BBC Radio Five Live, and parts of BBC Future Media and Technology) to a new development on Pier 9 called MediaCityUK (see Figure 11). The arrival of the BBC is expected to attract other media, broadcasting, and film-making companies to the area. Constructed at a cost of £550 million, MediaCityUK created 10,000 jobs and added an estimated £1 billion to the regional economy by 2013.

▲ **Figure 11** Aerial view of the BBC's MediaCityUK

There have been several residential developments in Salford Quays, including traditional low-rise flats and town houses in Grain Wharf and Merchants Quay. Some high-rise buildings have also been constructed to make use of the limited pier space.

Other developments in Salford Quays include:

- A £90 million retail and leisure facility called the Lowry Outlet
- The construction of the Imperial War Museum North
- In 1999, the construction of a new line of the city's light rapid transit (LRT)/tram system, Metrolink, linking Salford Quays with the centre of Manchester and beyond.

Salford City Council aims to establish Salford as a 'modern global city' by 2025, with Salford Quays being very much at the heart of its regeneration plans.

▲ **Figure 12** Aerial view of Salford Quays

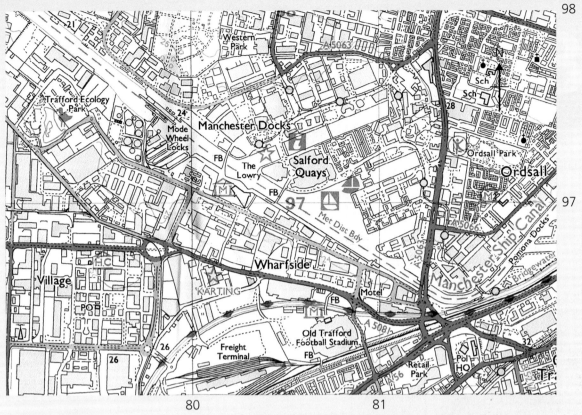

98

97

80   81

▲ **Figure 13** OS Explorer 1:25,000 map 277. © Crown copyright and/or database right. All rights reserved. Licence number 100036470

Activities

1. Study Figure 12, an aerial view of Salford Quays, and Figure 13, a 1:25,000 map extract of Salford Quays. The photo was taken from approximately 798974 looking east-southeast.

   a. Look at Figure 12. Which of the two footbridges is the Lowry Bridge? Use Figure 10 on page 53 to help you.

   b. What is the number of the road that crosses the Manchester Ship Canal in the distance?

   c. What is the name and function of the building labelled A? Use Figure 10 on page 53 to help you.

   d. Give the six-figure reference of footbridge B.

   e. Use the map to calculate the distance between the two footbridges. Give your answer to the nearest 100 m.

   f. What is the development at C? Use Figure 11 on page 53 to help you.

   g. Use Figure 13 to identify the public transport system that links the development at C with the city.

   h. What is the function of the building at D?

   i. What are the attractions of Salford Quay for tourists?

   j. How do you think the land at E should be developed in the future? Justify your answer.

   k. Use the photos and the map to suggest how the environment of Salford Quays has been improved to make it a more attractive area.

2. Complete a summary table using all the resources to describe the consequences of both economic growth and decline of Salford Quays. Consider economic, social and environmental consequences.

CHAPTER 8

The UK's changing population

Key idea: The UK's population is changing.

→ **In this chapter you will study:**

→ the changes in the UK's population structure from 1900 to the present day, including its changing position on the Demographic Transition Model

→ the causes and the effects of, and responses to, an ageing population

→ outline flows of immigration into the UK in the twenty-first century including an overview of the social and economic impacts on the UK.

Measuring population – the census

The population of a country is measured by a survey called a census. In most countries of the world, including the UK, a census is carried out every ten years. The most recent UK census took place on 27 March 2011.

The UK census, run separately by the Office for National Statistics (England and Wales), National Records of Scotland and the Northern Ireland Statistics & Research Agency, paints a picture of the nation and how we live (see Figure 1). It provides a valuable snapshot of the population and its characteristics, helping the government to plan funding and public services for the future (see Figure 3).

UK area	Population (million)	Percentage
England and Wales	53	84
Scotland	5.3	8
Wales	3.1	5
Northern Ireland	1.8	3
Total	63.2	100

▲ **Figure 1** UK Population 2011

Year	UK population (million)
1901	38.2
1911	42.1
1921	44.0
1931	46.0
1951	50.2
1961	52.7
1971	55.9
1981	56.4
1991	57.4
2001	59.1
2011	63.2
2021	67.6 (projected)

▲ **Figure 2** Population of the UK (million)

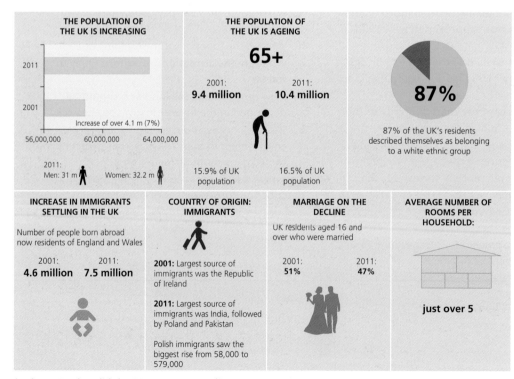

▲ **Figure 3** What did the 2011 UK census discover?

The UK's population structure

The breakdown of a population by age and sex is called the **population structure**. It is commonly illustrated by a diagram called a **population pyramid**. Bars are drawn to represent each five-year age band. The length of each bar relates to the number of people of that age in the population. Bars are drawn for both males and females.

Look at Figure 4. It shows the most recent population pyramid for the UK based on information from the 2011 census. Notice that there is an outline for 2001 to show how it has changed.

Population pyramids can be used to see trends in the population, such as declining birth rates or increases in the numbers of elderly people. These trends provide useful information for the government in helping to plan for future education, housing, employment and healthcare.

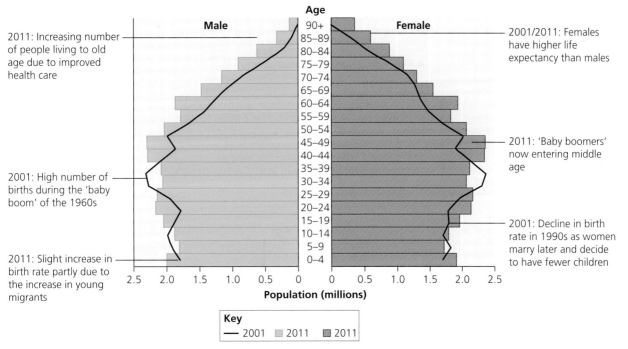

2011: Increasing number of people living to old age due to improved health care

2001: High number of births during the 'baby boom' of the 1960s

2011: Slight increase in birth rate partly due to the increase in young migrants

2001/2011: Females have higher life expectancy than males

2011: 'Baby boomers' now entering middle age

2001: Decline in birth rate in 1990s as women marry later and decide to have fewer children

Key
— 2001   ▨ 2011   ▨ 2011

▲ **Figure 4** Population pyramid for the UK, 2001–11

⚥ Geographical skills

Use the data in Figure 1 to produce a pie chart to show the population of the countries of the United Kingdom. To find the degrees, you will need to multiply by the final column by 3.6. Use colours to show each country and include a key.

Activities

1. Use the data in Figure 2 to draw a line graph to show the UK's population (1901-2021). Write a short description of the pattern of population growth.
2. Study Figure 4.
   a. What is a population pyramid?
   b. Identify three changes that have taken place between 2001 and 2011.
   c. Do you think the government should plan for more primary school places? Why?
   d. Is the government right to be concerned about growing numbers of pensioners in the future?
   e. Is the death rate likely to increase in the near future? Why?
   f. Why might there be a shortage of labour in the UK in 2021?

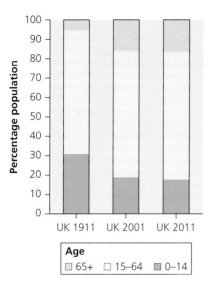

▲ **Figure 5** Divided bar graph showing the UK's population structure, 1911–2011

Activities

1. Study the information in Figure 5. Describe the trends in the UK's population structure from 1911–2011.

Changes in the UK's population structure since 1900

In 1900, the population of the UK was about 42 million and 30 per cent of people lived in the countryside, mostly engaged with farming. Farming was starting to become mechanised and increasing numbers of people were moving to work in factories in towns and cities.

Look at Figure 5. Notice that in 1911 about 30 per cent of the UK's population was aged 0–14 years. This high proportion of children reflected a relatively high birth rate. Children were needed to support the family – particularly those living in the countryside engaged with farming. Few women had careers at the time and contraception was not widely used. Relatively few people lived to old age due mainly to limited heathcare.

Age group	1911	2001	2011
0–14	30.8%	18.8%	17.6%
15–64	63.8%	65.4%	66%
65+	5.3%	15.9%	16.4%

▲ **Figure 6** UK's population structure, 1911–2011

Look at Figure 7. The population pyramid of 1921 clearly shows the bulk of the UK's population is towards the base. Notice, however, that the number of births is beginning to decline as the bars are becoming narrower towards the bottom. Notice the dip for men aged 20–30. This reflects the high death toll during the First World War. See how few people are living into old age.

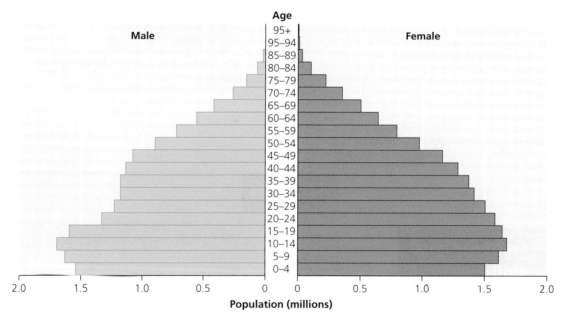

▲ **Figure 7** UK's population pyramid, 1921

By 1951 (see Figure 8), the structure of the UK's population was starting to change.

- The youthful population 'bulge' in 1921 had moved up the pyramid to become middle aged
- More people are now living into old age
- After a period of declining births, there is a sudden increase – this continues into the early 1960s and has become known as the 'baby-boomer generation'.
- By 1991, the 'baby boomers' were now aged 30–40 years. You can clearly see this bulge in the pyramid (see Figure 9). Births are generally low and steady. Women are now following careers and choosing to have smaller families later in life. The number of older people is continuing to increase, reflecting higher standards of living and high quality medical care.
- These trends have continued through to 2001 and 2011 (see Figure 4, page 57). Birth rate remains low and steady, the 'baby boomers' have moved into late middle age and the number of older people remains high and growing. Average life expectancy is now well into the 80s.

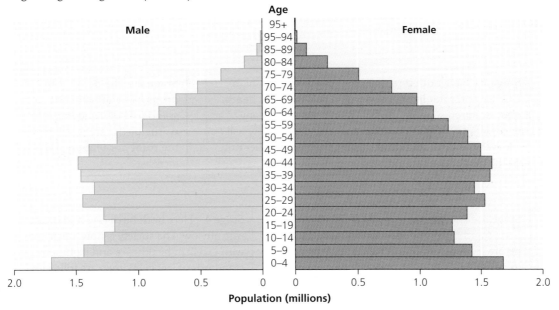

▲ **Figure 8** UK's population pyramid, 1951

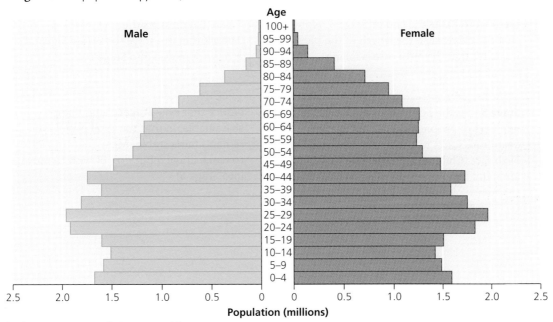

▲ **Figure 9** UK's population pyramid, 1991

The Demographic Transition Model

Look at Figure 10. It is a graph called the **Demographic Transition Model**. It shows changes in the population of the UK since 1700. Notice that there are three lines on the graph:

- birth rate – the number of live births per 1,000 of the population per year
- death rate – the number of deaths per 1,000 of the population per year
- total population – this is the total population of the country.

The difference between the birth rate and the death rate is called the **natural increase**. This is usually expressed as a percentage. Notice that the natural increase is shaded on the graph between the birth rate line and the death rate line.

The total population of a country is the natural increase +/- migration. In the UK migration has contributed quite a lot to the growth of the population.

Notice that the Demographic Transition Model can be divided into a number of stages. These can be related directly to changes in the UK's population structure.

Stage 1 – Here both birth rate and death rate are high. Disease and poor living standards result in a high death rate. Children support the family and, because many die in infancy, lots are born to guarantee that a few will survive. The birth and death rates cancel each other out, so the total population does not grow much.

Stage 2 – The death rate drops as healthcare and standards of living improve. As the birth rate is still high, the total population starts to increase.

Stage 3 – The birth rate declines during this period and the death rate continues to fall before levelling off. Infant mortality falls due to better healthcare, so fewer children need to be born. Women are being educated and are choosing to have fewer children. The total population continues to grow but starts to slow down. The population pyramid for 1921 (see Figure 7) fits the end of Stage 3. Notice that the decrease in the length of the bars indicates that the birth rate is falling.

Stage 4 – Here both birth rate and death rate are low. The society is now advanced with excellent healthcare and high standards of living. Women are following careers and choosing to have fewer children. Contraceptives are widely available. Infant mortality rates are very low. People are living longer. The total population levels off. Figure 8 represents the start of this period. The UK is in this stage today (see Figure 4). It has not moved into Stage 5.

Stage 5 – As the population ages, with large numbers of people reaching old age, the death rate starts to become higher than the birth rate. Children are expensive to look after and families are deciding to have fewer children.

Notice that only Stages 1 and 4 are sustainable, in that the total population remains fairly stable. Most countries strive to reach Stage 4 but do not wish to move into Stage 5!

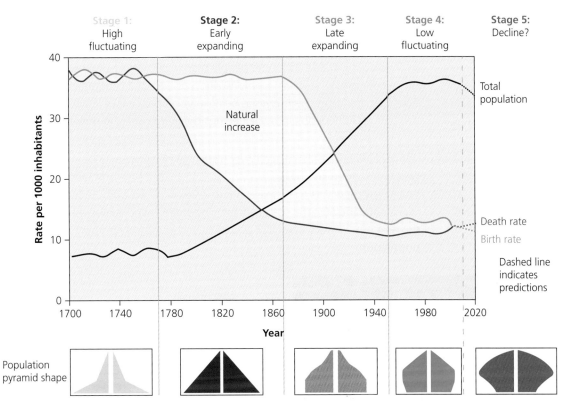

▲ **Figure 10** The Demographic Transition Model

Activities

1. Study Figure 10, which shows the Demographic Transition Model.
   a. Make a careful copy of Figure 10. Use separate colours to show the different parts for the graph.
   b. Add the following labels in their correct places.
      ● High death rate due to disease, poor healthcare and low standards of living.
      ● High birth rate due to high infant mortality and poor healthcare.
      ● Death rate falls as healthcare and standards of living improve.
      ● Birth rate falls as infant mortality drops.
      ● Total population increases rapidly.
      ● Low birth rate as women choose to have fewer children.
      ● Death rate starts to rise due to an ageing population.
      ● Total population levels off.
2. Study Figure 10 and the population pyramids (see Figures 4, 7–9).
   a. Suggest why the pyramid in Figure 7 belongs to Stage 3 of the Demographic Transition Model.
   b. Why does Figure 8 represent the start of Stage 4?
   c. How would the population pyramid for 2011 (see Figure 4) be different if the UK had entered Stage 5 of the Demographic Transition Model?

Ageing population in the UK

In 2011, 9.2 million people (16 per cent of the UK's population) were aged over 65. This is almost a million more people than in 2001. In England and Wales, of those people over 65 in 2011, only 10 per cent were still economically active. Over half described themselves as being in good health (see Figure 11). Some 14 per cent of older people provide free healthcare to others in their households.

Look back to the UK's population pyramid in Figure 4. Notice that the number of people (length of bars) aged over 65 increased between 2001 and 2011. Just below this group are the people who were born just after the Second World War when there was an increase in births. Below them is a bulge of people in their 40s and 50s (the so-called 'baby boomers') who will be turning 65 in the next 10–20 years. The UK is gradually becoming a country with an **ageing population**.

▲ **Figure 11** Older people in good health

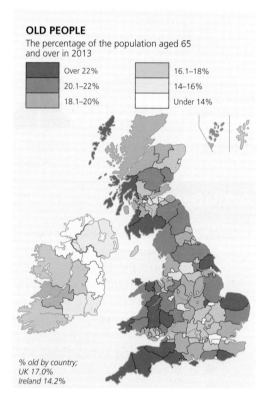

OLD PEOPLE
The percentage of the population aged 65 and over in 2013

Over 22%	16.1–18%
20.1–22%	14–16%
18.1–20%	Under 14%

% old by country;
UK 17.0%
Ireland 14.2%

▲ **Figure 12** Distribution of pensioners in the UK and Ireland, 2010

Activities

1. Study Figure 12, which shows the distribution of pensioners in the UK. It shows that elderly people are concentrated in certain parts of the UK.

   a. On a blank outline map of the UK, draw the high concentrations of elderly people (over 22 per cent).

   b. Use an atlas to locate some towns within these areas.

   c. Describe the distribution of the high concentrations of elderly people.

   d. Why do you think there are such high concentrations along the south coast of England?

   e. How might high concentrations of elderly people create challenges for local authorities?

▲ **Figure 13** Caring for the elderly

An ageing population – challenges and opportunities

An ageing population does present many challenges. Elderly people have greater medical needs and the costs of looking after them will increase in the future. They will need increasing amounts of care to enable them to stay in their own homes (see Figure 13). Their children – in middle age – will increasingly be responsible for their care.

However, an ageing population brings with it huge amounts of wisdom and compassion for others. Many older people give up their time to work as volunteers in the community and some continue to work in paid employment. Many newly retired people enjoy good health and have money to spend on travel, home improvements and hobbies such as gardening. Several businesses specialise in providing services for older people.

Causes	Effects	Responses
• The main reason is that a large number of people born after the Second World War and through into the 1960s ('baby boomers') are now moving into old age • Improved healthcare and new treatments prolong life, especially from diseases such as cancer and heart conditions • Reductions in smoking, which caused a huge early death toll in the past • Greater awareness of the benefits of a good diet • People living more active lives and benefiting from regular exercise • Many older people are reasonably well off financially so can afford a reasonable standard of life.	• Healthcare costs are very high and will increase as the elderly require support services and expensive treatments • Shortages of places in care homes, many of which are expensive • Many older people are looked after by their middle-aged children, often affecting their lives and their ability to remain in full-time employment • Older people are valued employees as they have high standards and are reliable • Older people act as volunteers in hospitals, advice centres, food banks, etc. • Many older people are keen to travel and to join clubs, societies, sports centres, etc. This helps to boost the economy and provide jobs.	• Government-issued pensioner bonds in 2015 to encourage older people to save money for the future • Pensioners receive support in the form of care, reduced transport costs and heating allowances (winter fuel payments), which is expensive for the government. This may be withdrawn from wealthy pensioners in the future. • Retirement age, which used to be 65, is being phased out to encourage people to continue working • State pension age is gradually being increased to 67 • The government could encourage people to take out private health insurance to cut NHS costs • Pronatalist policies to encourage an increase in birth rate to balance the population structure. This could include cheaper childcare, improved maternity and paternity leave and higher child benefit payments • Allowing more immigration would also address the need for a larger young workforce and higher birth rate, but this is controversial.

▲ **Figure 14** The UK's ageing population – causes, effects and responses

Activities

1. Study Figure 14.
   a. Look back to the UK's population pyramid (see Figure 4, page 57) and explain why the UK's population is ageing.
   b. What health and lifestyle changes are responsible for people living longer today than in the past?
   c. Choose **one** 'Effect' from Figure 14 and explain why an ageing population can cause problems for the country.
   d. Now choose **one** 'Effect' and explain why an ageing population can bring **benefits**.
   e. What 'Responses' are the government making to try to cut the costs of an ageing population?
   f. What are 'pronatal policies'? How can they help to balance the structure of the UK's population?
   g. How could more immigration help to balance the UK's population structure?
   h. Should the government encourage more immigration? Explain your answer.

→ Take it further

2. Work in pairs for this activity.
   a. Use the internet to obtain a selection of photos showing some challenges and opportunities associated with an ageing population in the UK.
   b. Use your photos, together with some text boxes, to produce a poster divided into two halves; challenges and opportunities.
   c. Give your poster a title 'Challenges and Opportunities of an Ageing Population in the UK'.

Immigration into the UK in the twenty-first century

Who are immigrants?

People have always migrated to the UK – they are called **immigrants**.
Emigrants are people who move out of a country. The UK has a diverse cultural
heritage. In the twentieth century, the UK welcomed people migrating from the
Caribbean and from India, Pakistan and Bangladesh. In the twenty-first century,
the UK has welcomed people migrating from other parts of Europe, Asia and
from war-torn countries such as Iraq, Afghanistan and Syria (see Figure 15).

▲ **Figure 15** Iraqi immigrants seeking asylum

Story of an immigrant

Hande (not her real name) escaped from her abusive
father in Istanbul, Turkey, when she was just 17. She
made her way to Paris where she got a good job and
rented a flat.

'During holidays in England I met the father of my three
children. It was a huge surprise when I found out I was
pregnant with my first child and I had no idea what to
do. I decided to stay in London. I wanted the baby to
grow up with the father and his family as I did not have
a family myself.

'We got married and went on to have three beautiful
and amazing children. They were born here and they are
British. I have not put them on a Turkish passport as I
still have nightmares about my father finding me and my
children. I have been working and paying taxes for years
and brought my three children up as a single mother
until my youngest child Hope got killed by a 18-ton
heavy goods vehicle on her way back from school.

'I did not come here for money or benefits; safety and
freedom were my main concerns. I am forever grateful
that I have had the opportunity to become a free citizen
who is entitled to a normal life. Bringing up our children
in a free country is priceless.'

What are the recent trends in immigration?

Look at Figure 16. It shows the recent trends in immigration and emigration. In the year to March 2015, net migration (the difference between immigration and emigration) reached 330,000, an all-time high. This was more than three times the government target.

One reason for the high level of net migration is a reduction in people wishing to leave the UK (emigration). However, the main cause has been the very large number of people wanting to enter the UK.

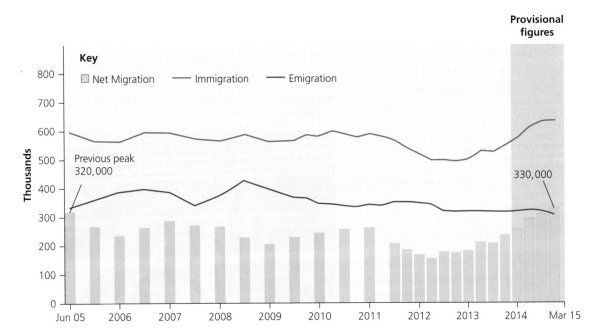

▲ **Figure 16** Long-term international migration to the UK, 2005–15

Why do people come to the UK?

Look at Figure 17. It shows the reasons why people have migrated to the UK. In the year to March 2015, net migration of EU citizens was 183,000. Most of these were seeking work, while others were students or wished to join family. About half of the migrants from outside the UK were students.

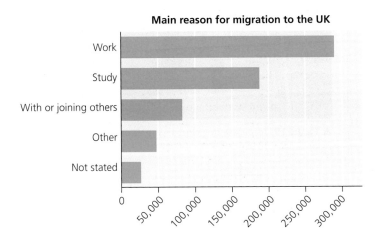

▲ **Figure 17** Migration to the UK, year ending March 2015

Activities

1. Study Figure 16.
   a. Describe the trend in immigration.
   b. With reference to immigration and emigration, explain why the net migration reached an all-time high in March 2015.
   c. What is the evidence from Figure 16 that net migration may start to fall soon?

Where do people come from?

Look at Figure 18. It shows recent trends in the countries of origin for migrants to the UK.

- Many immigrants continue to come from India and Pakistan, many seeking to join family who are already in the UK.
- Recently a large number of people from Poland have decided to move to the UK in search of better wages and improved opportunities.
- A considerable number of people have come to the UK from other European countries. Free movement is allowed within the EU to date.
- Migrants have arrived from across the world, including Africa, Asia, the USA and the Caribbean. Several countries are former colonial countries and current members of the Commonwealth.

In the year ending March 2015, the highest numbers of migrants from outside the EU were from China. From within the EU, large numbers migrated from Romania and Bulgaria, two of the poorest and most recent countries to join the EU.

In the past few years an increasing number of people have arrived from war-torn countries, such as Syria and Afghanistan. They are seeking asylum (safety) fearing for their lives if they return to their countries of origin. In the year to June 2015, the UK received over 25,000 asylum applications, an increase of 10 per cent on the previous year. Some people have resorted to desperate measures to reach the UK (see Figure 19).

2011 rank	Country of birth	2001 Census	2011 Census
1	India	456,000	694,000
2	Poland	58,000	579,000
3	Pakistan	308,000	482,000
4	Republic of Ireland	473,000	407,000
5	Germany	244,000	274,000
6	Bangladesh	153,000	212,000
7	Nigeria	87,000	191,000
8	South Africa	132,000	191,000
9	United States	144,000	177,000
10	Jamaica	146,000	160,000

▲ **Figure 18** Top ten countries for non-UK born residents in England and Wales, 2001 and 2011

▲ **Figure 19** Desperate migrants trying to catch a train to the UK from Calais, 2015

Activities

1. Study Figure 18, which shows the top ten countries for non-UK residents in 2001 and 2011.
   a. Draw a series of parallel bars to represent the data. For each country, draw two bars side by side to show the numbers for 2001 and 2011. Use two different colours to shade each bar. Do this for each of the ten countries to give you 20 bars in total.
   b. Which country has experienced the greatest growth between 2001 and 2011?
   c. Which other countries have shown a significant increase?
   d. Which country has experienced a fall?

→ Take it further

2. Use the internet to try to find out why there has been a big increase in migration from Poland and Nigeria.

What are the social and economic impacts of immigration on the UK?

Since the last census in 2011, immigration has become a very controversial issue. It was one of the main issues in the 2015 general election with people expressing very different views on the advantages and disadvantages of mass immigration (see Figure 20).

	Advantages	Disadvantages
Social	Introduction of different cultures including foods, music and fashion Immigrants bring skills that may be in short supply within the UK Immigrants are often keen to engage with local communities.	May be some tensions with local people or other ethnic groups May be some bad feeling about housing shortages leading to social unrest Some people feel that the UK is already overcrowded and that too many immigrants will lead to increased urban pollution and congestion.
Economic	Workers pay taxes to the government – the majority of immigrants work – more money is paid in taxes than received in benefits Immigrants often take low-paid jobs in farming, factories or support services such as cleaning. Semi-skilled workers have filled gaps in decorating and plumbing as well as working as nurses Some immigrants are well educated and highly trained Those immigrants who study in the UK pay a considerable amount to colleges and universities.	Extra costs for healthcare, education and social services House prices and rents may increase as demand outstrips supply Money may be sent home by immigrants so does not get spent in the UK Some people think that migrants are 'taking our jobs' and increasing unemployment – there is, however, no real evidence that immigration is linked to unemployment.

▲ **Figure 20** Advantages and disadvantages of immigration

Activities

1. Look back to Figure 4 (page 57). Suggest how recent migration has affected the shape of the UK's population pyramid in 2011.

→ Take it further

2. Access the interactive ONS website at www.ons.gov.uk/ons/interactive/census-3-1---country-of-birth/index.html to discover the population structure for immigrants to the UK. Compare the population structures for Poland, Ireland and India. Find out which countries have younger profiles and which ones have older profiles.

3. What are the arguments in favour and against allowing immigration to continue? Use the internet to help you research this question.

4. Use the internet to find an immigration story involving someone who has recently moved to the UK. Find out why the person has moved to the UK and what their experience has been like.

CHAPTER

9

Urban trends in the UK

Key idea: There are causes for and consequences of urban trends in the UK.

➜ **In this chapter you will study:**

➜ an overview of the causes for contrasting urban trends in the UK, including suburbanisation, counter-urbanisation and re-urbanisation

➜ an outline of the social, economic and environmental consequences of contrasting urban trends in the UK, including suburbanisation, counter-urbanisation and re-urbanisation.

👣 Fieldwork ideas

If your school is in an urban area, think about your journey to school and the changes that you may have noticed during your time at the school. Map the changes that have taken place, and keep an eye on local newspapers for proposed future plans.

The causes and consequences of different urban trends in the UK

There are a number of changes which take place in cities over time, including suburbanisation, counter-urbanisation and re-urbanisation.

What are the causes and consequences of suburbanisation?

Suburbanisation is the spread of cities outwards and the development of new residential areas. These areas are connected back to the city centre, but are distanced physically from it. Traditionally, they lie beyond the industrial and commercial activity of the city and the inner city housing which serviced that. The UK has a large and growing population and there are housing shortages. In recent years, land prices and property prices have risen sharply, particularly in London and the South. As land is cheaper in the suburbs, housing and commercial developments have been built there. Improvements in transport infrastructure, such as the London underground, as well as increasing trends for people to work from home have meant it is easier for commuters to live in the suburbs while working in the city.

In Newcastle upon Tyne, a new suburb is under development called Newcastle Great Park. It is in North Newcastle, four miles north of the city centre and has been built on the city's **green belt** as the government gave permission for the development to go ahead. It consists of a new housing development of 2,500 new homes and, as people moved in, services such as a supermarket, cafes, hotels and leisure facilities. It is also home to the headquarters of the software company Sage Group. It is situated on the A1, with nearby Metro stations and park and ride services into Newcastle's city centre. More housing is planned for the future increasing to 3,000 by 2030 and over 4,000 beyond 2030.

Suburbanisation has enabled more people to benefit from living in a particular city, even though in reality they may be separated from it by miles of sprawl and face long commutes on crowded highways to reach their place of employment. Cities such as this also place large demands on resources, particularly water. Another consequence is poor air quality caused by the large number of vehicles on the roads.

What are the causes and consequences of counter-urbanisation?

Counter-urbanisation refers to the movement of people from urban areas (back) into rural areas, particularly where those people had originally moved to the city. It is against the established pattern of movement, which has driven the growth of cities for the last few decades.

There has been an increase in the movement of people out towards the suburbs, and a 'hollowing out' of the central areas. This leads to decentralisation of people, employment and services towards the edges of urban areas. People who are moving out are often looking for a more peaceful place to live and perhaps to raise a family. They believe that crime rates may be lower and the cost of living less than in the city. People are encouraged to do this by improvements in the speed of rail links. Counter-urbanisation extends the usual urbanisation process beyond the city area and into smaller urban centres which are usually within commuting distance of the main centre as a result.

What are the key drivers of counter-urbanisation?

The people who move out of cities tend to be those who can afford to: the most affluent and also the most mobile. They are often those with young children, who have a notion that the countryside may be a 'better place' to bring them up. They may be driven out by traffic congestion, the higher cost of living, crime (or the perception of crime), the poor air quality, which might impact on their health, the dream of a rural idyll, or the marketing of estate agents and property companies, fostered by media. Deprivation scores vary across cities, but there are often clusters where multiple problems occur.

These demographic changes may continue to alter the character of the rural fringes of large cities for some time to come, particularly when there is a major difference in the price of property. An ageing population also means that there are more people reaching retirement and searching for a peaceful place to live. The designation of land around major UK cities as green belt land (see Figure 1) means that building is restricted in these areas, so developers sometimes leap-frog these areas and produce a new ring of developments further out.

Another trend is the migration of offices due to high costs of office space in London. Business and science parks often seek out-of-town locations, so that their workers can have a better quality of life and costs of land purchase are reduced.

There are two key trends in this movement. The first is a movement of employees out to rural areas. In many ACs, new industries have developed which are free to locate where they choose. The growth in the number of people who can work from home has also fuelled a demand for high-speed broadband for rural areas (see Figure 13, page 47). Businesses are realising the benefits of home-working. Software can log activity, so staff can still be monitored during working hours. Broadband internet is vital for industries to develop in many ACs, and this has improved, as has the use of mobile devices to maintain connectivity through VOIP services such as Skype. This is partly through the work of campaign groups who try to persuade companies to invest in rural broadband.

The second trend has been for people to live in the rural areas, but continue to commute back into the city for work. This has placed pressure on suburban rail services which are seeing an increase in passenger numbers. Ticket prices are particularly high on these lines as people have no choice but to use them to travel to work.

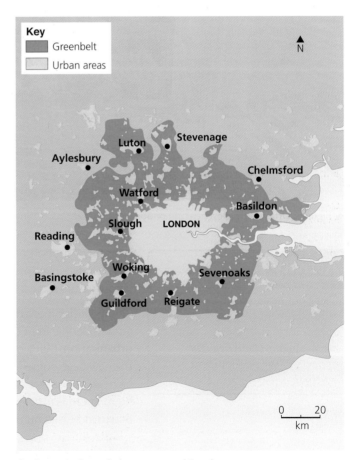

▲ **Figure 1:** Green belt area around London

What are the consequences of counter-urbanisation?

Counter-urbanisation results in 'dormitory villages', where many residents work in the city, but desire a more rural lifestyle. It has also led to changes in the character of villages which are just outside large urban areas. House prices in these locations have increased in recent years. Places such as Hemel Hempstead, for example, are benefiting from their relative proximity to London. Similarly, there has been a recent rise in property prices in Bury St Edmunds because of the access it offers to Cambridge via rail.

Not all of this change has been welcomed by longer-term residents, who fear that the character of these settlements is changing. Some areas are also changing as a result of gentrification: properties are bought and renovated by middle-class or wealthier people; this raises the profile of the area and causes property prices to rise. This can result in local people being priced out of the housing market.

What are the causes and consequences of re-urbanisation?

In 2015, London's population reached 8.6 million. This is the highest it has ever been and surpasses its previous peak in the 1950s (see Figure 2). This surprised some people, but was a sign that people are returning to live in the city and particularly in the inner city areas.

In many cities in AC countries there have been government initiatives to counter some of the problems created by inner city decline. These have often targeted the more deprived areas in the city for additional investment to support the growth of industry which might otherwise struggle to attract investment. Firms are paid a premium for new jobs created in these areas and are given other incentives to locate there. The EU has also offered a range of financial support through the years that the UK has been a member. This has included investment funds, support for new employment and support for infrastructure projects which draw in industry.

▲ **Figure 2** Urban redevelopment in London

This redevelopment of inner urban areas creates new homes and jobs, which attracts people from outside of the area to move in. This process is called **re-urbanisation**. Many of the people who move into these areas are pleased with the new developments, as are visitors and local government, however there can be negative aspects if developments are not well planned. A lack of affordable housing can lead to expensive apartments ending up empty. Traffic congestion due to increased numbers of residents can also be a problem.

Activity

Carry out research into a redevelopment of a rundown area in your local town or city. What are the positive and negative impacts of the development scheme?

CHAPTER

10

Leeds: a major city in the UK

Key idea: Cities have distinct challenges and ways of life, influenced by its people, cultures and geography.

➔ **In this chapter you will study:**

➔ a case study of Leeds, a major city in the UK, including the influences of: the city within its region, the country and the wider world; migration (national and international) and its impact on the city's growth and character; the ways of life within the city, such as culture, ethnicity, housing, leisure and consumption; contemporary challenges that affect urban change, including housing availability, transport provision and waste management; sustainable strategies to overcome one of the city's challenges.

Leeds is a city which has a long history of industry, but has had to reinvent itself as the traditional employment base has declined.

The city's location and importance

The city has a well-developed transport infrastructure and lies at the heart of a complex of motorways including the M1 (which connects it to London) and the M62 (a major east–west artery), along with major roads which connect it to other parts of the country. The city is well served by rail links, with a travel time to London of just over two hours. It has a canal and waterway network, as well as an international airport at Leeds–Bradford.

Leeds is the major city in West Yorkshire and lies at the heart of a conurbation which also includes cities such as Bradford and Huddersfield. It is the largest city in the Yorkshire and Humber region, which lies in the north of England.

It is the second largest metropolitan district in England behind Birmingham and covers an area of over 200 square miles in total.

The city's population is estimated at around 800,000 people, a rise of around 10 per cent in the last decade. This provides a large number of consumers as well as potential employees.

Leeds' economy has performed well in recent years and the city has not suffered as much as some nearby towns and cities, such as Hull and Bradford. It has succeeded in attracting investment and creating private-sector jobs.

Leeds acts as a shopping destination for the north of England and also has several major universities and the associated research activity that goes with them.

Culturally, Leeds is a centre for the arts, with a number of galleries and music venues. The football team has not enjoyed success recently, but was previously one of the top teams in the country.

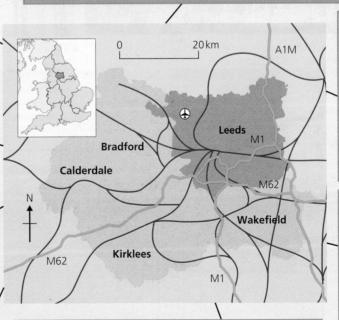

Internationally, Leeds has attracted interest through global connections between clothing firms and outsourced factories. There are good export links, with many of the firms operating within the city.

▲ **Figure 1** Location of Leeds.

How Leeds developed?

Leeds started out as a Saxon village, but grew quickly in medieval times, when many main roads that still exist today were named and set out. The early wealth of the city came from the wool industry. Wool from sheep grazing in Yorkshire and beyond was woven and dyed in the city. By the seventeenth century, the city was growing along the course of the River Aire, with markets and other trades moving in. Leeds was fought over during the English Civil War in 1643. As time passed, the textile industry was joined by pottery, brick making and various craft industries. The Leeds–Liverpool canal was completed in 1816, providing a route to and from the coast. The city grew to a population of 100,000 by 1850, at which time the railway arrived. The impressive Town Hall was built in 1858 (see Figure 2).

▲ **Figure 2** Leeds Town Hall

▲ **Figure 3** Shopping in Leeds

▲ **Figure 4** Civic Hall and Nelson Mandela Gardens in Leeds

The patterns of national and international migration in and out of the city

Leeds has grown in size in recent years as a result of new arrivals into the city as well as natural increase from its existing population (see Figure 5). Around 17 per cent of the city's population is from black and ethnic minority communities. The non-British population is higher than the average for the region. Those residents who are non-UK born tend to settle in the Gipton and Harehills wards of the city.

There was an influx of migrants, including 'new commonwealth' immigrants from the Caribbean, during the 1950s. Leeds claims to have the oldest Caribbean community in the UK, settling in areas like Harehills. The city has a West Indian carnival every year. Pakistan and India were also well represented at this time by a further influx.

Leeds has a large Irish community too, dating back to the early nineteenth century. The Irish settled in an area called 'the Bank' until the early twentieth century, when slum clearances forced the communities to disperse across the city. There was a second wave of Irish arrivals in the mid-twentieth century, when they mostly found work in labouring and manufacturing jobs, taking the numbers of Irish migrants to over 30,000.

After the Second World War, the city welcomed Polish, Ukrainian and Hungarian refugees and these also moved into inner-city Leeds. The extension of the EU in 2004 led to many new arrivals from countries such as Lithuania and Poland, although not in the same numbers as the previous arrivals. In 2013, the ONS estimated there were between 6000 and 9000 new long-term immigrants into the city, with net migration to the city of around 1700 in total.

The impacts of immigration on the character of the city

The character of the city is diverse as a result of these different groups. One large group of people is the student population, which numbers over 30,000, along with over 7000 staff at the University of Leeds, one of two universities in the city. These young people produce a great demand for housing stock and they are important for the local economy. The city has responded by providing a wealth of entertainment and food options, particularly close to the university, which can be recognised by the famous Parkinson building (see Figure 7). Around 18 per cent of the population of the city are aged 15 and under, compared with around 15 per cent for those aged over 65.

Year	Population
1801	94,421
1811	108,459
1821	137,476
1831	183,015
1841	222,189
1851	249,992
1861	311,197
1871	372,402
1881	433,607
1891	503,493
1901	552,479
1911	606,250
1921	625,854
1931	646,119
1941	668,667
1951	692,003
1961	715,260
1971	739,401
1981	696,732
1991	716,760
2001	715,404
2011	751,500

▲ **Figure 5** Population growth of Leeds

Ethnicity	Percentage of Population
White	85%
Mixed race	2.7%
Asian	7.7%
Black	3.5%
Arab	0.5%
other	0.6%

▲ **Figure 6** Ethnic mix of Leeds

▲ **Figure 7** The Parkinson building, University of Leeds

Leeds has a higher proportion of young people than the national average, which means that the city has as many people under 16 as it does over 60 years old. This creates a demand for services which are relevant for these age groups. Many of the retail and entertainment businesses in the city centre sell clothing and products for teenagers and young adults. There is a thriving café culture and lots of nightlife (see Figures 9 and 10).

Leeds is a city which shows great diversity in its population, although around 89 per cent of the population were born in the UK (see Figure 8). Between 1991 and 2011, the ethnic minority population in Leeds doubled in size, to reach 15 per cent of the total population. The largest groups within this were Pakistani and Indian. Some ethnic minority groups struggle to earn highly paid work. The Pakistani group also shows more clustering, with a preference for living in the same areas of Leeds.

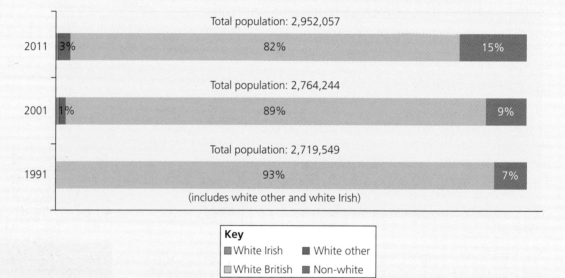

Key
- White Irish
- White other
- White British
- Non-white

▲ **Figure 8** Ethnic diversity in the Leeds City region

▲ **Figure 9** Cafe in Trinity Centre

▲ **Figure 10** Queens Arcade

What is life like for people in Leeds?

Leeds is very diverse with many different cultures, languages, faiths and races, and this is seen as one of the strengths of the city. There are, however, groups who may require additional support, such as help with the English language or with financial matters.

Leeds is already important for many industries, with companies such as the supermarket chain ASDA and the Danish food company ARLA having their headquarters there. There are also TV production companies and financial institutions. It has a well-developed digital infrastructure, which is attracting new businesses, as well as a rich industrial heritage. Many of the creative industries work from hubs, which are often based in old industrial buildings with attractive Victorian architecture. The supermarket founders Marks and Spencer opened their first penny arcade in Leeds in 1884, and grew from there to become a household name.

In 2014, the Tour de France cyclists lined up to start the first main stage of the famous race. Instead of France, they set out from Leeds, and were watched by millions of spectators lining the road and many more watching on television. This was part of a strategy by the Yorkshire tourism agency to raise the profile of the region. The city already attracts many visitors to its retail districts, such as the revamped Trinity Leeds mall (see Figure 11), but the Tour de France offered a chance for the city (and region) to sell itself on a global scale. Sport is also well represented in the city. Its football team and two rugby teams have enjoyed great success at the highest level. Leeds also has a cricket ground, which attracts test cricket, and is the 'home' of the county cricket team, Yorkshire.

The city sits close to the Yorkshire Dales and North York Moors National Park, and there are other Areas of Outstanding Natural Beauty (AONB) within a short distance of the city.

Leeds has been through a number of changes over the last decade and, like any city, is constantly evolving. New buildings are going up along the waterfront and in the canal basin. The city council plans to build new affordable housing to tackle some of the homelessness issues and bring in further investment. Redevelopment has already taken place on a large scale in some areas of the city, although not all of these developments currently have full occupancy. The city centre has changed dramatically over the last few decades. Taxi drivers in the city have to cope with regular changes to street patterns. Some businesses, such as nightclubs, even change their names at night or on different days of the week to provide a different experience for their young customers.

Major employers include the Leeds General Infirmary, which employs 7000 people, and local industries. The city makes a significant contribution to the country's economy (see Figure 12). It sits at the heart of a city region which has an economy worth over £50 billion and a workforce of over 1.4 million. Figure 12 shows that Leeds is the third most important urban area in this respect.

▲ **Figure 11** The Trinity Centre Leeds

Activities

1. Leeds comes third in terms of economic importance compared to London and Manchester. What industries have contributed to its position in Figure 12?
2. How can the city ensure it maintains this position?

	GVA, £ millions	GVA per head
Inner London	237,356	71,162
Greater Manchester South	38,645	25,950
Leeds	20,362	26,741
Greater Manchester North	17,620	14,375

* GVA measures the contribution to the economy of each individual producer, industry or sector in the UK

▲ **Figure 12** Leeds' economic importance

What challenges does Leeds face?

Leeds faces a series of challenges, many of which are common to all AC cities. The city has introduced a strategy called 'Leeds 2030' in which it proposes 'to be the best city in the UK' by this date. This strategy targets the major issues facing many large cities such as:

- affordability of housing
- unemployment, particularly among young people
- social inequality, including deprivation and poverty facing young people.

Most city councils have strategies for dealing with these issues, with varying degrees of success.

The city faces some environmental challenges, which include the quality of water in the city's rivers. There is also environmental monitoring of the air quality.

Is Leeds a divided city?

One issue that faces all AC cities is **social inequality**: the division between the wealthier and poorer residents. These residents are not necessarily divided by long distances; some of the more prosperous areas are located very close to areas going through tough times. The wealthy areas of Leeds include Moseley Wood and Cookridge. Gipton and Harehills are among those areas which have not shared in Leeds' prosperity and deprivation is ingrained. Some of these have a history of housing migrant arrivals. In Holbeck, over 15 per cent of residents were on Jobseekers' Allowance and similar benefits in 2015, whereas in Weatwood, the figure was just 0.2%.

Leeds is recovering well from the financial crisis of 2008, but not all communities share equally in the city's prosperity. A 2015 report by Cities Outlook showed that over 20 per cent of children in Leeds were living in poverty, including **fuel poverty**, particularly in the Leeds Central constituency. According to the same report, Leeds has the third highest levels of inequality of any city in the UK.

Edie

I can't recognise the city as it was when I was a young girl. A lot of the old buildings have gone and been replaced by modern ones.

Ruth

The shopping in Leeds is great now. The new arcades mean I don't even need to worry about the weather.

Dessy

The mix of people in Leeds has always been one of its strengths.

Luke

I'm struggling to find somewhere affordable to live, and yet there are quite a few new flats sitting empty which are outside of many people's price range.

Traci

It takes me quite a long time to travel into work these days.

▲ **Figure 13** What do residents think of Leeds as a city?

> ### Definitions
>
> **Child poverty:** in the UK child poverty is defined as living in a household with an income below 60 per cent of the national average (although this definition is under review).
>
> **Fuel poverty:** a situation in which spending money to heat your home would take you below the official poverty line, or if you have required fuel costs that are above average.

Studying the problem?

There are large student areas to the north of the city centre which are not necessarily struggling financially, but have been affected by a process called 'studentification' (see Figure 14). This means that the local community has been replaced by a student community. This is true of South Headingley and Hyde Park, where many rely on the private rented sector. This results in demographic imbalance, as well as rent and property price inflation. There will often be more pubs and takeaway restaurants in these areas, but the demand is seasonal, with quieter periods in the university holidays. Some work is provided, however, by the need for student property maintenance. Services such as schools are not needed to the level that one would expect. Crime levels in such areas can also be high, with offences ranging from theft of property to antisocial behaviour, such as noise.

Pride in the community and the fabric of housing tends to be reduced in these areas, so there can be a problem with blight. There are also problems with car parking, from 'Gridlock Sunday' (when students return for the start of the new term) onwards, as students look for places to park their cars without charge. Any streets within reasonable walking distance of the university will fill with cars, causing resentment among residents. Despite this, the students bring millions of pounds into the local economy and the universities are major employers.

▲ **Figure 14** Leeds University

▲ **Figure 15** Royal Armouries, Leeds

▲ **Figure 16** Anti-homeless spikes

Waste management

Every household in Leeds produces 590g of household waste per year, which equates to 166,100 tonnes of waste per year! In 2013, Leeds council recycled nearly 44% of their waste but introduced plans to reduce waste further and improve recycling. Waste and recycling is now collected every two weeks rather than weekly, and a new recycling facility was built in 2016, see www.veolia.co.uk/leeds. This uses modern technology to recover recyclable materials and energy from waste which would otherwise have gone to landfill sites.

In the past, there has been a lot of development along the river and the Leeds–Liverpool Canal. The Royal Armouries area was an area of development, associated with the move of a national museum to the city (see Figure 15). This has resulted in a number of new housing developments along the canal, sometimes in regenerated warehouses and wharfs. Some larger retail and cultural developments such as Trinity, Eastgate and Leeds Arena have been likened to 'enormous hoovers' which suck up any available investment at the expense of local businesses. This threatens to remove some of the original 'soul' of the city. There have also been calls for a better mass transportation system in Leeds than at present. Fares are rising and there is a need for a well-developed tram system which could reach more areas of the city.

In general, cities are becoming more, rather than less, unequal. House prices, employment and the quality of services are all changing dramatically, but cities are not homogenous. These differences are reflected in the algorithms used by insurance companies to provide quotes for car and house insurance based on postcodes. Policies can vary by hundreds of pounds depending on location within a city, sometimes for places just a few hundred metres apart.

Another trend has been the rise in gated communities, where the rich hide behind walls and gated security. At the same time, concrete 'anti-homeless spikes' discourage people from staying overnight near prestigious developments (see Figure 16), and many public spaces are becoming private property.

Activities

1. Explore the website of Leeds City Council (www.leeds.gov.uk) to see what is planned for the future.
   a. i. If you were a young person living in Leeds, what do you think might persuade you to stay in the city?
      ii. What challenges do you think might persuade you to leave the city?
   b. Do the same activity but for a different group. Choose from:
      - a recently retired person
      - an unemployed person
      - a newly arrived refugee
      - an investor looking for a location for a new start-up company.

What lies in the future for Leeds?

One word that crops up in a lot of official documents is the word 'sustainable'. For a city to be sustainable, it needs to provide people with a good quality of life in a way that is:

- socially
- economically
- environmentally sustainable.

This means that the quality of life that people enjoy today needs to be protected for future generations, but in such a way that it does not risk the health of the city. This is a challenge for any city, requiring investment in technologies and the promotion of lifestyle changes. A focus on primary healthcare, investment in renewable technology and money spent on improving public transport would all help. Leeds City Council is focusing on these and many other areas.

HS2 and Leeds

In 2014, the government announced that it was considering extending the planned HS2 (High Speed railway line, which was due to finish in Birmingham) as far as Leeds, which already has a reasonably fast service to the capital (see Figure 17). HS2 is planned to arrive

in the city in 2032. Although this is a long way off, the city is already considering the potential benefits of being part of what the government has called the 'Northern powerhouse'. This refers to the government's plans to invest in the cities which lie in the north of England as part of a plan to reduce the dominance of London in the economy. It is feared that if London starts to lose investment, the country's economy could suffer unduly.

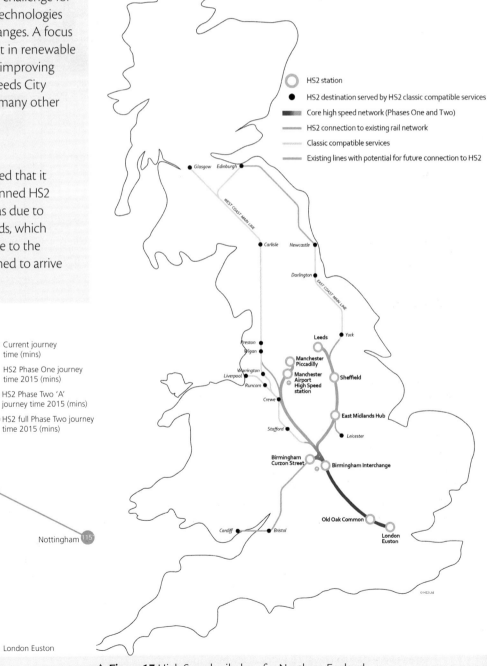

▲ **Figure 17** High Speed rail plans for Northern England

Leeds South Bank: a sustainable development?

Before the possible changes that HS2 might bring (which are some years away), there are major plans for an area called the South Bank of the city. This area is due to undergo the next major development in the city (see Figure 18).

▲ **Figure 18** Leeds South Bank development

Plans for the South Bank

→ A focus on infrastructure and investment, including a new HS2 station, which means that public transport is prioritised for residents

→ Retail, leisure, financial and professional services are supported

→ Incorporates previous developments at Royal Armouries

→ A cultural centre at the old Tetley brewery will support contemporary art

→ Educational improvements linked to Leeds City College, which will transform the former Alf Cooke Printworks into a vocational campus

→ Hub for new creative and digital industries

→ A new 3.5 hectare park and open space along the waterfront

→ Over 300,000 m² of development land available

→ Creation of Holbeck Urban Village: digital technology and living spaces close to the waterfront, which have won awards for their improvements in economic, social and physical environment

→ Developments will include former mills and the Temple Works

→ New pedestrian and cycle bridges will connect new open spaces to improve connectivity

→ Clarence Dock will become Leeds Dock, hoping to build on success of similar developments in cities such as Liverpool and Birmingham, providing entertainment and restaurants alongside retail developments

→ Water taxi and shuttle-bus services will connect the area to the station, and reduce carbon emissions

Activities

1. Take a look at the planned development for the South Bank in the information box above.
   a. How sustainable are these developments? Consider the three elements of sustainability. Try to give each one an overall rating.
   b. What are the costs and benefits of developments like this for the city?

→ Take it further

2. List the adjectives used to describe the Leeds South Bank project. How does the language of documents like this match the reality of living in a city like Leeds?

3. Use a house price website such as Zoopla or Rightmove to compare prices for similar houses in different Leeds possicode areas.

Assessing sustainability

In order for a development to be sustainable, we might expect it to meet certain conditions.

→ **Social sustainability:** measures in place to improve the quality of life and the way that people who live in the area interact

→ **Economic sustainability:** providing employment and training for residents, so that they don't have to leave the area every day to travel to work elsewhere in the city

→ **Environmental sustainability:** development needs to offer buildings which are energy efficient, with an eye to renewable energy, low emissions from activities and protection of local habitats

Practice questions

1. Describe the difference between 'imports' and 'exports'. **[1 mark]**

2. Study Figures 2a and 2b on page 39 that describe imports to the UK. Which of the following statements is *incorrect*?
   a) Imports from China are worth less than imports from the USA
   b) The value of imports from Germany has increased by £16bn
   c) Imports of road vehicles are worth about £17bn
   d) Apparel and clothing accessories are worth half as much as imports of petroleum and products. **[1 mark]**

3. Describe **two** recent trends in employment in the UK **[4 marks]**

4. Study Figure 4 on page 42. Describe the pattern of employment in manufacturing in the UK. **[4 marks]**

5. Study Figure 6 on page 43. Calculate the range of disposable incomes for London. **[1 mark]**

6. Study Figure 7 on page 44. To what extent does life expectancy illustrate a north-south divide in the UK? **[4 marks]**

7. Study Figure 9 on page 45. Which one of the following correctly ranks the regions shown in Figure 9 from highest to lowest for the *most deprived* students? **[1 mark]**

Highest %		Lowest %	
A London	Yorkshire and The Humber	North East	West Midlands
B South East	Yorkshire and The Humber	South West	East Midlands
C South West	North West	South East	East Midlands
D London	North West	East Midlands	East

Tips

- For question 4, describe the overall pattern using supporting information from the map, and refer to any anomalies.
- When you are doing calculations like the one in question 5, make sure you double-check your calculation to ensure you haven't made a mistake.

8. a) Define the term 'ethnicity'. **[1 mark]**
   b) Assess the advantages and disadvantages of increased ethnicity in UK cities such as London. **[4 marks]**

9. The term 'north-south divide' is used to describe uneven levels of development in the UK. Evaluate the causes of uneven development in the UK. **[6 marks]**

Tips

- For question 8 b), make sure your answer is balanced and that you refer to both advantages and disadvantages.
- For question 9, make sure that in evaluating you weigh up the relative importance of the various causes.

10. Evaluate the UK government's strategies aimed at overcoming regional imbalance. **[6 marks]**

11. With reference to a named case study (Salford Quays), describe the responses to economic decline and evaluate the level of success. **[6 marks]**

12. a) What is a 'census' **[1 mark]**
    b) State two reasons why a census is of value to a government planning for the future? **[2 marks]**

13. Study Figure 4 on page 57 which shows the UK's population structure.
    a) Describe the shape of the population pyramid for 2011. **[4 marks]**
    b) For males, explain the changes that have taken place between 2001 and 2011. **[4 marks]**
    c) Consider what the UK's population pyramid might look like in 2021. Draw a sketch to show the shape of the pyramid and use detailed annotations to explain the changes between 2011 and 2021. **[6 marks]**

14. Evaluate the challenges and opportunities of an ageing population. **[6 marks]**

15. a) Define the terms 'immigration' and 'emigration'. **[2 marks]**
    b) Why has the rate of immigration into the UK increased in recent years? **[4 marks]**
    c) Discuss the social impacts of immigration into the UK. **[6 marks]**

THEME UK Environmental Challenges

3

The UK faces many challenges through people's interaction with the physical environment and the use of resources. This theme investigates some of the environmental challenges faced by the UK. It explores extreme weather events in the UK, looking at the links between extreme weather and flooding. It investigates the factors affecting the UK's energy use and security, including the decision makers involved, as well as the issues of sustainability and management.

Chapter 11: Extreme weather in the UK

Key idea: The UK has a unique climate for its latitude which can create extreme weather conditions.

Key idea: Extreme flood hazard events are becoming more commonplace in the UK.

In this chapter you will study:

→ how air masses, the North Atlantic Drift and continentality influence the weather in the UK

→ how air masses cause extreme weather conditions in the UK, including extremes of wind, temperature and precipitation

→ a case study of flooding on the Somerset Levels including: causes of the flood event, including the extreme weather conditions which led to the event; effects of the flood event on people and the environment; the management of the flood event at a variety of scales.

Chapter 12: Resources and UK ecosystems

Key idea: Humans use, modify and change ecosystems and environments to obtain food, energy and water.

In this chapter you will study:

→ how environments and ecosystems in the UK are used and modified by humans, including: mechanisation of farming and commercial fishing to provide food; wind farms and fracking to provide energy; reservoirs and water transfer schemes to provide water.

Chapter 13: Energy sources in the UK

Key idea: There are a range of energy sources available to the UK.

In this chapter you will study:

→ renewable and non-renewable energy sources

→ the contribution of renewable and non-renewable sources to energy supply in the UK.

Chapter 14: Energy management

Key idea: Energy in the UK is affected by a number of factors and requires careful management and consideration of future supplies.

In this chapter you will study:

→ the changing patterns of energy supply and demand in the UK from 1950 to the present day, and how changes have been influenced by government decision making and international organisations

→ the strategies for sustainable use and management of energy at local and UK national scales, including the success of these strategies

→ the development of renewable energy in the UK and the impacts on people and the environment

→ the extent to which non-renewable energy could and should contribute to the UK's future energy supply

→ the economic, political and environmental factors affecting UK energy supply in the future.

CHAPTER

11

Extreme weather in the UK

The **weather** is a description of the day-to-day conditions of the atmosphere. This refers to temperature, cloud cover, wind strength and direction, and precipitation. The **climate** is the average weather over a long period of time. Data is used over a 30-year period to describe the climate of a place.

Key idea: The UK has a unique climate for its latitude which can create extreme weather conditions.

Key idea: Extreme flood hazard events are becoming more commonplace in the UK.

→ In this chapter you will study:

→ how air masses, the North Atlantic Drift and continentality influence the weather in the UK

→ how air masses cause extreme weather conditions in the UK, including extremes of wind, temperature and precipitation

→ a case study of flooding on the Somerset Level

What affects the weather in the UK?

There are several factors that affect the weather in the UK (see Figure 1). Notice that the UK is positioned in the mid-latitudes, with cold Arctic air to the north and warm tropical air to the south. We are also influenced by the Atlantic Ocean to the west and the drier European continent to the east. It is no wonder that the UK is known for its changeable weather!

Prevailing wind

In the UK, the dominant, or prevailing wind direction is from the southwest. This is the direction from which winds blow most of the time. This is an extremely important influence over our weather and climate as it brings mild, moist air towards the UK from the southwest. This explains why we get so much rain!

Air masses

An air mass is a large body of air that has particular characteristics of temperature and moisture. Air masses have their source over stable areas such as the Arctic or Northern Africa. They acquire their unique characteristics while remaining stationary over their source areas for several weeks. As they move towards the UK, these characteristics are modified. For example, the cold and dry Arctic air mass warms up as it moves south. It also becomes more humid as it travels over the ocean. Look at Figure 1 and notice that the UK is like a giant roundabout, with air masses arriving from several different directions!

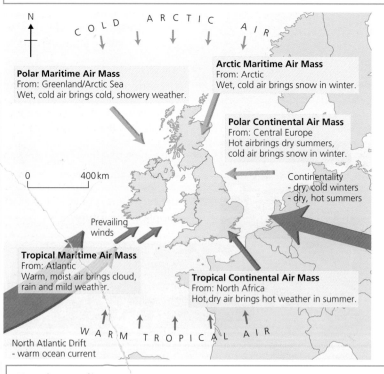

North Atlantic Drift

The North Atlantic Drift is a warm ocean current that originates from the Caribbean. It is extremely important in maintaining warm conditions throughout the year and particularly in the winter. The North Atlantic Drift takes warm waters up the west coast of the UK and towards Norway where it keeps the coast ice free.

Continentality

Large areas of land, such as the European continent, respond quickly to changes in temperature. This explains why continental Europe experiences very cold winters and hot summers. Air masses from Europe may transfer these conditions to the UK.

Continental areas also tend to be drier than maritime (coastal) areas. This explains why the west of the UK – with its southwesterly prevailing winds off the sea – tends to be wetter than the south east, which is more likely to be influenced by drier continental conditions.

▲ **Figure 1** Air masses affecting the UK

How do air masses cause extreme weather events?

Extreme weather events in the UK are rare but can lead to considerable damage and disruption, and occasionally cause injuries and loss of life. Here are a few examples of some recent extreme weather events than can be directly linked to air masses.

Tropical Maritime: Strong winds 2014

In February 2014, the UK was battered by a succession of winter storms from the Atlantic, driven onshore by strong westerly winds. This was the stormiest period of weather experienced by the UK for 20 years. Strong winds and huge waves made conditions extremely dangerous around exposed coastlines – particularly in the south and west, and caused widespread transport disruption (see Figure 2).

▲ **Figure 2** Waves batter the Welsh coast at Aberystwyth, 12 February 2014

- The South West mainline railway was severely damaged at Dawlish, Devon, during the storm of 4–5 February, severing a key transport link to the South West of England for many weeks.
- Huge waves overtopped coastal flood defences and many coastal communities in Cornwall, Devon and Dorset experienced coastal flooding and damage to infrastructure, buildings and sea defences.
- Roofs were damaged in Porthmadog, Gwynedd, and a member of the public was killed on 13 February after trees brought down power lines in Wiltshire.
- The Met Office issued a red warning for wind – the highest level of warning – for parts of North Wales and North West England for the storm of 12 February 2014 (see Figure 3).

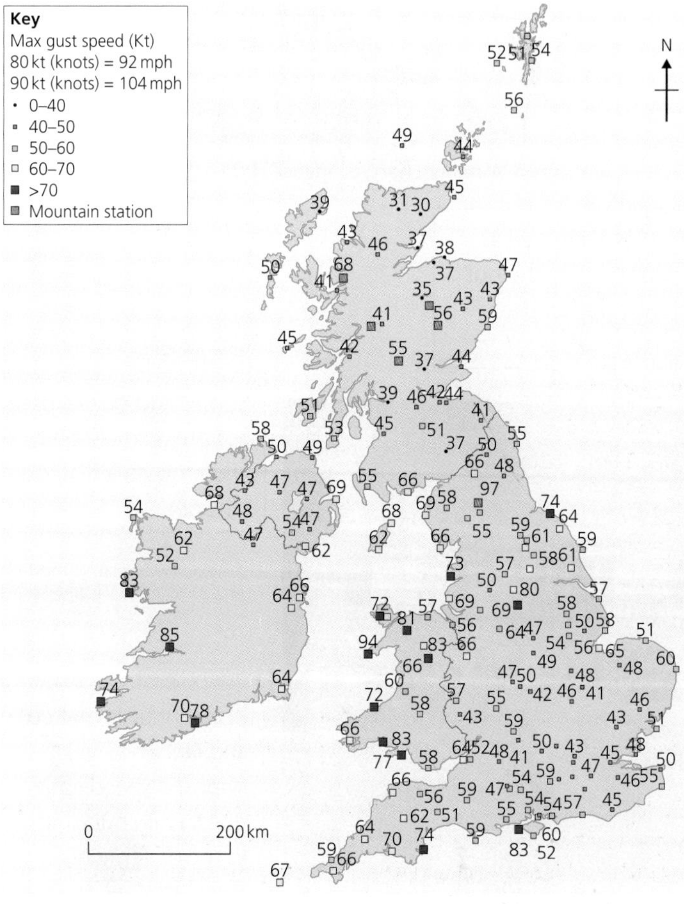

Key
Max gust speed (Kt)
80 kt (knots) = 92 mph
90 kt (knots) = 104 mph
- · 0–40
- ▪ 40–50
- ◻ 50–60
- ◻ 60–70
- ■ >70
- ◼ Mountain station

0   200 km

▲ **Figure 3** Maximum wind gusts, 12–13 February 2014

Activities

1. Study Figure 1.
   a. Which air mass has its source in North Africa?
   b. Where is the source area of the Polar Maritime air mass?
   c. Describe the typical weather associated with the Polar Continental air mass.
   d. Explain why the UK is frequently affected by mild and wet weather from the Atlantic Ocean?
   e. What is meant by the term 'continentality' and how does it affect the UK's weather?

2. Study Figure 2. Imagine that this photo was to be used in a newspaper. Write a few sentences to describe the scene and suggest the impact of the high waves on people living at the coast. You have a maximum of 100 words.

3. Study Figure 3.
   a. What was the highest wind gust? Use an atlas to identify its location.
   b. To what extent did the highest wind gusts occur along the west coast of the UK?
   c. Is there any evidence that upland areas experienced very high wind gusts?
   d. Which parts of the UK experienced the lowest wind gusts? Suggest reasons for your answer.

▲ **Figure 4** Somerset Floods, 2014

Tropical continental: Heatwave, 2003

The tropical continental air mass can introduce very warm and dry weather to Western Europe and the UK. In 2003, much of Europe suffered the most extreme heatwave for 500 years (see Figure 6). Over 20,000 people died across Europe and several countries including the UK recorded their highest ever temperatures. Wildfires broke out, rivers ran dry and some reservoirs became dangerously low, affecting water supplies and wildlife.

Tropical maritime: Flooding, 2014

The winter of 2014 was extremely wet, with wave after wave of depressions (rain-bearing weather systems) bearing down on southern England from the Atlantic. It was the wettest January since records began in 1910. About 350 mm of rain fell in January and February, about 100 mm above average.

One area that was badly affected was the Somerset Levels. In the worst floods ever recorded, some 600 properties were flooded and several villages were cut off (see Figure 4). Roads and railway lines were inundated and over 14,000 hectares of agricultural land were underwater for several weeks. The cost of the floods was over £10 million.

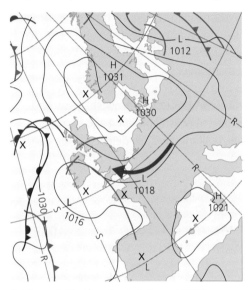

▲ **Figure 5** Weather chart, 5 August 2003

Tourism in the UK increased as people decided to enjoy the hot weather in the UK rather then travelling abroad.

Drinking water supplies were affected and hosepipe bans were introduced.

Some food prices rose as farm animals died and crops failed across Europe.

A UK record temperature of 38.5°C was recorded in text on 10 August 2003.

Road surfaces melted and Network Rail imposed speed limits due to rails buckling in the extreme heat.

▲ **Figure 6** The 2003 heatwave

Arctic maritime: Heavy snow, 2009–10

The Arctic maritime air mass can bring heavy snow and extremely cold conditions particularly to Scotland and northern England. The period from mid-December 2009 to mid-January 2010, brought very low temperatures and heavy snowfall to much of the UK (see Figure 7). It was the most severe period of winter weather since 1981–82.

- Night-time temperatures regularly fell to below -10°C in Scotland.
- Widespread snow fell across the UK with up 10–20 cm across parts of England and Wales and up to 30 cm in Scotland.
- Transport was badly affected – roads were blocked, trains were cancelled and airports disrupted (see Figure 8).
- Ice brought down power lines, disrupting electricity supplies to over 25,000 homes.
- Several people died in accidents caused by ice and snow.
- Farm animals across the UK were also severely impacted particularly sheep in mountainous areas.

▲ **Figure 7** Recorded snow depths (in cm) at 0900 on 7 January 2010

Activity

1. Study Figure 4. Describe the impacts of the Somerset Levels floods in 2014. Consider both short-term and longer-term impacts.
2. Study Figure 7.
   a. Which parts of the UK recorded the greatest depths of snow? Use an atlas to enable you to give precise locations.
   b. With reference to the Arctic air mass (see Figure 1) explain why Scotland experienced the heaviest snowfalls.
3. How does extreme weather affect transport communications in the UK?

▲ **Figure 8** Travel disruption on the M25

Case study: a UK flood event caused by extreme weather conditions

The Somerset Levels: a flood disaster waiting to happen?

Where are the Somerset Levels?

The Somerset Levels are located in South West England (see Figure 9). They cover an area of 650 km² in the northern and central part of the county. It is a unique, flat landscape between the Quantock and Mendip hills. It is so low that much of the land is below sea level with the maximum altitude being only 8 m.

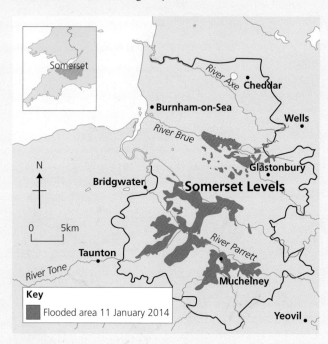

▲ **Figure 9** Location map of the Somerset Levels

Why is it such a unique landscape?

The Somerset Levels have historically been drained for agricultural and residential purposes. Thousands of years ago, the area was covered by the sea, but today it is a landscape of rivers and wetlands. In Roman times, artificial flood defences were built to keep out the tides of the River Severn. Dutch engineers helped to drain the levels in the seventeenth century. Ditches were dug to create a network of channels to allow productive farming on what was marshy land either side of the channels. This land is known as the floodplain. The Levels are therefore vulnerable to both river and tidal flooding.

What happened?

In early 2014, the UK was hit by the worst storms for twenty years. The Somerset Levels experienced widespread flooding of the Parrett and Tone. More than 65 million m³ of floodwater covered an area of 65 km².

What were the causes of the flood?

Physical causes:

- Prolonged rain, hurricane-force wind speeds and tidal surges caused widespread flooding.
- The storms were caused by a powerful **jet stream** driving low-pressure systems and their storms across the Atlantic Ocean. A jet stream is a narrow band of very strong wind currents that circle the globe several km above the earth.
- From mid-December 2013 to mid-February 2014, there were twelve major storms.

Human causes:

- The river has not been dredged properly for twenty years. This process involves digging up weeds, mud and rubbish from the riverbeds. The River Parrett, in particular, was blocked and in desperate need of dredging. The process of dredging used to happen every five years at a cost of £4 million.
- Campaigners believe that, if the river had been dredged, then the river would have been deeper and wider. This would have created more capacity to carry away the floodwater.
- Farmers warned the government that dredging was needed.
- Building has developed on the floodplain, much of which is below sea level.

What were the social, economic and environmental consequences of the flood?

Social
● 600 homes were affected
● Villages such as Muchelney, were completely cut off (see Figure 9)
● Journey times were longer as roads were inaccessible

Economic
● The financial cost to the Somerset economy was between £82 million and £147 million
● Many of the livestock had to be moved out of the area and sold
● Businesses in the local area lost trade.

Environmental
● 6,900 hectares of agricultural land was underwater for over a month
● Natural England reported that the floods seemed to have little impact on wildlife.

▲ **Figure 10** The consequences of the flooding for people, the economy and the environment

How did different stakeholders respond to the flood?

The Environment Agency installed 62 pumps, working 24 hours a day, to remove 1.5 millon tonnes of water. Giant pumps were also brought in from the Netherlands to bolster the effort (see Figure 11). Royal Marines were deployed to help residents of villages cut off by the floodwater, and the police increased their patrols.

There were nearly 50 defences across Somerset that were in need of repair, including embankments, pumping stations, sluices, floodgates and coastal defences.

A range of options for the future management of the Somerset Levels have been explored. The removal of silts and weeds from the riverbed is important (see Figure 12), as is reducing run-off from housing developments and a consideration of whether farmers could be paid to store floodwater on their land.

In March 2014, the government wrote a twenty-year flood action plan for Somerset. The Prime Minister at that time, David Cameron, said that 'money is no object' in sorting out the flooding problems. The plan suggested several responses, including:

- dredging more of the River Tone and the River Parrett
- repairing damaged flood banks
- raising of the road into Muchelney
- making the pumps permanent
- building a tidal barrier, similar to the Thames Barrier in London, to hold back tidal surges.

These approaches are all examples of **hard engineering** which means that they are expensive and man-made approaches. But, could there be other, more sustainable solutions? Some areas could be changed back to natural wetlands, rather than agricultural land; and local farmers could be encouraged to invest in more flood-tolerant activities. Homeowners in the most vulnerable areas could be given government compensation to relocate to a less flood-prone area.

▲ **Figure 11** Pumps at Burrowbridge reducing floodwater levels

▲ **Figure 12** Dredging the River Parrett after the floods

Activities

1. Draw a sketch map to show the case study location.
   a. Using a map of the UK to help you, add the following labels:
      - Severn Estuary
      - Quantock and Mendip hills
      - Fordgate, Moorland, Burrowbridge, Muchelney
   b. Add the following rivers to your map:
      - Axe, Brue, Tone and Parrett
2. Give three reasons why the Somerset Levels are prone to flooding.

3. Describe how human activity made the flooding worse.
4. Create a mind map of each of the stakeholders who responded to the flood and explain how they helped. Colour-code each explanation according to whether it was a short-term or long-term response.

→ Take it further

5. Should the Somerset Levels be allowed to return to a natural wetland?

CHAPTER

12

Resources and UK ecosystems

Key idea: Humans use, modify and change ecosystems and environments to obtain food, energy and water.

→ In this chapter you will study:

→ how environments and ecosystems in the UK are used and modified by humans, including: mechanisation of farming and commercial fishing to provide food; wind farms and fracking to provide energy; reservoirs and water transfer schemes to provide water.

How environments and ecosystems in the UK are used and modified by humans

Most of the UK is made up of land which humans have heavily modified to help them to grow food, produce energy and obtain water. The UK used to be covered by woodland, which over time has been cut down to be used for fuel and to make space for land for housing, farm animals and growing crops. This chapter investigates how UK ecosystems have been changed for the essential needs of humans: food, energy and water.

Providing food

Mechanisation of farming

Over time, farming practices have changed dramatically. Traditional subsistence agriculture that relied upon human and animal manual labour (through ploughing, weeding, sowing and watering) has become largely industrialised through changing technology (see Figure 1). This **mechanisation** has led to the introduction of large-scale farming and the use of tractors, combine harvesters, mechanical ploughs, motor vehicle transport (for importing materials like fertilisers and exporting goods) and even aircraft and satellite technology.

▲ **Figure 1** How farming has changed

How are ecosystems and the environment affected?

Some of the implications of modern farming are shown in Figure 2.

- In order to house machinery and produce food on a large scale, farms have increased in size. This has led to the destruction of hedgerows, which affects the small mammals which live there and the food webs they are part of.
- Farming is now a year-round process with consumers wanting produce out of season. As a result, fields are not given time to recover. The traditional farming practice of 'fallowing' allowed fields to recover nutrients. This is no longer an option and as a result soils become exhausted.
- The increase in use of chemical fertilisers and pesticides not only costs farmers but can also cause problems for local water supplies if **eutrophication** occurs where chemicals wash into water.

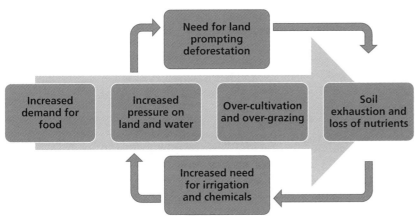

▲ **Figure 2** Needs and impacts of modern farming

Commercial fishing

Commercial fishing has increased throughout the twentieth and twenty-first centuries, with over 1 billion people relying on fish for their primary food source. In the UK, fish and chips has been a popular takeaway food since the nineteenth century, and its popularity caused the rapid development of commercial fishing in the North sea. Commercial fishing utilises large trawlers rather than small boats, with thermal sensors and digital imagery helping workers to identify where fish stocks are located.

How are ecosystems and the environment affected?

Commercial fishing techniques have led to over-fishing of popular species such as cod. Too many young fish are caught, and there are not enough left in the sea to breed and produce new fish to replace those which have been taken for food. Although cod is popular, it takes four years for cod to reach breeding age, and many were taken from the sea before they reached this stage. In the UK, there are now minimum sizes of certain fish that are allowed to be taken from the sea, to prevent depleting stock levels. Consumers are also encouraged to be aware of other fish that are more sustainable, for example choosing pollock over cod, and organisations such as the Marine Stewardship Council publish guidance on how to choose sustainable fish.

▲ **Figure 3** Fish and chips – a popular takeaway meal in the UK

Commercial fishing also causes the accidental death of other, unplanned species (such as dolphins caught by mistake in large nets meant for tuna, or coral reefs being snagged by deep trawlers). The average fish catch has been declining for ten years; tuna and cod are particularly threatened. This means fishing boats have to travel further, as stocks migrate away. As a result, they use more diesel fuel, causing water pollution and an increase in the use of fossil fuels.

Activities

1. Suggest how the mechanisation of farming and commercial fishing can impact the environment in the UK, both in the long term and the short term.
2. What is eutrophication?
3. How can eutrophication affect ecosystems?
4. Create an information pamphlet aimed at customers to encourage them to eat sustainable fish.

➡ Take it further

5. Research and investigate how the EU manages the fish stocks around Europe.

Providing energy

The different types of energy sources that are available in the UK are described in detail in Chapter 13.

- Wind power is a renewable energy source. Power is produced by wind turbines on land or at sea which are turned by the wind to generate electricity.
- 'Fracking' (hydraulic fracturing) is a modern process which pumps a mixture of water, sand and chemicals under high pressure into deep shale rocks in order to split them apart and force gas or oil rapidly to the surface. More detail on this process can be found on page 113.

Wind farms

Wind farms can be found on land (onshore wind farms) or out to sea (offshore wind farms). Wind farms are cheap to produce compared to other sources of energy, and wind power has recently developed as a major source of electricity in the UK.

How are ecosystems and the environment affected?

Most onshore wind farms are found in areas of open countryside on high ground. This is because this is where the wind is strongest. Some people find wind turbines are unsightly and affect the quality of the landscape. Some wind turbines create a lot of noise, although newer versions are quieter. Wind turbines need to be manufactured and transported to their site, whether on land or on sea. Greenhouse gases are emitted during this process. However, wind turbines do not emit greenhouse gases once they are in use and are seen as 'green' energy.

Offshore wind farms are less environmentally polluting, however, they may disturb the migration patterns of birds.

Fracking

In the USA in 2015, 49 per cent of all gas and oil extracted was through fracking, which has reduced the country's CO2 emissions. The UK currently imports oil and gas from overseas, yet we have shale reserves across the country, such as in Yorkshire and the Mendips. The UK ban on fracking has ended and, in 2015, the government formally offered up licences to allow companies to frack natural shale in areas inland.

How are ecosystems and the environment affected?

Fracking uses less water than coal power stations, and emits fewer greenhouse gases. However, there are concerns about groundwater supplied becoming toxic. The fracking fluid remains in the ground, and could contaminate water and soil with bromide, diesel, methane, lead or hydrochloric acid. In 2012, over 1 trillion litres of toxic waste water from fracking processes across the world had to be treated.

There are many concerns from the public about fracking. Some claim the process leads to seismic activity with 'microquakes'. In Oklahoma, earthquakes increased by 100 times during fracking regimes. However, the UK does not have major seismic risks.

▲ **Figure 4** Wind farm at the village of Bothel in Cumbria, Lake District

Providing water

Water supply is an issue in the UK. This is because most rain falls in the west and north whereas the greatest demand for water – for domestic use, industry and agriculture – is in the south and east. Currently, around 40 per cent of all blue water abstraction in the UK is for domestic use, 40 per cent is for energy, 20 per cent is for industry and just one per cent is for agriculture. We spend £82 million a year on irrigation and water transport to industry. Two solutions are to construct reservoirs, and to build water transfer schemes.

Reservoirs

Reservoirs are large areas of water, often created by building a dam to alter the flow of a river. They are specifically created for the capture and storage of water. They are very expensive to construct, and changing the flow of the river is also costly.

How are ecosystems and the environment affected?

Flooding of landscapes to create reservoirs can lead to the loss of settlements and farming land. Sediment can accumulate against dams in reservoirs. This can result in a chemical imbalance leading to either excessive plant growth (as with eutrophication) or limited growth. It disrupts the natural processes at work in the river valley. Reservoirs require energy during their construction from concrete, and they can disrupt local ecology and affect life cycles.

Water transfer schemes

Since water supply is unequally spread across the UK, one possible solution involves the transfer of water from a region where there is plenty to a region without. This could involve rivers, canals or pipelines.

One example of a successful UK water transfer scheme is the transfer from Norfolk's River Ely Ouse to the River Stour in Essex. This has been running since 1972 but was expanded in 2014 by enlarging the Abberton reservoir. Tunnels and pipes bring water to the reservoir from Norfolk's excess in order to supply 400 million litres of water per day to Essex, one of the driest counties in the UK and home to a high-density population.

Similarly, the Elan Valley water transfer has been successfully supplying Birmingham with water from 100 miles away in Wales via the Craig Goch dam and reservoir. This provides 160 million litres of water per day. This scheme is to be expanded and may one day even supply the River Thames and London.

How are ecosystems and the environment affected?

- The transfer of water from one region to another does have a potential implication for local ecology since the chemistry of the water in each area is different.
- Water transfer can lead to nutrient imbalances which can affect aquatic plant and animal life.
- As with reservoirs, sediment can accumulate within pipelines, which can lead to excessive or limited plant growth.
- These schemes rely heavily on the hard engineering of rivers through pipe networks and dams. This alters natural floods and can reduce water access for the donor area.
- River channels can silt up or have an increased saline content.
- The introduction of water to a new area can also spread non-native invasive species which can threaten the new ecosystem.

Activities

1. Produce a table to compare the environmental implications of wind farms and fracking.
2. Is fracking a sustainable solution to the UK's energy crisis?
3. Consider water transfer schemes. Create a table to compare benefits and costs to the donor area and the receiving area. Are these schemes sustainable?

→ Take it further

4. Carry out some internet research to see if there have been any recent developments in fracking in the UK. Using the information on this page, as well as further research, suggest how this has affected the local environment and ecosystems.
5. Research and investigate one of the following water transfer schemes:
   - the Ely Ouse to Essex transfer scheme
   - the Elan Valley transfer scheme
   - the Severn–Thames transfer scheme.
   Describe and evaluate the positives and negatives of the scheme.

Energy sources in the UK

Key idea: There are a range of energy sources available to the UK.

→ In this chapter you will study:

→ renewable and non-renewable energy sources

→ the contribution of these sources to energy supply in the UK.

What are the energy sources in the UK?

Energy is used to power machinery and provide light and heat. In the UK we are fortunate in having several different sources of energy. There are two broad types of energy source in the UK: renewable and non-renewable.

Renewable energy

Renewable energy sources can be used to generate power over and over again without being used up. They are generally non-polluting. Apart from biomass, they do not directly involve the emission of harmful greenhouse gases. Figure 1 describes the main types of renewable energy in the UK.

Renewable energy source	How does it work?	Importance in the UK
Biomass	Energy produced from organic matter. It includes burning dung or plant matter and the production of biofuels, by processing specially grown plants such as sugar cane and maize.	Some biofuels are produced and used in transportation (about 3 per cent of total road transport fuel). Biofuels and waste account for over 5 per cent of the UK's electricity generation.
Wind	Turbines on land or at sea are turned by the wind to generate electricity. The UK is one of Europe's windiest countries!	In 2014, wind power accounted for just below 10 per cent of the UK's electricity demand. Despite being unpopular, wind energy does have considerable potential for the future.
Hydro (HEP)	Large-scale dams and smaller micro-dams create a head of water that can spin turbines to generate electricity.	Large dams are expensive and controversial. Micro-dams are becoming popular options at the local level. HEP currently supplies just 1.4 per cent of the UK's electricity production.
Geothermal	Water heated underground when in contact with hot rocks creates steam that drives turbines to generate electricity.	There are some small geothermal projects in the UK, for example in Southampton's city centre.
Tidal	Turbines within barrages (dams) constructed across river estuaries can use rising and falling tides to generate electricity.	There are no existing tidal power barrages in the UK due to the high costs and environmental concerns. Tidal power could generate up to 10 per cent of the UK's electricity. In the future, sites such as Swansea Bay and Bridgwater Bay might be developed for tidal power.
Wave	One method involves waves forcing air into a chamber where it turns a turbine linked to a generator.	Portugal has installed the world's first wave farm, which started generating electricity in 2008. There are some experimental wave sites in the UK but costs are high and there are environmental concerns.
Solar	Most commonly, this involves photovoltaic cells mounted on solar panels which convert light from the sun into electricity.	During the summer, solar power can generate considerable amounts of electricity. There are increasing numbers of solar farms in the UK and many homes have solar panels on their roofs. Solar power almost doubled during 2014.

▲ **Figure 1** Renewable energy sources

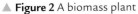

▲ **Figure 2** A biomass plant

▲ **Figure 3** Wind turbines

▲ **Figure 4** Solar panels

Activities

1. What is the difference between a renewable and a non-renewable energy source?
2. Why are non-renewable energy sources also called 'fossil fuels'?
3. Why is there a strong desire to develop renewable energy sources in the future?

→ **Take it further**

4. Study Figure 1. Use the table and your own research to answer the following questions.
   a. Why is there potential for wind energy in the UK?

b. Suggest why some people object to the construction of wind farms.
c. Why is HEP generated in upland regions of the UK like Scotland and Wales?
d. Suggest why tidal and wave energy have yet to be exploited in the UK.
e. Find out more about biomass in the UK. Where does it come from?
f. What are the advantages and disadvantages of turning huge fields into 'solar farms'?

Non-renewable energy

Also known as 'fossil fuels', **non-renewable** energy sources were formed millions of years ago and have to be extracted from the ground. They include hydrocarbons such as coal, oil and natural gas. These non-renewable energy sources are finite. They will eventually 'run out' when they become too expensive (economically or environmentally) to extract. Hydrocarbons emit large quantities of greenhouse gases – especially carbon dioxide – and pollute the air.

Coal

Coal used to be the main energy source in the UK. One hundred years ago, the industry employed over 3 million coal miners, mostly working deep underground.

Today just a few thousand work in the industry and, in December 2015, the last deep-shaft pit at Kellingley near Castleford closed. Coal is now only extracted from huge opencast pits (see Figure 5).

▲ **Figure 5** Opencast coal mine near Leeds

Oil and natural gas

In the UK, oil is not expected to produce any of the UK's electricity beyond 2015. By this time, the last oil-fired power station should have closed down. Nearly half of the UK's electricity comes from natural gas. In the past, this has mostly come from the North Sea but, as supplies run down, it is increasingly imported (see Figure 6). By 2019, the UK is expected to import 69 per cent of its gas required for electricity generation.

▲ **Figure 6** Gas platform in the North Sea

Nuclear

Nuclear power is also a non-renewable energy source because it uses uranium as a raw material. It is an extremely important source of power in the UK. There are currently sixteen reactors generating about 20 per cent of the UK's total electricity. Figure 7 shows the location of the UK's nuclear power plants. Notice that they are located at the coast. This is because they require huge quantities of water for cooling. Some are close to ports where imported uranium arrives. Several new reactors are planned in the future, including two each at Hinkley Point in Somerset (see Figure 8) and Sizewell in Suffolk. These should be up and running in the 2020s and will replace reactors reaching the end of their useful life.

Activities

1. Should the UK continue to use fossil fuels despite their harmful greenhouse gas emissions?
2. Developing nuclear power is extremely expensive and controversial.
   a. Find out about the latest developments at either Hinkley Point or Sizewell.
   b. Consider the pros and cons of building new reactors.

Key
Nuclear power plants in United Kingdom
● Established
● New sites

Torness
Hunterston
Hartlepool
Moorside
Heysham
Wylfa
Sizewell
London
Hinkley Point
Dungeness

0   200 km

▲ **Figure 7** Nuclear power plants in the UK

▲ **Figure 8** Hinkley Point nuclear reactor, Somerset

The energy mix in the UK

The UK has a good **energy mix**, making use of several different sources of energy. Look at Figure 9. Notice that almost 50 per cent of the UK's energy comes from natural gas. Coal is still important despite the closure in 2015 of the last deep-shaft mine. Together, natural gas, coal and nuclear energy provide the majority of the UK's energy. Only a relatively small amount comes from renewable sources. A reduction in oil and gas reserves, and in the production of coal, means that the UK is now increasingly reliant on imported fossil fuels.

Figure 10 shows energy used to produce electricity in the UK. The pattern is much the same with coal, gas and nuclear producing the vast majority of the UK's electricity.

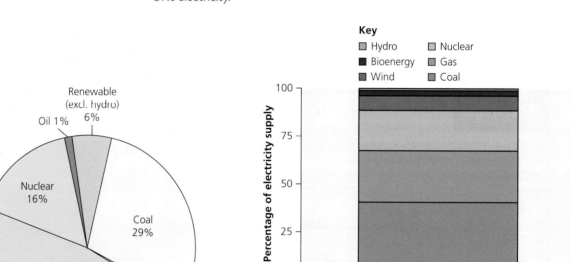

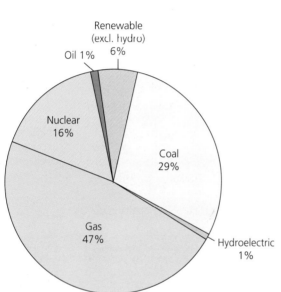

▲ **Figure 9** Energy sources in the UK, 2010

▲ **Figure 10** The UK's electricity supply, 2013

Activities

1. Study Figure 9.
   a. What percentage of the UK's energy comes from coal, gas and nuclear combined?
   b. What percentage comes from renewable sources?
   c. Do you think the UK has a good energy mix? Explain your answer.
2. Use the information in Figure 11 to draw a pie chart to show the energy sources for electricity production in the UK.

Energy Source	Percentage of the UK's energy
Coal	36%
Nuclear	19.7%
Gas	27%
Wind	7.7%
Biofuels and wastes	5.7%
Others (hydro, solar, imports from France and Netherlands)	3.9%

▲ **Figure 11** Electricity production in the UK, 2013

14

Energy management

Key idea: Energy in the UK is affected by a number of factors and requires careful management and consideration of future supplies

→ **In this chapter you will study:**

→ the changing patterns of energy supply and demand in the UK from 1950 to the present day

→ the strategies for sustainable use and management of energy at local and UK national scales

→ the development of renewable energy in the UK and the impacts on people and the environment

→ the extent to which non-renewable energy could and should contribute to the UK's future energy supply

→ the economic, political and environmental factors affecting UK energy supply in the future.

Energy supply changes since 1950

Today, natural gas supplies almost 50 per cent of the UK's energy supply. Coal supplies nearly 30 per cent and nuclear 16 per cent. The UK has a reasonably balanced energy mix. However, this has not always been the case.

Look at Figure 1. Primary fuels were either used directly to provide energy or indirectly to generate electricity. In 1950, almost all energy in the UK came from coal that was mined in the UK. In 1947, the coal industry was nationalised, bringing it under state control. From then on the government controlled coal production, until very recently when some mines have been privatised. Coal was used directly in industry and in the home to provide heating and hot water. It was used to fuel steam trains and to produce 'town gas', a strong smelling gas that was used in many homes for cooking. Coal generated almost all of the UK's electricity, apart from a small amount of hydro-electricity in Scotland.

Look at Figure 2, which plots the UK energy sources from 1961–2009. Notice the dramatic decline of coal over the years and the growth of natural gas and nuclear. See how oil has been very erratic and how renewables continue to make only a small contribution.

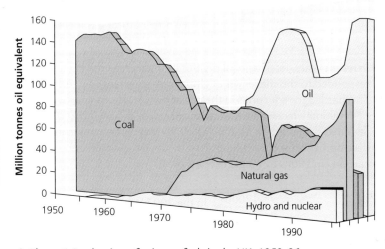

▲ **Figure 1** Production of primary fuels in the UK, 1950–96

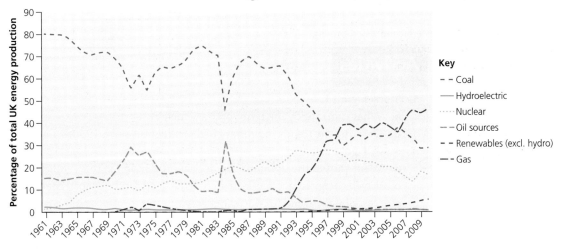

▲ **Figure 2** Trends in UK energy sources, 1961–2009

Many of the changes that have taken place since the 1950s reflect government decisions and the role of international organisations.

1961

In 1961, coal accounted for 80 per cent of the UK's energy supply. Since then, it has declined erratically to its current level of about 30 per cent. Notice the sudden dip in the 1980s. This was due to a prolonged miners' strike in 1984–85 over mine closures and job losses. Since then, coal production declined rapidly. It had become increasingly expensive to mine and alternative energy sources were becoming available, particularly oil and gas from the Middle East.

1974

In 1974, the international organisation OPEC (Organization of the Petroleum Exporting Countries) quadrupled the price of oil on the world markets. OPEC had a huge amount of collective power at the time and this had a massive impact on the world economy.

1975

Fortunately, the UK had started to develop its North Sea oil and gas, with the first oil being produced in 1975. The government recognised the potential power of OPEC in determining world prices, so wanted to make the UK as self-sufficient as possible in energy production. Multinational oil companies were involved in exploration and production, with the UK government taking money through taxation.

1990s

In the early 1990s, the EU's 'Gas Burn' directive was repealed. Up until then, the EU's Gas Burn Directive had imposed restrictions on the use of gas. Once repealed, the gas industry was able to grow rapidly. Look at Figure 1 to see how natural gas increased dramatically in the 1990s.

2000s

In recent years, international organisations such as the EU and the United Nations have responded to the challenges of global climate change by setting limits on carbon emissions. This has led to reductions in the use of hydrocarbons (particularly coal and oil) in favour of developing renewable sources of energy, such as wind and solar. Natural gas is the favoured hydrocarbon as it has relatively low carbon and sulphur emissions. Many of these developments have been supported by the UK government, which has a target of reducing carbon emissions by 60 per cent by 2050.

2000+

In the 2007 White Paper 'Meeting the Energy Challenge', the government recognised the need to build new electricity power stations to replace those built in the 1960s and 1970s. This accounts for plans to build new nuclear reactors, for example, at Hinkley Point in Somerset. Foreign investment from countries such as China is now being encouraged.

Activities

1. Study Figure 1.
   a. What is meant by the term 'primary fuels'?
   b. Describe the trends in primary fuel production since 1950.
2. Study Figure 2.
   a. What caused the dramatic dip in coal production in the 1980s?
   b. Which energy source was increased to make up for the drop in coal?
   c. Describe the trend for nuclear energy.
   d. Suggest why natural gas production increased rapidly in the 1990s.
   e. Contrast the energy mix in the UK between 1961 and 2009.

Energy demand changes since 1950

Energy consumption in the UK has steadily risen since the 1950s. This reflected the growth in the UK's population and increasing energy demands in the home (see Figure 3) as well as growing demand from industry and transport. In the period 1970–2000 energy consumption increased by about 15 per cent. Since 1990, it has increased by about 1 per cent per year. Figure 4 shows the increasing trend in energy consumption since 1970.

▲ **Figure 3** Housewife in a 'modern' electric kitchen in the 1950s

Activity

Study Figure 3. Suggest some of the 'modern' kitchen appliances that led to an increase in the demand for energy in the 1950s.

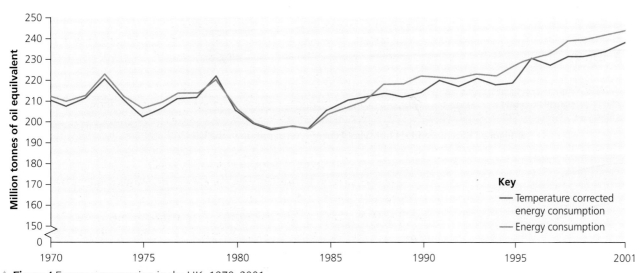

▲ **Figure 4** Energy consumption in the UK, 1970–2001

Look at Figure 5. It shows household energy consumption. Notice that since 2003 energy consumption has actually started to decrease. Between 2005 and 2011, overall energy consumption in UK homes fell by more than 25 per cent. This coincided with a sharp increase in the cost of energy. However, other factors help to explain this recent trend:

- Government insulation policy. Under CERT (Carbon Emissions Reduction Target), one of the large-scale energy efficiency schemes, 5.3 million homes received free loft insulation and 2.6 million had their cavity walls filled. The scheme finished in 2012.
- Since 2007, buildings in England and Wales have had to undergo an Energy Performance Certification before they are sold or let. This identifies how efficient the building is in its use of energy.
- New standards set by the government. Since 2005, all new boilers have at least a B rating (see Figure 7). National Grid thinks that this could account for more than a 40 per cent of the overall drop in household demand.
- People are living in smaller properties and more shared accommodation, reducing the use for energy.
- Environmentalism. Awareness of our carbon footprint and efforts by the Energy Saving Trust and other international organisations such as the United Nations to encourage people to use less energy.

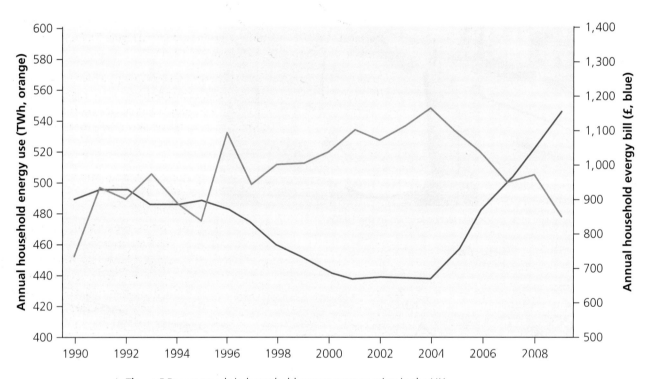

▲ **Figure 5** Recent trends in household energy consumption in the UK

In the future demand is expected to fall further (see Figure 6). This will reflect greater fuel efficiency along with increased energy conservation in the home, more efficient energy production and a greater sense of environmental awareness.

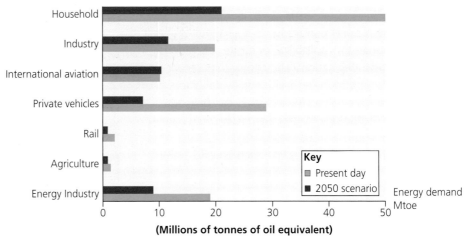

▲ **Figure 6** Projected future reductions in UK energy demand

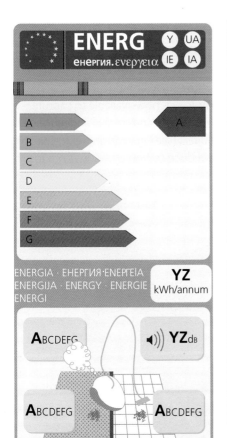

▲ **Figure 7** EU energy label for a fridge

The EU has a target of reducing carbon emissions by 40 per cent by 2030. It too is encouraging reductions in energy use:

● EU 'energy label' details the energy efficiency of products such as light bulbs, refrigerators and washing machines, giving consumers more information about energy use. Products are rated from A–G, with A being the most efficient and having a green colour (see Figure 7). From 2017, there will be seven categories from A*** to D.

● In 2011, the EU adopted the Energy Efficiency Plan, which encourages the construction of more energy-efficient houses, encourages industry to produce more energy-efficient products and promotes the use of 'smart meters' for customers to assess their own energy use to enable them to make savings

Heating	60%
Hot water	24%
Cold appliances	3%
Electronics	3%
Cooking	3%
Lighting	3%
Wet appliances	2%
Miscellaneous	2%

▲ **Figure 8** Household energy consumption

Activities

1. Present the data in Figure 8 in the form of a pie chart.
2. Suggest how government and EU policies have led to a reduction in household energy demand since 2003.

Sustainable energy solutions

The **sustainable** use of energy resources is all about ensuring their long-term availability for future generations. It is also about ensuring national and community security and avoiding damage to the environment. By definition, fossil fuels are unsustainable. However, they can be made to last longer if technology enables them to be used more efficiently. For the future, sustainable energy solutions involve developing renewable sources such as wind, water and heat from the Earth.

National strategies

The UK government wants to create a low-carbon, sustainable future that helps to address climate change. In seeking greater energy security, the government wants the UK to be less dependent upon the import of fossil fuels.

There are four key aspects of this vision for a sustainable future.

1. **Increase the contribution of renewable sources.** The government's Renewable Energy Strategy (2009) identified a target of 15 per cent of the UK's energy to come from renewable sources by 2020. In 2013, it was just over 5 per cent.

2. **Encourage energy saving and conservation.** Grants have been available for loft insulation and all homes need to have an energy efficiency survey before being sold or rented. The EU requires energy labelling for appliances such as fridges. Technology is being encouraged to develop ever more efficient household appliances.

3. **Develop nuclear energy.** While not strictly renewable, nuclear power uses very small amounts of raw material and some of this can be re-processed for further use. It also has very low carbon emissions. Renewable energy will not address all of the UK's energy needs and nuclear energy represents a long-term alternative that is reasonably sustainable. It is, however, very controversial. Radioactive waste needs to be disposed of safely and the costs involved in constructing nuclear power plants are very high. Foreign money from China is being used to support recent developments at Hinkley Point in Somerset, Bradwell in Essex and Sizewell in Suffolk.

4. **Develop carbon capture and storage.** This involves capturing carbon rather than emitting it into the atmosphere. Technology is now available to capture carbon from power stations and store it underground within rocks or aquifers (see Figure 9). In the future, this could significantly reduce carbon emissions from fossil fuel-burning power stations.

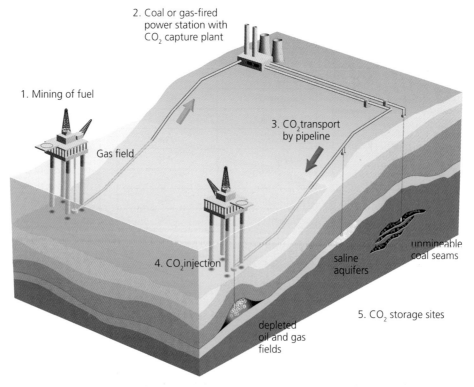

2. Coal or gas-fired power station with CO_2 capture plant

1. Mining of fuel

Gas field

3. CO_2 transport by pipeline

4. CO_2 injection

unmineable coal seams

saline aquifers

5. CO_2 storage sites

depleted oil and gas fields

▲ **Figure 9** Carbon capture and storage

Figure 10 presents the key points from the government's Renewable Energy Strategy.

- Achieve a target of 15 per cent of UK energy to come from renewable sources by 2020

- Provide financial support for renewable electricity and heat, supporting renewable energy projects, encouraging the use of biofuels in transport and supporting the use of electric cars

- Reduce the UK's carbon emissions by reducing dependence on fossil fuels

- Reduce the need for foreign imports of fossil fuels

- Create up to 500,00 jobs in the renewable sector by 2020

- Promote the use of offshore wind farms and research the potential for wave energy

- Encourage households and communities to generate their own electricity through the introduction of a Renewable Heat Incentive and 'feed-in tariffs'

- Make the planning process easier and quicker for local renewable energy schemes.

▲ **Figure 10** The UK government's Renewable Energy Strategy, 2009

Recent developments

Between 2010 and 2013 the Department of Energy and Climate Change recorded £31 billion of private sector investment in renewable electricity generation supporting over 35,000 jobs. In 2014, £10 billion was invested in renewable electricity generation. This included the Pen y Cymoedd wind project in Wales and the world's largest gasification plant on Teesside.

In 2015, the government published plans to cut subsidies for renewables such as solar and wind. This may lead to job losses in the industry and the closure of solar panel companies. Some new wind and solar projects may be in jeopardy.

Activities

1. What is meant by a 'sustainable energy strategy'?
2. To what extent can nuclear power be considered a sustainable option for the future?

→ Take it further

3. Design an information poster to outline the four main aspects of the UK government's vision for sustainable energy management. Use the internet to find some photos or diagrams to illustrate the points. Find out more about schemes such as the Renewable Heat Incentive.

Local solutions

In the UK, there are many local sustainable energy projects involving private individuals and small communities. These range from wind turbines through to micro-hydro schemes and anaerobic digesters. While most schemes involve private funding, financial and technical support is available from the government and from other organisations and businesses.

PlanLoCaL is a support organisation developed by the Centre for Sustainable Energy in 2009. It receives financial support from the government's Department for Communities and Local Government, and Department of Energy and Climate Change. PlanLoCaL provides advice and support for communities wishing to develop sustainable energy solutions.

Anaerobic digestion, Silloth, Cumbria

In 2011, an anaerobic digestion system was installed at Dryholme Farm near Silloth, an isolated farming community on the Cumbrian coast in North West England (see Figure 11). The digester uses farm slurry and silage made from locally grown grass and maize to generate enough electricity to power 4,000 homes. The cost of the project was about £4 million. Money came from a variety of sources including government grants, loans and private investments.

Anaerobic digestion works much like a cow's stomach! In the absence of oxygen (hence the term 'anaerobic') bacteria is used to break down the slurry and silage, creating a methane-rich biogas (see Figure 12). As methane is a very powerful greenhouse gas, it is captured and then burned as a fuel to generate electricity. This is sold to the National Grid to make a profit.

▲ **Figure 11** Anaerobic digester at Dryholme Farm, Silloth

In addition to the electricity generated by the plant, the waste organic matter (digestate) forms a valuable liquid fertiliser that farmers can spread onto their land. For every tonne of slurry and silage, 0.8 tonne of digestate is produced. This is worth about £4 a tonne. Heat is also produced by the plant, which can be used locally.

Anaerobic digesters are increasingly being used to make the most of farm waste by turning it into renewable energy. It benefits many different groups including the local community, farmers, energy entrepreneurs who develop the technology and the environment. Despite some initial concerns about smell, noise and visual impact, most local communities welcome the new schemes.

Activities

1. Study Figure 12.
   a. What is an anaerobic digester and how does it work?
   b. Suggest why this has become a popular sustainable energy option for local communities and private individuals.
   c. Assuming that 30,000 tonnes of slurry and silage are used each year, how much money is this worth as digestate?

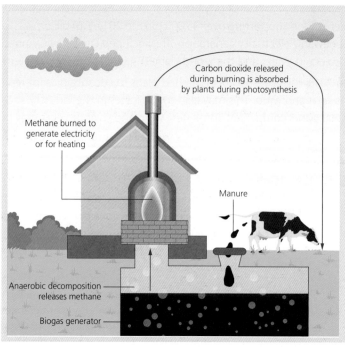

▲ **Figure 12** How anaerobic digestion works

▲ **Figure 13** At the Trelowarren Estate in Cornwall, they have installed a district heating system fuelled by a single woodchip-powered bio-mass boiler. The boiler provides heating for twenty cottages. Find out more at http://trelowarren.com

Hoathly Hill district heating, West Sussex

Hoathly Hill is a small community of 27 homes in a rural part of the High Weald in West Sussex. Since 2007 the community has benefited from the installation of a district heating system to supply hot water to each house through insulated pipes.

→ The system uses a central low-maintenance woodchip boiler to generate the heat, similar to the one shown in Figure 13

→ Each house is fitted with a meter and homeowners can monitor and regulate the amount of heat used

→ The cost of the project was £400,000. Some of the cost was covered by national and local grants with the balance being paid by the local community.

The project has brought several benefits:

→ The contract to supply woodchip for the boiler has created new employment opportunities at the local sawmill

→ The use of woodchip rather than LPG (liquefied petroleum gas) has reduced carbon emissions

→ Increased community cohesion, as the community worked together to make the project happen.

Activities

1. How has the Hoathly Hill district heating system brought benefits to the local community?

→ Take it further

2. Access the Centre for Sustainable Energy's website at www.cse.org.uk to find information about other case studies of small-scale local renewable energy projects. Choose one that interests you and write a short summary.

The development of renewable energy in the UK

The history of renewable energy

In the 1950s, almost all of the UK's energy supply was coal (see page 96). Only a very small amount of energy came from another source – hydroelectric power (HEP). Although wind and water mills had harnessed the power of nature for several centuries, HEP was the first form of renewable energy to generate electricity on a large scale.

In the 1960s, coal accounted for over 80 per cent of the UK's electricity generation. Most of the rest was oil. In 1967, the world's first pumped storage HEP station at Cruachan Loch in Argyll and Bute, Scotland, began operations (see Figures 14 and 15). Here water passes from Cruachan Loch through generating turbines to a lower lake, Loch Awe. At night, when demand is less, water is pumped back to the top lake so that it can be used again. Cruachan Loch is one of one four pumped storage schemes in the UK.

▲ **Figure 14** Cruachan Loch pumped storage HEP scheme

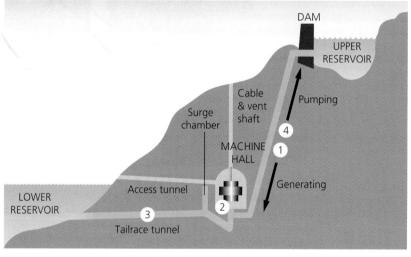

▲ **Figure 15** Diagram of Cruachan Loch pumped storage HEP scheme

In the 1970s, a sudden rise in oil prices and miners' strikes sparked government research into renewable energy. At first this involved investigating wave power. After several experiments, this was considered too expensive.

In the 1980s, solar energy started to be explored as a possibility. In 1986, Southampton started to use geothermal heat to pump hot water through a district heating system. By the late 1980s, several wind turbines had been constructed, and in 1991, the first wind farm began operating at Delabole in Cornwall (see Figure 16).

In 1990, renewables contributed less than 2 per cent of the UK's electricity generation. This grew rapidly to reach 15 per cent in 2013, and 25 per cent in 2015. Government targets aimed at reducing greenhouse gas emissions led to generous subsidies being available and, together with falling prices, this explains why there has been a rapid recent growth in renewable energy.

▲ **Figure 16** Delabole wind farm, Cornwall

Recent trends in renewable energy

Look at Figure 17. It shows the steady increase in renewable energy since 2006. Notice the rapid increase that has taken place since 2010, as the UK strives to meet its targets for carbon reduction. Notice that wind accounts for almost half of the electricity generated by renewables. You can see that there is a wide range of renewable energy sources that includes using landfill gas, sewage sludge and anaerobic digestion (see page 94).

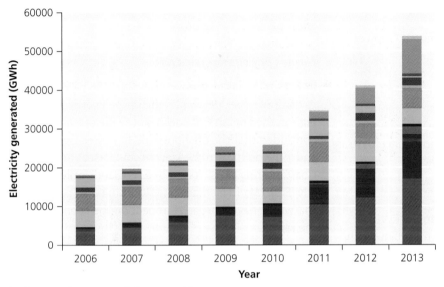

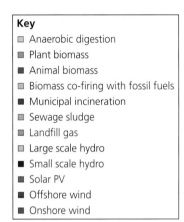

Key
- ☐ Anaerobic digestion
- ◪ Plant biomass
- ■ Animal biomass
- ☐ Biomass co-firing with fossil fuels
- ■ Municipal incineration
- ◪ Sewage sludge
- ◪ Landfill gas
- ☐ Large scale hydro
- ■ Small scale hydro
- ◪ Solar PV
- ■ Offshore wind
- ◪ Onshore wind

▲ **Figure 17** Recent trends in renewable energy

Activities

1. Study Figures 14 and 15.
   a. Describe how pumped storage works at Cruachan Loch.
   b. Why might some people object to the construction of a new dam and reservoir to produce HEP?
2. Draw a timeline to show the historical development of renewable energy in the UK.
3. Study Figure 17.
   a. What was the amount of electricity generated in 2006 and 2013?
   b. In 2013 what proportion of electricity generated came from onshore wind?
   c. Describe and suggest reasons for the trend for offshore wind from 2006–13.
   d. Why do you think there are a greater number of renewable energy sources in 2013 compared with 2006?

What are the impacts on people and the environment?

Many people are in favour of renewable energy as an alternative to using polluting fossil fuels. However, people often object if the developments are close to where they live! Such people are sometimes referred to as 'nimbys' – an acronym for 'not in my back yard'!

Wind farms

Most objections are for proposed wind farms. Onshore wind farms are often planned to be sited in areas of open countryside on high ground so that they can catch the strongest wind. These same areas are much cherished for their natural beauty and local residents are often unhappy about any proposed construction. While some people are concerned about the operating noise, most concerns relate to visual pollution and the possible impact on tourism.

Kirkby Moor wind farm, Cumbria

In 2015, local councillors objected to plans by RWE Innogy Ltd to replace twelve existing 42 m turbines with six huge turbines 115 m tall. They were concerned about the impact of the new turbines on the quality of the Lake District landscape and feared that tourism would be affected.

Many people travel to the Lake District to see the same views that inspired artists and writers such as William Wordsworth. Local people are concerned that visitors will stop visiting if these views are spoiled. This would have a harmful impact on the economy of the area and would affect people's livelihoods.

Navitus Bay offshore wind farm

In 2015, ministers rejected an ambitious £3.5 billion plan to construct over 190 wind turbines, each nearly 200 m high, in the English Channel near the Isle of Wight. They concluded that the offshore wind farm (see Figures 18 and 19) would harm the views from Dorset's Jurassic Coast, putting at risk its status as England's only natural UNESCO World Heritage Site. Tourism could suffer and this would have a negative impact on the economy of the region.

◀ **Figure 18** Artist's impression of the Navitus Bay wind farm

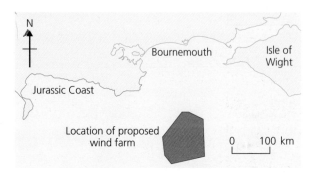

◀ **Figure 19** Location of proposed wind farm

Solar Farms

Look at Figure 20. It shows a field used for giant solar panels. Have you noticed that these developments have become increasingly popular in the past few years? The main reason for this trend has been the availability of generous government subsidies, which has made solar farms more profitable than farming. In 2015 this subsidy was significantly reduced which means that there will probably be fewer solar farms in the near future.

Hacheston solar park

In 2014 a proposal for a huge solar farm at Hacheston in Suffolk was rejected by the government. The proposed solar farm would cover an area equivalent to 75 football pitches with 100,000 solar panels. The project was rejected because it would have a negative impact on the landscape and would be a waste of valuable arable farmland. Had the development gone ahead, it would have produced enough renewable energy to power 25,000 homes.

▲ **Figure 20** Field with giant solar panels

Activities

1. Why are there often public objections to new wind farms and solar farms? Refer to examples in your answer.
2. If the government is to reach its targets for renewable energy, at what stage will it have to overrule these objections and force through new developments?

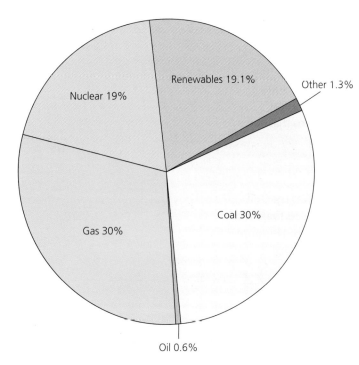

Renewables 19.1%

Other 1.3%

Nuclear 19%

Coal 30%

Gas 30%

Oil 0.6%

▲ **Figure 21** The UK electricity mix

UK energy futures

Is there a place for non-renewable energy sources?

Despite the recent growth in renewables, the UK is still dependent on fossil fuels to satisfy our energy needs. With no major renewable projects on the horizon and recent rejections of proposed wind and solar farms, it seems likely that growth in renewables will start to slow down. So, can the UK balance the need to use non-renewable energy sources with the desire to reduce carbon emissions?

Look at Figure 21. Notice that the UK has a balanced electricity mix, making use of a variety of fuel sources to generate electricity. Renewables are unlikely to change a great deal in the near future, and coal is likely to decline given its high emissions of greenhouse gases. Both natural gas and nuclear energy have low carbon emissions and are efficient ways of producing electricity. For these reasons, there is a strong argument for the UK continuing to use non-renewable energy sources in the future.

The story of natural gas

Natural gas was formed millions of years ago when the remains of plants and animals were buried and subjected to high temperatures and pressure. Natural gas is mostly methane. Today, natural gas accounts for about 50 per cent of the UK's energy supply. About 45 per cent of this is imported. As the UK's own North Sea gas reserves start to decline, imports will probably rise.

Look at Figure 22. Notice that in addition to generating electricity, natural gas is an important domestic fuel for providing heat and hot water to UK homes and businesses.

Uses	Gigawatt hours (GWh)
Electricity generation	218,395
Domestic	278,101
Industry	92,493
Energy industry	49,379
Public administration	36,969
Commercial	48,443
Miscellaneous	41,560
Total consumption	765,340

▲ **Figure 22** Natural gas consumption in the UK, 2014

Gas plays an important role in providing a reliable supply of electricity (see Figure 23). Compared with coal and oil, gas burns cleanly and it is far less polluting. Carbon capture and storage may be introduced in the future to reduce carbon emissions, though this will be expensive.

● When the gas is burned it produces combustion gases.
● Under pressure, this gas turns blades in the gas turbine and generates some electricity in the gas generator.
● The hot gases pass into the heat recovery steam turbine where pipes of water are heated.
● The steam from the heated water is then used to generate electricity in the steam turbine generator.
● The steam cools and condenses and can be reused time and time again.

In terms of energy security, natural gas is reasonably secure. The UK has its own North Sea reserves and imports come from a range of different countries (see Figure 24). This means that gas is likely to remain an important source of energy for some time to come.

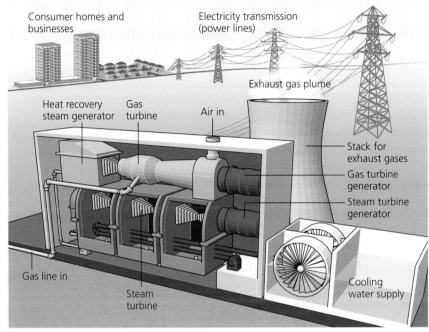

▲ **Figure 23** How a gas-fired power station works

Source of UK gas import	Percentage of total UK gas imported
Pipeline Norway	57.4%
LNG Qatar	24.5%
Pipeline Netherlands	15.1%
Pipeline Belgium	0.8%
LNG Algeria	1.2%
LNG Trinidad & Tobago	0.9%
LNG Nigeria	0.1%

▲ **Figure 24** Where the UK's imported gas comes from, 2014

The fracking debate

Large quantities of oil and gas are trapped deep underground in shale formations. Shale is a black sedimentary rock rich in organic hydrocarbons. One method of extracting both oil and gas from shale involves hydraulic fracturing, commonly known as 'fracking'. This involves pumping water, sand and chemicals into the shale under high pressure. It fractures the rock and enables the oil and gas to escape and be extracted.

Fracking is used in the USA and elsewhere in the world but it is controversial (see Figure 25). Fracking can cause minor earthquakes and possible pollution of groundwater. In the UK, several licences have been granted for experimental investigations but no commercial fracking is taking place.

▲ **Figure 25** Public protest at Balcombe, West Sussex, at the proposed site for shale gas drilling, 2014

Nuclear energy

Nuclear energy currently accounts for about 16 per cent of the UK's energy supply and generates about 19 per cent of the UK's electricity. Many of the country's nuclear power stations were constructed in the 1960s and 1970s, and some are now reaching the end of their lives.

Nuclear power stations are extremely expensive to build, yet they do offer relatively efficient and sustainable power for the future. The government is committed to developing nuclear power to secure the UK's energy supply. This means commissioning new power stations. The UK's most recent nuclear power station – Sizewell B in Suffolk – began operating in 1995, over twenty years ago!

In 2015, the Chinese announced that it would invest in the UK's nuclear programme by supporting new developments at Hinkley Point in Somerset, Bradwell in Essex and Sizewell.

▲ **Figure 26** Construction site at Hinkley Point C, Somerset

Hinkley Point C power station, Somerset

The new nuclear power station, Hinkley Point C, will be the third to be sited on the North Somerset coast (see Figure 26).

● Hinkley Point A was completed in 1965 but was decommissioned (stopped producing electricity) in 2000.
● Hinkley Point B was commissioned in 1976 and is expected to remain operational until 2023. It is operated by the French energy company EDF.

In 2015, China agreed to fund about a third of the costs of constructing a new nuclear power plant at Hinkley Point in Somerset. The total cost of the project is estimated to be £18 billion. The plant will be run by the French company EDF and is expected to start generating electricity in 2025.

The high costs involved mean that electricity will cost about twice the current amount, and this could lead to price rises for consumers. However, an estimated 25,000 jobs will be created and the government expects the power station to generate enough electricity to supply over 5 million homes (see Figure 27).

▶ **Figure 27** Hinkley Point C in numbers

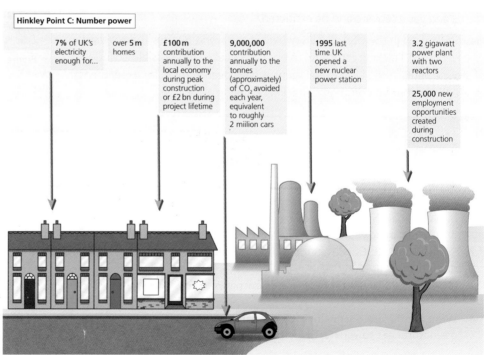

Hinkley Point C: Number power

- 7% of UK's electricity enough for...
- over 5 m homes
- £100 m contribution annually to the local economy during peak construction or £2 bn during project lifetime
- 9,000,000 contribution annually to the tonnes (approximately) of CO_2 avoided each year, equivalent to roughly 2 million cars
- 1995 last time UK opened a new nuclear power station
- 3.2 gigawatt power plant with two reactors
- 25,000 new employment opportunities created during construction

What are the factors affecting the UK's future energy supply?

The future of the UK's energy supply depends upon economic, political and environmental factors. Many of these have been covered already but Figure 28 gives you a summary.

Economic
- The high cost of building new nuclear and gas-fired power stations, as well as the decommissioning of old power stations.
- New power stations may result in more expensive electricity which could hit businesses and consumers.
- With North Sea supplies starting to dwindle, it will become increasingly expensive to extract oil and gas.
- High cost of constructing renewable energy alternatives, such as wind farms, tidal barrages and HEP.
- For individuals and local communities, small-scale renewable projects have to be cost-effective. Most require grants or loans.

Political
- Fracking could become a political issue with political parties adopting a different stance.
- Imports of natural gas, ensuring energy security by having a wide import base involving agreements with stable nations.
- To what extent should foreign countries own, operate or invest in UK energy, such as the Chinese investing in new nuclear power stations?
- Will the government continue to support and encourage the renewable sector with grants and subsidies? The solar industry may suffer as its subsidy has been cut.

Environmental
- The UK is committed to reducing carbon emissions, so will need to ensure low carbon fuels are used to provide energy in the future.
- Fracking may have environmental impacts, particularly involving pollution of groundwater aquifers.
- Many people are concerned about nuclear power – the radioactive waste and the dangers of a radioactive leak. Terrorism, too, is a concern.
- Environmental concerns may prevent expansion of the renewable sector by preventing the construction of wind farms and solar farms.

▲ **Figure 28** What are the economic, political and environmental factors affecting the UK's future energy supply?

Activities

1. Work in pairs to complete a table listing the advantages and disadvantages of developing nuclear power in the UK. Do you think the government is right to encourage foreign investment in future nuclear power stations? Justify your decision, giving evidence.
2. Study Figure 28.
   a. Can you suggest other economic, political or environmental factors that will affect the UK's energy supply in the future?
   b. Select one example for each of the three factors. For each one, suggest how it might affect the UK's future energy supply.

Practice questions

1. What is meant by the term 'prevailing wind'? **[1 mark]**

2. Describe the influence of the North Atlantic Drift on the weather of the UK? **[4 marks]**

3. Study Figure 1 on page 84 which shows the air masses affecting the UK.
   a) What is an air mass? **[1 mark]**
   b) Which air mass brings warm and moist conditions to the UK throughout the year? **[1 mark]**
   c) What are the characteristics of the Arctic Maritime air mass? **[1 mark]**
   d) From what direction does the Polar Maritime air mass travel towards the UK? **[1 mark]**

4. With reference to one air mass, describe how it can bring extreme weather to the UK. **[6 marks]**

5. With reference to a case study, evaluate the physical and human causes of flooding. **[6 marks]**

6. To what extent can future flooding be controlled by hard engineering techniques? **[6 marks]**

7. Describe how modern farming has impacted on natural ecosystems. **[4 marks]**

8. Outline the causes and ecological impacts of over-fishing. **[4 marks]**

9. Describe the advantages and disadvantages of wind farms in contributing towards the UK's future energy demands. **[4 marks]**

10. 'The process of fracking is an effective way of extracting oil and gas and its environmental impacts are minimal'. To what extent do you agree with this statement? **[6 marks]**

11. Explain the impacts of reservoirs and water transfer schemes on ecosystems and the environment. **[6 marks]**

12. Identify the renewable energy source that matches each of the following definitions:
    a) Water heated underground when in contact with hot rocks **[1 mark]**
    b) Energy produced from organic matter **[1 mark]**
    c) Energy produced using photovoltaic cells **[1 mark]**

13. Assess the importance of non-renewable energy sources in contributing towards the UK's energy mix. **[6 marks]**

14. Study Figure 2 on page 99 which shows trends in UK energy sources 1961–2009. Which of the following statements is *incorrect*? **[1 mark]**
    a) In 1961 80% of energy came from coal.
    b) Since 2005, natural gas has been the most important source of energy.
    c) Hydroelectricity has shown a steady increase since 1961.
    d) In 2009 nuclear power is the third most important energy source.

15. Assess the role of the government and international organisations in changing the UK's energy supply since 1950. **[6 marks]**

16. 'In the future, demand for energy in the UK will fall'. To what extent do you agree with this statement? **[6 marks]**

17. Evaluate the UK government's strategies for creating a low-carbon energy future. **[6 marks]**

18. With reference to one type of renewable energy, describe the impacts on people and the environment. **[6 marks]**

19. Study Figure 27 on page 114 which illustrates some facts about the proposed Hinkley Point C nuclear reactor. Outline the advantages and disadvantages of constructing a new nuclear power station at Hinkley Point. **[4 marks]**

20. Describe the environmental factors affecting the UK's future energy supply. **[4 marks]**

Tip

For question 3, make sure that you focus on a single air mass only in your answer.

Tip

Look at question 5. Make sure that you weigh up the relative importance of physical and human causes and refer in detail to a case study.

Tip

Look at question 10. You need to decide to what extent you agree with this statement and then justify your position.

Tip

For multiple choice questions, such as question 14, select the correct answer by a process of elimination.

Tip

When evaluating, like in question 17, make sure that you weigh up the advantages and disadvantages of each strategy.

Tip

For question 20, make sure that you focus entirely on environmental factors.

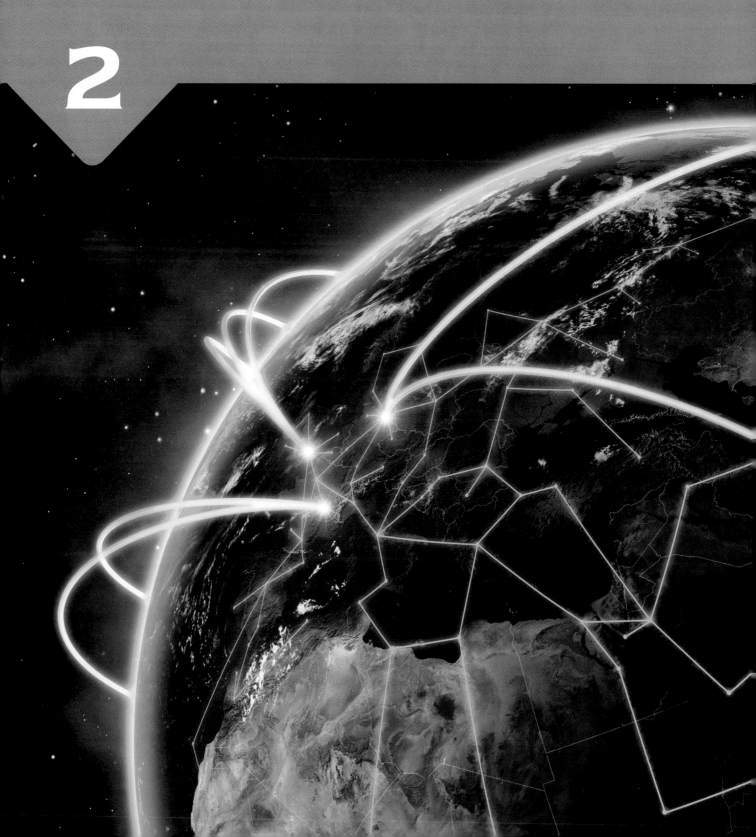

The World Around Us

THEME Ecosystems of the Planet
1

A variety of ecosystems are spread across the world and these have a number of interacting components and characteristics. This theme explores a number of these ecosystems, before looking at coral reefs and tropical rainforests in detail.

Chapter 15: Global ecosystems

Key idea: Ecosystems consist of interdependent components.
Key idea: Ecosystems have distinct distributions and characteristics.

In this chapter you will study:

→ how ecosystems include abiotic (weather, climate, soil) and biotic (plants, animals, humans) components which are interdependent

→ an overview of the global distribution of polar regions, coral reefs, grasslands, temperate forests, tropical rainforests, and hot deserts

→ an overview of the climate, plants and animals within these ecosystems.

Chapter 16: Tropical rainforests

Key idea: There are major tropical rainforests in the world.
Key idea: Biodiverse ecosystems are under threat from human activity.

In this chapter you will study:

→ the location of the tropical rainforests including the Amazon, Central American, Congo River Basin, Madagascan, South East Asian and Australasian

→ the processes that operate within tropical rainforests, including nutrient and water cycles

→ a case study of the Peruvian Amazon to investigate: the interdependence of climate, soil, water, plants, animals and humans; the value of rainforests to humans and the planet; threats to biodiversity and attempts to mitigate these through sustainable use and management.

Chapter 17: **Coral reefs**

Key idea: There are major coral reefs in the world.
Key idea: Biodiverse ecosystems are under threat from human activity.

In this chapter you will study:

→ the location of warm water coral reefs including the Great Barrier Reef, Red Sea Coral Reef, New Caledonia Barrier Reef, the Mesoamerican Barrier Reef, Florida Reef and Andros Coral Reef

→ the process of nutrient cycling that operates within coral reefs

→ a case study of the Andros Barrier Reef to explore: the interdependence of climate, soil, water, plants, animals and humans; their value to humans and to the planet; threats to biodiversity and attempts to mitigate these through sustainable use and management.

CHAPTER

15

Global ecosystems

Key idea: Ecosystems consist of interdependent components.
Key idea: Ecosystems have distinct distributions and characteristics

➜ **In this chapter you will study:**

➜ how ecosystems include abiotic and biotic components which are interdependent

➜ an overview of the global distribution of polar regions, coral reefs, grasslands, temperate forests, tropical rain forests and hot deserts

➜ an overview of the climate, plants and animals within these ecosystems.

What is an ecosystem?

Ecosystems are natural areas in which plants, animals and other organisms are linked to each other, and to the non-living elements of the environment, to form a natural system. Each ecosystem is made up of **biotic** and **abiotic** elements (see Figure 2).

- Biotic elements comprise all of the living parts of the ecosystem including plants, animals and bacteria. In the natural world, plants are known as **flora** and animals are known as **fauna**.
- Abiotic elements are the physical, non-living parts of the ecosystem, including temperature, water and light.

Large-scale ecosystems, known as **biomes**, spread across continents and have types of plants and animals that are unique to them. For example, polar bears are unique to the Arctic tundra and orang-utans are unique to the tropical rainforest. Biomes cover a wide area and are identified by their climate, soils, plants and animal species. Each of these factors is reliant upon all the others. This is known as **interdependence** (see Figure 1). Climate has the greatest influence over vegetation and soil within an ecosystem. During a period of low rainfall, less vegetation will grow, meaning that there is less food for some animals. Increasingly, however, ecosystems are being changed by human activity.

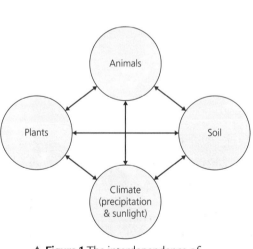

▲ **Figure 1** The interdependence of ecosystems

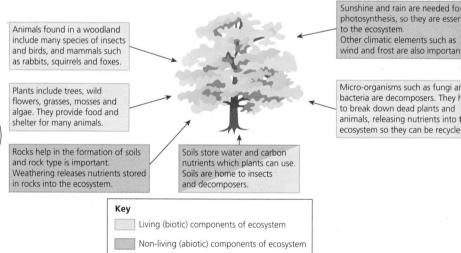

Animals found in a woodland include many species of insects and birds, and mammals such as rabbits, squirrels and foxes.

Plants include trees, wild flowers, grasses, mosses and algae. They provide food and shelter for many animals.

Rocks help in the formation of soils and rock type is important. Weathering releases nutrients stored in rocks into the ecosystem.

Soils store water and carbon nutrients which plants can use. Soils are home to insects and decomposers.

Sunshine and rain are needed for photosynthesis, so they are essential to the ecosystem. Other climatic elements such as wind and frost are also important.

Micro-organisms such as fungi and bacteria are decomposers. They help to break down dead plants and animals, releasing nutrients into the ecosystem so they can be recycled.

Key

Living (biotic) components of ecosystem

Non-living (abiotic) components of ecosystem

▲ **Figure 2** The biotic and abiotic components of an ecosystem

Where in the world are the major biomes?

Climate and latitude are important factors that contribute to the location of the world's major biomes, which broadly match the world's climate zones (see Chapter 27, pages 212–213). The world contains eight major biomes (see Figure 3). Each biome has its own climate characteristics which create distinct environments for a range of plants and animals to survive.

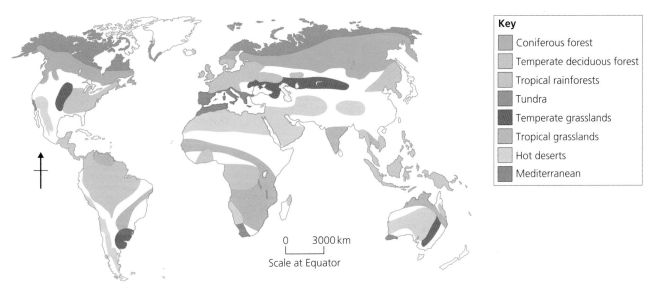

Key

- Coniferous forest
- Temperate deciduous forest
- Tropical rainforests
- Tundra
- Temperate grasslands
- Tropical grasslands
- Hot deserts
- Mediterranean

0   3000 km

Scale at Equator

▲ **Figure 3** Global distribution of the major biomes

Figure 4 shows the distribution of biomes according to temperature. **Temperate** simply means a region characterised by milder temperature; they are neither hot nor cold regions.

Temperature	World ecosystem
Tropical	1. Tropical rainforests
	2. Tropical grasslands
	3. Hot deserts
Warm temperate	4. Mediterranean
Cool temperate	5. Temperate deciduous forest
	6. Temperate grasslands
Cold	7. Coniferous forest
	8. Tundra

▲ **Figure 4** Classification of world ecosystems

Activities

1. Research the places in the world that contain the ecosystems listed in Figure 4.
2. Describe the global distribution of two contrasting ecosystems using Figure 3 and an atlas to help you.

From pole to pole: how do the two polar regions vary?

How does their location vary?

> Antarctica: a continent that covers the South Pole region. It is covered by an immense ice shelf.

> Arctic: located in the north polar ocean, including several larger islands such as Greenland and various other countries including Russia and Canada.

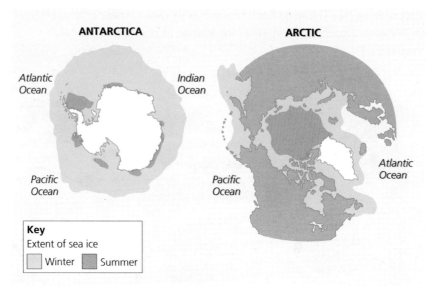

▲ **Figure 5** The polar regions – Antarctica and Arctic

What is the climate like in the polar regions?

The climate of both polar regions consists of long, cold winters and short, cool summers. They are covered by snow and ice throughout the year, though the extent of this ice varies with the seasons (see Figure 5). Antarctica is covered by an ice sheet 2.8 miles thick in some places. Temperatures rarely rise above freezing in these high-latitude regions. This is largely due to the low angle of the Sun in the sky. Owing to the tilt of the Earth, the polar regions spend half of the year in darkness and half of the year in daylight. Polar regions tend to be dry, receiving as little as 250 mm of rainfall per year. This is because the descending air is unable to pick up moisture to form clouds and snowfall.

The Arctic is much warmer than Antarctica. The North Pole winter temperatures vary from −46 °C to −26 °C whereas the South Pole temperatures range from −62 °C to −55 °C. But why is there such a difference in temperature?

- The sea in the Arctic does not fall below −2 °C, which means that the whole Arctic region stays warmer than Antarctica.
- The weather in the Arctic travels south and relatively warm weather from the south travels north into the Arctic region. This is known as the Gulf Stream.
- All of the weather in Antarctica is kept within the continent due to the circumpolar winds and currents travelling around the coastline.
- Antarctica has an average height of 2300 m, making it the highest of all the continents in the world. Temperature falls as altitude increases. In fact, with every 100 m in altitude, the temperature falls by 1°C.

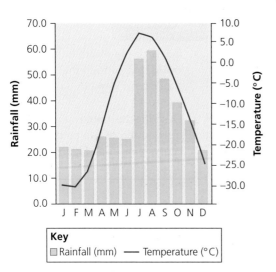

▲ **Figure 6** Climate graph for Iqaluit in Canada

What flora and fauna are found in the polar regions?

The polar region to the north is characterised by what can grow in the tundra. This is a vast area of 11.5 million km² that consists of permafrost, which means that the ground is permanently frozen. Consequently, it is a treeless area. There are, however, low shrubs, reaching a height of around 2 m, along with mosses, grasses and alpine-like flowering plants. There are approximately 1700 species of plant living in the tundra. Land mammals include polar bears, wolves, foxes and reindeer and sea mammals include walruses and whales. As the Arctic is part of a land mass, some animals are able to migrate southwards during the winter months.

Plant life in Antarctica is much less plentiful due to only about one per cent of the continent being ice free. There are some exposed rocks on which the hardiest of plants can grow. There are around 100 species of moss and 300–400 species of lichen. Both the Arctic and Antarctica have very productive seas due to large volumes of phytoplankton. Many animals that feed in the sea come onto land for part or most of the time, including large numbers of penguin species such as gentoo, emperor and Adélie. Likewise, fur seals, Weddell seals and elephant seals live in Antarctica (some of which are prey for killer whales, see Figure 7).

▲ **Figure 7** A killer whale hunting a seal in the Antarctic

Activities

1. Draw a climate graph for Vostok, Antarctica, using the data below (see Chapter 27, Figure 7 on page 213 for an example).

	Jan	Feb	Mar	Apr	May	Jun	July	Aug	Sept	Oct	Nov	Dec
Average temperature (°C)	−32	−44	−58	−65	−66	−65	−67	−68	−66	−57	−43	−32
Rainfall (mm)	0.1	0.0	0.7	0.5	0.4	0.5	0.6	0.7	0.3	0.2	0.1	0.0

2. Compare the climate graph for Iqaluit, Canada (see Figure 6) with your graph for Vostok, Antarctica.
3. Explain why Antarctica is a colder polar region than the Arctic.

What are the characteristics of tropical rainforests?

Where are they located?

Tropical rainforests are found within the Tropics of Cancer and Capricorn (23.5° north and south of the Equator) (see Figure 8).

Tropical rainforests are found in:

- South America in the Amazon River basin
- Africa (Zaire basin, small area in West Africa and eastern Madagascar)
- Southeast Asia
- New Guinea
- Queensland in Australia
- west coast of India.

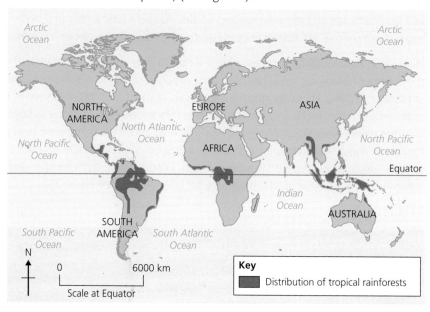

▲ **Figure 8** Locations of tropical rainforests

Rainforests now cover less than six per cent of the Earth's land surface, though this figure was once much higher. Despite this small area, it is thought that the tropical rainforests contain 50 per cent of all plant and animal species.

Tropical rainforests are being destroyed at an alarming rate, with trees cut down on a large scale. This is known as **deforestation** (see Chapter 16, page 139).

What is the climate like?

Temperatures in the tropical rainforest are high and remain constant throughout the year because the Sun is always high in the sky. It is a hot and wet climate (see Figure 9). There are no seasons like you would find in the temperate forest (see page 131). In fact, the mean monthly temperatures only vary by 2°C from 26°C to 28°C. Each day has a reliable 12 hours of daylight and 12 hours of darkness.

Annual rainfall totals are very high; often over 2000 mm. A heavy, thundery downpour can be expected most afternoons in the rainforest. This is because of the meeting of trade winds at the ITCZ where warm, moist air is forced to rise rapidly, cool and condense to form frequent rain. Owing to the large amounts of moisture in the air from both rainfall and transpiration from the dense vegetation, the atmosphere is very humid and sticky. This can make it a rather unbearable climate for even the most intrepid of explorers.

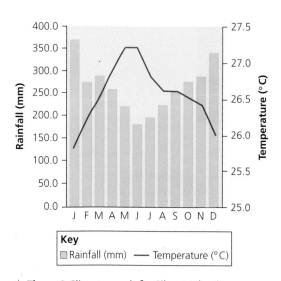

▲ **Figure 9** Climate graph for Sibu, Malaysia

What flora and fauna are found in tropical rainforests?

The climate creates the perfect environment for a wide variety of species to survive. The growing season is constant throughout the year as the climate does not vary. Fifteen million plant and animal species have been identified successfully and many more have yet to be discovered.

Vegetation consists mainly of trees. In Amazonia, there may be as many as 300 species of tree in any one square kilometre, including mahogany, ebony and rosewood. There are distinct layers to the vegetation of the tropical rainforest, as shown in Figure 10.

- The tallest trees are known as **emergents** and can reach as high as 50 m. Below this are three layers that compete for sunlight.
- The **canopy** is the next layer below the emergent layer and receives 70 per cent of the sunlight and 80 per cent of the rainfall. It is a continuous blanket of leaves. These trees are approximately 30 m high.
- The next layer is the **under canopy**, consisting of trees growing up to 20 m.
- The **shrub layer** is the lowest layer where only small trees and shrubs that have adapted to living in the shade can survive. Less than five per cent of sunlight reaches the forest floor.

The tallest trees are supported by buttress roots (see Figure 11). These emerge over 3 m above the ground level to give the tree support. Trunks are usually thin and branchless as they compete for space. Leaves are dark green and smooth and often have 'drip-tips' to shed excess water. Vine-like plants, called lianas, grow around and between tree trunks and can reach lengths of 200 m. These vines help to connect layers of the rainforest for the many animals that live there.

The tropical rainforest is filled with beautiful colours and patterns. Most of the birds, animals and insects live in the canopy layer. Insects make up the largest single group of animals, ranging from camouflaged stick insects to vast colonies of ants. Other species found in the tropical rainforest include toucans, jaguars, monkeys, chameleons, frogs and snakes. The rainforests of Borneo are one of the last habitats of the orang-utan.

There is an abundance of amphibian species. The poison dart frog is brightly coloured to warn predators. It has poison on its back and, when touched, can kill almost instantly. A single poison dart frog has enough poison to kill ten full-grown men!

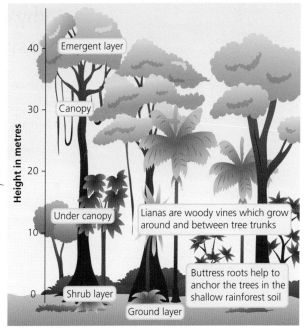

▲ **Figure 10** Structure of the rainforest

▲ **Figure 11** Buttress roots in the Amazon rainforest, Ecuador

- Rainforests have 170,000 of the world's 250,000 known plant species.
- More than 2000 different species of butterfly live in South America.
- Around 8000 different species of plant are found in Central Africa.

Activities

1. In which of these locations would you **not** find tropical rainforests?
   A. Amazon River basin
   B. Southeast Asia
   C. Namibia in southern Africa
   D. Queensland, Australia
2. Describe, using examples, how plants have adapted to survive in the tropical rainforest.

Why are coral reefs such a unique ecosystem?

Where are coral reefs found in the world?

Coral reefs are found within 30° north and south of the Equator in tropical and sub-tropical oceans (see Figure 12). Locations include:

- the western Atlantic Ocean including Bermuda, the Bahamas, Belize, Florida and the Gulf of Mexico
- an Indian and Pacific Ocean region extending from the Red Sea and Persian Gulf through to the western coast of Panama
- some areas of the Gulf of California
- the Great Barrier Reef off the eastern coast of Australia. This is the largest reef at 1500 km long and covering an area of 284,300 km². It is broken up into 2900 different reefs.

In total, 109 countries in the world have coral reefs in their waters.

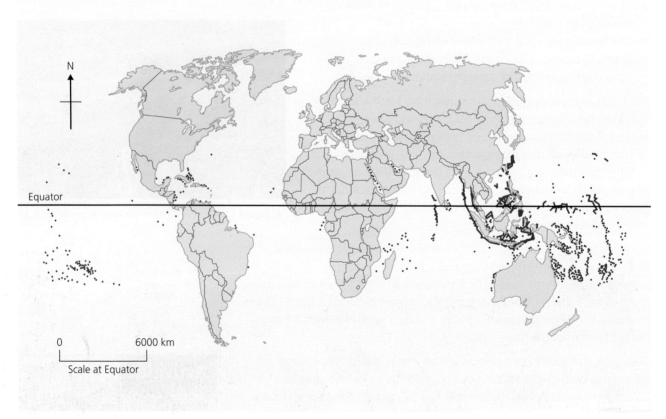

▲ **Figure 12** Global distribution of coral reefs

What are the ideal environmental conditions for coral reefs to grow?

For coral to grow, there needs to be warm water all year around with a mean temperature of 18°C. The water also needs to be clear and shallow – no deeper than 30 m. Beyond this, there is not enough sunlight for photosynthesis. Coral reefs are located on the seabed around the land, before the water depth increases. This is known as the **continental shelf**.

What flora and fauna are found in coral reefs?

Coral reefs are some of the most productive and diverse ecosystems on Earth. In fact, they are known as the 'rainforests of the oceans'. Less than one per cent (about the size of France) of the world's ocean surface is made up of coral reefs, yet it is estimated that they contain 25 per cent of all marine life. These species depend on the reef for food and shelter.

Coral reefs are made up of thousands of coral polyps which live together in reefs or colonies (see Figure 13). Although coral may look like a plant, it is actually an animal related to the jellyfish. A single polyp is 2–3 cm in length and feeds on tiny organisms such as plankton. Each polyp is a small and simple organism consisting of a stomach topped with a mouth and tentacles. They can secrete calcium carbonate to make a mineral skeleton which helps to build the structure of the reef. Corals take a long time to grow, averaging between 0.5 cm and 2 cm per year.

There is a relatively small range of plant life in coral reefs. The algae on the coral produce energy through photosynthesis, giving the coral its vibrant range of colours. Sea grasses such as turtle grass and manatee grass are commonly found in the Caribbean Sea. Unlike algae, sea grasses are flowering plants. They provide shelter and a habitat for reef animals such as the young of lobsters and provide food for herbivores such as reef fish.

Some estimates suggest that there are up to two million species living in coral reefs and 4000 species of fish alone. Some species include:

- parrot fish – feed directly on polyps, tearing coral to get to them
- starfish – produce digestive juices that they squirt into the polyps; they then suck out the middle like a soup
- clams – settle on the coral bed and filter plankton from seawater
- eels – live within the coral, pouncing on small fish
- molluscs, worms, crustaceans and sponges
- larger mammals such as dugongs, which are related to elephants; they consume large quantities of sea grass.

▼ **Figure 13** Coral sea, Queensland in Australia

Activities

1. Annotate a world map with the main locations of coral reefs in the world. Add the lines of latitude.
2. Describe the distribution shown on your map.
3. What is a polyp?
4. Suggest how **two** species have adapted to survive in the coral reef.
5. Why are coral reefs often compared to tropical rainforests?

What is a grassland?

A grassland is a region where the annual average precipitation is high enough to cause grass to grow. In some areas, there might also be occasional small trees and shrubs.

What are the characteristics of tropical grasslands?

Where are they located?

Tropical grasslands, also known as savannah, are located between the latitudes of 5° and 30° north and south of the Equator, within central parts of continents. This includes:

- most of central Africa surrounding the Congo Basin
- parts of Venezuela
- the Brazilian highlands
- Mexico
- northern Australia.

What is the climate of the tropical grasslands?

The savannah region ranges from the fringes of the rainforest to the beginnings of the desert ecosystem. Consequently, the climate can range from tropical wet to tropical dry. Temperatures are high throughout the year. Cloud cover is limited for most of the year, allowing for daily temperatures of 25°C. The main characteristic of the climate in tropical grasslands is that there are two seasons: a longer dry season and a shorter wet season (see Figure 14).

The annual range of temperatures is slightly larger than that of tropical rainforests as a result of the reduced angle of the Sun in the sky for part of the year. The wet, or rainy, season occurs when the Sun moves overhead, bringing with it the ITCZ. This is a belt of low pressure which brings bursts of heavy rainfall. In fact, 80 per cent of the annual rainfall occurs in the 4–5 months of the wet season. As the ITCZ moves away, the dry season begins (see Figure 15). During the longer dry season, rainfall can be as low as 100 mm. Figure 15 shows how the ITCZ shifts to create the two seasons.

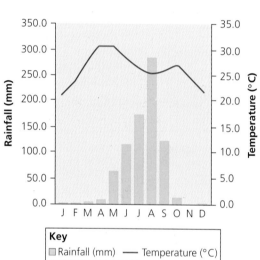

▲ **Figure 14** Climate graph for Kano, Nigeria

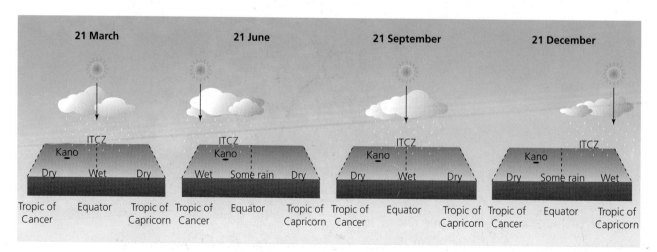

▲ **Figure 15** The movement of the ITCZ, creating wet and dry seasons

What flora and fauna are found in tropical grasslands?

The length of the growing season depends on how long the rainy season lasts. With the summer rain, the grasses, such as the tall and spiky pampas grass, grow very quickly to over 3 m in height. The baobab tree has adapted to the climate of the tropical grasslands by growing large swollen stems and a trunk with a diameter of 10 m (see Figure 16). The root-like branches hold only a small number of leaves to reduce the loss of water vapour by a process called transpiration. The bark of baobab trees is thick to retain moisture and roots are long to tap into supplies of water deep within the ground. Many trees are also drought-resistant (xerophytic) or fire-resistant (pyrophytic) as a means of surviving the long dry season.

The savannah grasslands of Africa contain the world's greatest diversity of hoofed animals with over 40 different species. The grasslands are home to herds of plant-eating animals known as **herbivores**. Antelopes are very diverse, and include gazelles and impalas. Up to 16 grazing species can live in the same area of grassland, including elephants, giraffes, wildebeest, zebras and rhinos (see Figure 17). African elephants are the largest mammals in the world. The **carnivores** in this ecosystem stalk the herds; these include cats such as cheetahs, lions and leopards, as well as dogs and hyenas.

▲ **Figure 16** Baobab trees in Madagascar, Africa

Activities

1. How does the baobab tree survive in the tropical grasslands?
2. What is the difference between xerophytic and pyrophytic trees?
3. Using Figures 14 and 15, explain how the movement of the ITCZ affects the climate.

▲ **Figure 17** Elephants at a waterhole in Etosha National Park, Namibia

What are the characteristics of temperate grasslands?

Where are they located?

Temperate grasslands lie in the centre of continents, between the latitudes of around 40–60° north and south of the Equator. The major temperate grasslands include the:

- plains of North America
- veldts of Africa
- pampas of South America
- steppes of Eurasia.

What is the climate of the temperate grasslands?

The climate of the temperate grasslands is cooler than that of the savannah. It is an ecosystem of extremes. Summers are very hot and winters are very cold. Summer temperatures can reach over 38°C and winter temperatures can plummer as low as −40°C. Average rainfall varies from 250 mm to 750 mm (see Figure 18). Around 75 per cent of this rainfall occurs during the summer growing season. Snow acts as a reservoir of moisture to help the start of the summer growing season as it melts. The summer months can bring periods of drought and the occasional fire which helps to maintain the grasslands.

▲ **Figure 18** Climate graph for Topeka, Kansas, USA

What flora and fauna are found in temperate grasslands?

The length of the growing season depends on the temperature. Vegetation does not grow as rapidly or as tall as that of the tropical grasslands. Trees and shrubs struggle to grow, but some trees, such as willow and oak, grow along river valleys where more water is available. Tussock grasses reach heights of 2 m and are found in clumps on the landscapes. Grasses, such as buffalo and feather grass, grow more evenly across the land, up to around 50 cm in height. Flowers including sunflowers and wild indigos can grow among the grasses.

The grasses provide a good habitat for burrowing animals such as gophers and rabbits and large herbivores such as kangaroos, bison and antelopes. Bison are typically found in the prairies of North America (see Figure 19). The carnivores in temperate grasslands include coyotes and wolves as well as large birds such as eagles and hawks.

Activity

Copy and complete the following table by summarising the key characteristics of tropical and temperate grasslands.

	Tropical grasslands	Temperate grasslands
Location		
Temperature		
Rainfall		
Flora		
Fauna		

▲ **Figure 19** American bison grazing in South Dakota, USA

What are the characteristics of the temperate forest ecosystem?

Where are temperate forests found?

Temperate forests are found between 40° and 60° north and south of the equator. Temperate refers to the temperature; it gets neither too hot nor too cold. It means 'not to extremes'. Temperate forest covers a wide range of forest types and their native flora and fauna, but the forests are mostly made up of deciduous or evergreen trees (see Figure 20). It is also possible to find temperate rainforests and temperate coniferous (needle-like leaves) forests in the world.

	Deciduous	Evergreen
Temperature	Moist, warm summers and frosty winters	Mild, nearly frost-free winters
Rainfall	Reliably high, year-round rainfall	Lower, more unreliable rainfall
Locations	Northern hemisphere including eastern North America, eastern Asia and western Europe (including the British Isles)	New Zealand, parts of South America, eastern Australia, southern China, Korea and Japan

▲ **Figure 20** Comparisons between different types of temperate forest

What is the climate like in temperate forests?

Owing to the tilt of the Earth, the Sun's rays hit different parts of the planet more directly at different times of the year. This has created four seasons of equal length: winter, spring, summer and autumn. This is where temperate forests thrive. Summers are warm and winters are mild. Rainfall ranges from 750 mm to 1500 mm and the average annual temperature is 10 °C (see Figure 21). An insulating layer of cloud cover helps to keep the temperature mostly above freezing. Precipitation falls throughout the year. Snow is common in mountainous areas during the winter, but is unlikely to settle at lower levels.

The temperate forest ecosystem has the second highest rainfall after tropical rainforests. This is largely due to their location at the meeting point of the Ferrell and polar cells. The warm tropical air is forced to rise over the denser, cold polar air. This creates an area of low pressure and subsequent rainfall (see Chapter 27, page 215).

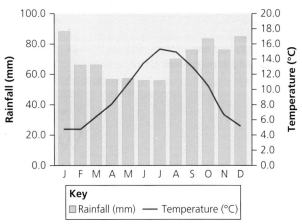

▲ **Figure 21** Climate graph for Kilkenny, Ireland

Activities

1. Describe the climate of the temperate deciduous forest.
2. Draw an annotated diagram similar to Figure 10 to show the layers of the temperate forest.

▲ **Figure 22** Black bear in western Montana, USA

▲ **Figure 23** Red deer under an oak tree in Richmond Park, England

What flora and fauna are found in temperate forests?

There are relatively few tree species when compared with the rainforest. Trees have a growing season of 6–8 months and may grow only 50 cm per year. Deciduous trees shed their leaves during the winter season. Leaves turn a spectacular range of reds, oranges and yellows during the autumn before they fall to the ground. In Britain, oak trees can reach heights of 30–40 m. A single oak tree can produce 90,000 acorns in one year. Elm, beech, sycamore and chestnut trees grow less tall and have broad, thin leaves. Beneath this canopy is a lower shrub layer, known as the understorey. Trees and shrubs here vary in height from 5 m for hawthorns to 20 m for ash and birch trees. Unlike the rainforest, branches of the higher trees are more open and allow enough sunlight through to enable smaller trees to grow. The forest floor is often covered with brambles, grass, bracken and thorns.

Animals must adapt to cope with the colder winters and warmer summer months. Some animals migrate to warmer places and others hibernate to escape the cold. The types of fauna often depend on the region of the world. Many species are native to certain places, so they may only be found there. For example, Australia's temperate forests contain marsupial species such as koalas and opossums which are not found anywhere else in the world.

Black bears are found in the temperate forests of North America (see Figure 22). They have adapted well to the conditions here. They have a heavy coat made of many layers of fur and build up a five-inch layer of fat before hibernating for the winter. Black bears also have long claws to climb trees and are **omnivores**. This means that they eat can plants and animals.

In the northern hemisphere, squirrels are widespread. Owls and pigeons are found in almost all temperate forests as are an abundance of other bird species. In Britain, rabbits, deer, mice and foxes are commonly found animal species (see Figure 23).

What are the characteristics of the hot deserts?

Where are deserts found?

Deserts cover one-fifth of the Earth's land surface. They are located between 5° and 30° north and south of the Equator, around the Tropic of Cancer and the Tropic of Capricorn. They are usually found on the west coast of continents. The extensive Sahara and the Arabian desert cover the African and Asian land mass, respectively. The Sahara covers a staggering land area of 9 million km²; that is 37 times the size of the UK.

What is the climate like in hot deserts?

Owing to their location near the tropics, deserts experience a fairly high number of daylight hours ranging from 14 hours in the summer to 10 hours in the winter. During the day, temperatures can reach 36°C, with extremes of 50°C recorded (see Figure 24). At night, however, temperatures plummet to well below freezing. During the day, high levels of input from the Sun raise the temperatures. Bare rock and

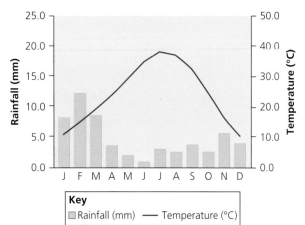

▲ **Figure 24** Climate graph for Death Valley, California, USA

sand will also heat up. The lack of clouds in the sky means that the heat from the day escapes readily into the atmosphere during the night, causing temperatures to fall dramatically to −12°C or lower.

Annual precipitation is around 40 mm and extremely unreliable. In Death Valley in California, rain may fall only once every 2–3 years. The baked ground makes infiltration, the process where water passes through the surface of the ground, very limited. As a result, the water sits on the surface and evaporates rapidly in the heat of the day.

What flora and fauna are found in hot deserts?

In desert climates, vegetation needs to be resistant to the lack of moisture and intense heat. Most plants are **xerophytic**, meaning that they have adapted to an environment with very little water. Cacti and yucca plants are found in the driest and hottest places (see Figure 25). Where the rainfall is slightly higher, thin grasses grow. Where bushes grow, they are far apart to avoid competition for water.

Cacti absorb large amounts of water during the rare periods of rain. They have thick, spiky, waxy leaves to reduce the loss of water through transpiration and to prevent animals from trying to eat them. Roots of xerophytes do one of two things. They are either very long, like those of the acacia tree with roots exceeding 15 m to tap into groundwater supplies, or they are near the ground's surface and spread over a large area to take advantage of any rain that falls.

When a storm occurs, the desert bursts into life. Plant seeds then lie dormant for many months or years, awaiting the next downpour.

The lack of food in the form of plants makes it difficult for deserts to support many animal species. The desert ecosystem is very fragile as animals do not have alternative food sources which may be available in other ecosystems. Many animals are small and nocturnal, meaning that they only come out at night. With the exception of camels, animals would not be able to survive in hot sun so are likely to burrow into the sand during the heat of the day.

Animals have adapted considerably to survive in the desert.

- Meerkats, which live in the harsh land of the Kalahari Desert in southern Africa, occupy complex underground tunnel systems. They have adapted to the limited food sources by feeding on scorpions, whose venom they are immune to. They also eat lizards and small rodents.
- Camels have humps on their backs that store fat and water. They also have thick hair on their ears, long eyelashes for keeping out the sand and wide feet that act like snowshoes.
- Sidewinder rattlesnakes are found in the Mojave Desert in southwest USA and the Namib Desert in southern Africa. Their unusual sideways motion helps them to keep moving in shifting sands and ensures that only two parts of their body are touching the hot ground at any one time.

▲ **Figure 25** Cacti in the Sonoran Desert, Tucson, Arizona, USA

Activities

1. Suggest two reasons to explain why the temperature varies so much during a day in the desert.
2. For either flora or fauna, explain how species have adapted to survive in the hostile desert climate.

→ Take it further

3. Choose one major desert in the world. Create a fact file, or a class presentation, about your chosen desert. Create three to five of your own enquiry questions to guide your research.

CHAPTER

16

Tropical rainforests

Key idea: There are major tropical rainforests in the world.

Key idea: Biodiverse ecosystems are under threat from human activity.

➡ In this chapter you will study:

➡ the location of the tropical rainforests in the world

➡ the processes that operate within tropical rainforests, including nutrient and water cycles

➡ a case study of the Peruvian Amazon to investigate:

— the interdependence of climate, soil, water, plants, animals and humans

— the value of rainforests to humans and the planet

— threats to biodiversity and attempts to mitigate these through sustainable use and management.

The location of tropical rainforests

Tropical rainforests are found in a broad belt through the Tropics, from Central and South America through central parts of Africa, South East Asia and into the northern part of Australia (see Figure 2). This biome is characterised by a plentiful supply of rainfall (over 2,000 mm a year) and high temperatures (averaging about 27°C) throughout the year. This climate provides ideal conditions for plant growth, accounting for the astonishing biodiversity of tropical rainforests.

▲ **Figure 1** Mist evaporating off the rainforest-covered highlands of Malaysia

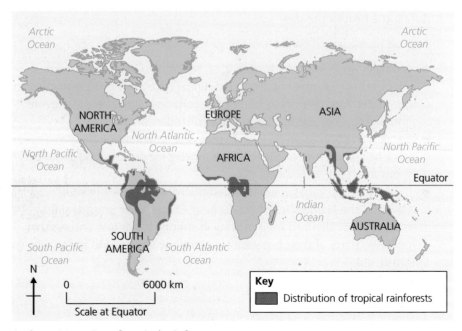

▲ **Figure 2** Location of tropical rainforests

Processes within tropical rainforests

Nutrient cycle

Nutrient cycling is rapid in the rainforest. Figure 3 shows the relationship between **biomass**, soil and **litter**. The size of the circles indicates the amount of nutrients held in each store.

- The forest floor is hot and damp, which enables dead plant leaves to decompose quickly. This explains the small circle for the leaf litter. This decomposition can occur within three to four months in the rainforest, whereas in the UK, it can take two or more years for leaves to decompose.
- As organic material, such as leaves, decays, it is recycled so quickly by the nutrient-hungry plants and trees that few nutrients ever reach the soil. The circle for the soil is even smaller than the litter. This is why many trees have their roots close to or above the surface of the ground, so that they are poised to take advantage of any nutrients available.
- The greatest store of nutrients is in the biomass, the living plants and animals.

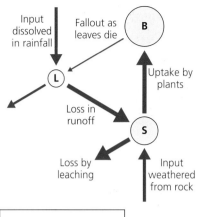

Key
- ○ Store of nutrients
- → Transfer of nutrients
- B Biomass
- L Litter
- S Soil

▲ **Figure 3** Nutrient cycle in the tropical rainforest ecosystem

Litter – total amount of organic matter, including humus (decomposed material) and leaf litter

Biomass – the total mass of plants and animals in the ecosystem.

Water cycle

Rainforests produce their own rainfall. As the rainforest heats up during the morning, the water evaporates into the atmosphere and forms clouds to make the rainfall for the next day. This is called **convectional rainfall**.

Water is lost through pores in leaves and then evaporated by heat in a process known as **evapotranspiration**. The roots of plants take up some moisture through **transpiration**, but much of the water is evaporated from the canopy later. The canopy also intercepts most of the rainfall (see Figure 4)

The removal of trees by exploitative practices means that there is less moisture in the atmosphere and rainfall declines. This can sometimes lead to drought, as can happen is the Amazon region.

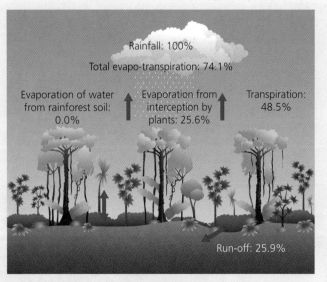

▲ **Figure 4** Water cycle in the tropical rainforest ecosystem

Activity

Represent Figure 4 as a flow diagram.

Case study: a tropical rainforest

Tropical rainforest case study: the Peruvian Amazon

Where is the Peruvian Amazon?

Most people assume that the Amazon rainforest is located solely in Brazil. In fact, the Amazon rainforest is spread across several countries in South America (see Figure 5). Peru has the second largest portion after Brazil. Tropical rainforest makes up some 60 per cent of Peru, yet only 5 per cent of Peruvians actually live in this region. The Peruvian Amazon is the third largest rainforest in the world.

▲ **Figure 5** The location of the Amazon rainforest

What are the characteristics of the Peruvian Amazon?

The tropical rainforest biome in Peru is one of the most diverse in the world. About 44 per cent of all bird species and 63 per cent of all mammals live in the Peruvian rainforest. It is, however, a surprisingly fragile ecosystem that involves complex interrelationships and considerable interdependence between abiotic (non-living) factors such as climate, soils and water and biotic (living) factors such as plants, animals and humans.

▲ **Figure 6** Peruvian jaguar

Look at Figure 7. It shows the interdependence that exists within the Peruvian Amazon rainforest.

The hot and wet tropical climate is ideal for the rapid and luxuriant growth of vegetation. The average temperature is 28°C and annual rainfall is 2600 mm. Among the many tropical hardwood trees in the Peruvian Amazon is the rare and highly valued big-leafed mahogany prized for its timber for furniture and construction.

The Peruvian Amazon is home to some of the world's most spectacular wildlife such as the jaguar, harpy eagle, scarlet macaw, giant river otter and black spider monkey (see Figure 6). They thrive in the rainforest where there is plenty to eat and many suitable places to live (habitats).

There are few nutrients in the soil – most are stored within the trees and plants. This is because fungi and bacteria thrive in warm and humid conditions. They cause the rapid decomposition of dead organic matter, such as leaves. The newly released nutrients are rapidly absorbed by the plants and trees.

Many people live and depend on the Peruvian Amazon. If people cut down and remove trees, they take away the valuable rainforest nutrients and the ecosystem will suffer. Illegal logging in the Peruvian Amazon is a major threat to the environment and the people that live there.

▲ **Figure 7** Interdependence in a tropical rainforest

Activity

Make a large copy of Figure 7. Describe the important links and connections (interdependence) that exist between the various components of the Peruvian Amazon rainforest.

How is the Peruvian Amazon valuable to humans and the planet?

The Peruvian Amazon is extremely valuable to people for all sorts of reasons.

- **Biodiversity** – Peru has some 2937 known species of amphibians, birds, mammals, and reptiles; 16 per cent exist in no other country.
- **Timber** – there are many highly valued hardwood trees in Peru and logging is widespread.
- **Minerals** – there are valuable minerals including oil, natural gas and gold. The exploitation of these resources poses a considerable threat to the rainforest and its people.
- **Hydro-electricity** – there are plans to construct fifteen large dams in the Peruvian Amazon, primarily to export electricity to supply Brazil's giant aluminium and extractive industries.
- **Archaeology** – there are many archaeological remains of buildings constructed by ancient civilisations, such as the Chachapoya, the so-called 'Cloud Forest People' (see Figure 8).
- **Indigenous tribes** – many traditional tribes live in the Peruvian Amazon, some of which have never been contacted. They live a simple but sustainable life, deep in the jungle. Unfortunately, their land is being destroyed by others and their future is threatened.
- **Medicinal plants** – the Peruvian Amazon has been described as a 'pharmacy' because of all the medical plants that exist. Scientists believe that some rainforest plants can help cure diseases such as cancer, aid digestion and even help cure addiction, and the possibility of more plants as yet to be discovered.

▲ **Figure 8** The ancient ruins of the walled city of Kuelap, constructed by the Chachapoyans in the sixth century AD

Rainforests, such as the Peruvian Amazon, are very important for the planet as a whole. They have a vital role to play in regulating the Earth's water and carbon cycles.

Water cycle – rainforests give off water from their leaves during the process of transpiration. This increases humidity in the atmosphere and increases rainfall. When rainforests are cut down the climate becomes drier.

Carbon cycle – rainforests take in carbon dioxide from the air as they grow and photosynthesise. With their large leaves, photosynthesis is very effective and trees store a lot of carbon. Carbon dioxide is a greenhouse gas which is partly responsible for climate change and global warming. Rainforests have an important role to play in storing carbon and reducing the amount of carbon in the atmosphere. If the trees are burned, then the carbon is released back into the atmosphere enhancing the greenhouse effect.

Threats to biodiversity

Rainforests across the world are under threat from a variety of pressures and deforestation is a global concern. The main threats in the Peruvian Amazon are:

- **Timber** – the many valuable hardwood trees in the rainforest, in particular the mahogany tree, has resulted in extensive logging. Up to 95 per cent is thought to be unregulated and illegal. Profits are so high that trees are even being felled in protected areas such as National Parks. Deforestation is a brutal operation that often takes out great swathes of forest, severely affecting biodiversity.
- **Energy** – there are valuable reserves of oil and natural gas in the Peruvian Amazon. China has invested in oil exploitation in Madre de Dios region, an area that is home to more than 10 per cent of the world's bird species and a popular destination for eco-tourists. The extraction of oil can lead to oil leaks and serious pollution of water courses (see Figure 9).

▲ **Figure 9** Oil pollution and fires resulting from an oil spill

Camisea natural gas project

The Camisea natural gas project is designed to exploit a huge gas field in the Peruvian Amazon that could save Peru $4 billion in energy costs and earn it several billion more in exports.

This project is, however, located in one of the most biodiverse parts of the rainforest. It is also home to several tribes. The extraction plant, together with pipelines and roads, has led to deforestation, landslides and water pollution.

Activity

Figures 9 and 10 show impacts on the environment of oil spills and gold mining.

a. Use evidence from the photos to describe the likely impacts on the rainforest ecosystem and on biodiversity.

b. Suggest impacts on the local indigenous people.

- **Gold mining** – gold is found in alluvial (river) deposits in the Peruvian Amazon. This is exploited by huge machines and often involves the blasting of river banks and the removal of rainforest to provide access to remote areas. Mercury is used in the operation and this is highly toxic, causing considerable harm to aquatic ecosystems and poisoning local tribes who depend upon rivers for food and water (see Figure 10).

▲ **Figure 10** The impact of gold mining on the Peruvian Amazon

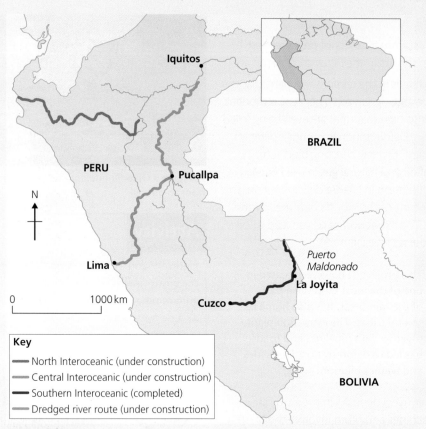

▲ Figure 11 Construction routes through the Peruvian Amazon

- **Highways** – one of the most significant threats to Peru's rainforests in the southeastern part of the country is the Trans-oceanic Highway, a road project that will connect Pacific ports to a major highway in Brazil. Environmentalists and local indigenous groups are concerned that the improved road will lead to deforestation and will worsen illegal logging in the region's protected areas. In 2015, plans were announced to extend Peru's 'jungle highway' through Manu National Park (see Figure 11), described by UNESCO as a place where biodiversity 'exceeds that of any other place on earth'.
- **Agriculture** – increasingly lowland areas are being deforested to create land for farming, particularly for growing soybeans and for rearing cattle. Fires used to clear land can sometimes burn out of control, wiping out valuable habitats and killing animals.

Managing Peru's rainforest

Despite its economic riches, the Peruvian government is acutely aware of the need to conserve its rainforest for future generations. Several NGOs, such as the World Wide Fund for Nature, are working with the government to encourage sustainable management and conservation of forest resources and wildlife in the Peruvian Amazon.

- Since 2000, management plans are required for all forest-related harvesting activities. The emphasis is on sustainable management in line with the requirements of the Forest Stewardship Council (FSC). With so much illegal logging and such a vast area to police, implementation of this law faces huge problems.
- Indigenous community reserves have been established, giving local communities land ownership and rights over the extraction of materials from their land. These communities have their own sustainable management plans.
- National Parks and National Reserves have been established to protect certain areas of high biodiversity.

Activity

Draw a large spider diagram or produce an information poster to describe the uses and value of the Peruvian Amazon to people. Use the internet to find a selection of photos to illustrate your work.

The Purus-Manu Conservation Corridor

Look at Figure 12. It shows the so-called Purus-Manu Conservation Corridor in the Madre de Dios region in southeast Peru close to the border with Brazil. It is made up of the Alto Purus and Manu National Parks together with several territorial reserves for indigenous communities.

The Purus-Manu Conservation Corridor project supports long-term biodiversity conservation in benefiting the native communities living in the Corridor. Comprising an area of over 10 million hectares, this is the largest preserved area in the Peruvian Amazon. It is recognised as being one of the most biodiverse regions in the world.

The 60 or so local communities depend on the rainforest for water, food, medicine, clothing and housing. Some of these communities are among the most isolated in the rainforest and wish to remain so (see Figure 13). Elsewhere, they have been driven out by illegal logging, ranching and highway construction. It is the largest area of responsibly managed forest in Peru and functions as a refuge for threatened species, such as river dolphins, red howler monkeys, spectacled bears and mahogany.

Management strategies to control developments and protect indigenous communities were put in place in 2015, to enable the Corridor to be managed in a sustainable way for the future.

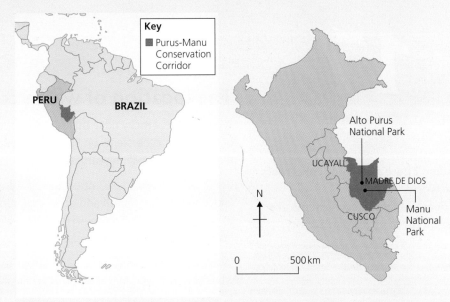

▲ **Figure 12** Location of the Purus-Manu Conservation Corridor

▲ **Figure 13** A village on Rio Madre de Dios, Peru

Land use	Percentage of total land use
Natural protected areas (e.g. National Parks)	50
Indigenous territorial reserves	17
Timber forest concessions	14
Native communities	10
Conservation and ecotourism concessions	2
Others	7
Total	100

▲ **Figure 14** Land use in Purus-Manu Conservation Corridor

Activities

1. Study Figure 12.
   a. Describe the location of the Purus-Manu Conservation Corridor in Peru.
   b. Look back through the section on 'Threats to biodiversity' and see if you can find any threats located within the Purus-Manu Conservation Corridor.
   c. Suggest why this area has been identified as needing sustainable management.
   d. Use the data in Figure 14 to draw a pie chart to show the land use within the Purus-Manu Conservation Corridor.
   e. Look at Figure 13. How will the generation of children in this village benefit from sustainable management of the rainforest?

CHAPTER

17

Coral reefs

Key idea: There are major coral reefs in the world.

Key idea: Biodiverse ecosystems are under threat from human activity.

→ **In this chapter you will study:**

→ the location of warm water coral reefs

→ the process of nutrient cycling within coral reefs

→ a case study of the Andros Barrier Reef to explore:

— the interdependence of climate, soil, water, plants, animals and humans

— their value to humans and to the planet

— threats to biodiversity and attempts to mitigate these through sustainable use and management.

The location of warm coral reefs

A coral reef is a rocky ridge built up from the seabed by coral animals. It is one of the richest ecosystems on Earth and is extremely biodiverse. Some living reefs are several million years old.

Coral reefs are extremely important ecosystems. They support a great number and a huge variety of fish and other organisms. Millions of people living close to coral reefs depend on them for their livelihoods, and from their protection from tropical storms and tsunami.

Warm coral reefs need certain conditions to survive and thrive. This explains why they are found in the Tropics (see Figure 1).

There are three main conditions needed for coral reefs to form.

- **Temperature** – they only live in seawater that has an average temperature of 18°C and over. The ideal temperature is between 23°C and 25°C. This explains why coral reefs are found in the Tropics.
- **Light** – corals feed on tiny algae and the algae need light to photosynthesise and grow. If there is not enough light, there will be no algae and if there is no algae there will be no coral! This explains why coral reefs are found in relatively shallow water where there is maximum light available.
- **Clear water** – corals survive best in clear unpolluted water. Sediment in the water affects the coral's ability to feed as well as reducing the amount of light. This explains the lack of extensive reefs close to river mouths.

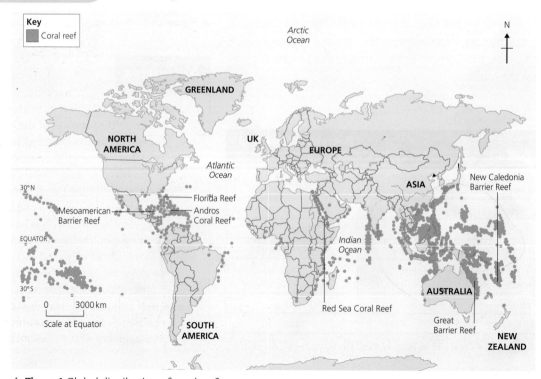

▲ **Figure 1** Global distribution of coral reefs

Nutrient cycling in coral reefs

Nutrient cycling involves the flows of nutrients (foods) within an ecosystem. Coral reefs are one of the most diverse and complex ecosystems in the world. Described as the 'tropical rainforest of the sea', in common with rainforests, their interrelationships are very fragile. The slightest change can have serious knock-on effects.

Corals live in nutrient-poor waters. It is only through very efficient nutrient recycling that corals maintain such a diverse ecosystem. At the heart of the recycling is a **symbiotic** relationship that exists between coral and algae. Symbiotic means that both organisms benefit from an association with each other.

- Zooxanthellae (plant-like algae) live within the tissues of the coral polyp (see Figure 2). They are able to harness the light from the sun, converting it into energy, just like plants, to provide nutrients to the corals.
- In exchange, the zooxanthellae benefit by having exclusive access to the waste nutrients produced by the coral. These wastes (nitrogen and phosphorus) fertilize the algae. They also have somewhere to live!

The most important nutrient is nitrogen. The symbiotic relationship between the algae and the coral captures and retains nitrogen very effectively. It is simply passed back and forth between the two organisms. In open waters, free-floating algae and marine animals lose nitrogen to the water, so nitrogen recycling is less effective.

The close relationship between coral and algae is supported by nutrients obtained from the water and from the consumption of microscopic prey called zooplankton (see Figure 3). Zooplankton obtains nutrients by consuming phytoplankton, a primary producer living in the ocean that converts light from the sun directly into energy. Corals are also able to digest bacteria and edible detritus that often enter the system by upwelling from the ocean floor.

Fish also have a role to play. They constantly excrete ammonia (a dissolved form of nitrogen) into the water and this can be absorbed by corals and algae. Fish also benefit from coral reefs in finding both food and shelter.

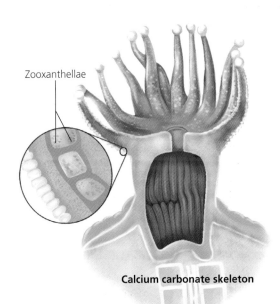

Zooxanthellae

Calcium carbonate skeleton

▲ **Figure 2** Coral polyp and zooxanthellae

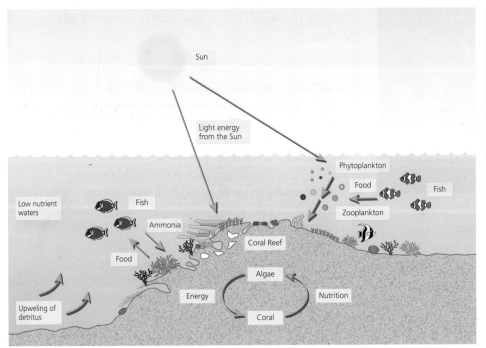

▲ **Figure 3** Simplified coral reef nutrient cycle

Activities

1. Study Figure 3.
   a. What are the sources for nutrients in the coral reef ecosystem?
   b. What is meant by the term 'symbiotic'?
   c. Describe the symbiotic relationship that exists between the corals and zooxanthellae.
   d. How does the coral reef ecosystem maintain such biodiversity in low nutrient waters?
   e. Describe the important relationship that exists between coral and fish.

Case study: a coral reef

The Andros Barrier Reef

The Andros Barrier Reef is part of an extensive coral reef system in the Bahamas, off the southeast coast of Florida, USA (see Figure 4). The entire reef is the third most extensive coral reef system in the world. The Andros reef, centred on Andros Island, is called a 'barrier reef' because it forms a linear feature parallel to the shoreline separated from it by a lagoon.

The Andros Barrier Reef stretches for approximately 200 km (see Figure 5). A shallow lagoon with mangrove forests separates the land from the main reef itself. The outer edge of the reef is marked by a steep drop to a depth of over 2000 m known as the 'Tongue of the Ocean'!

The Andros Barrier Reef ecosystem

Over 164 species of fish and coral make up the reef community. They include the red snapper, reef shark, rock lobster, sharp nose puffer and the green turtle, together with many colourful species of coral (see Figure 6).

The different species are closely interrelated in this unique habitat. The fish benefit from the safety and shelter of the reef for breeding. They obtain their food from the plankton, crustaceans and other fish. Coral benefits from nitrogen excreted through the gills of fish and from detritus swept up by the swirling fish shoals.

▲ Figure 4 Location of the Andros Barrier Reef

The warm tropical climate is ideal for reef formation and the waters are relatively clean and clear. This enables sunlight to penetrate into the water so that zooxanthellae and phytoplankton can photosynthesise effectively. Phytoplankton is at the bottom of the food chain. Without it, the ecosystem would not survive.

Humans are an important part of the coral reef ecosystem. They can cause damage to the ecosystem through over-fishing, tourism and mining. Coastal developments can lead to silt being washed into the reef system, clouding the waters and choking the corals. On the positive side, people can act as stewards monitoring coral reefs and helping to protect and preserve them.

What are the values of the coral reef to humans and the planet?

The Andros Barrier Reef is important for several reasons:

- **Coastal protection** – Coral reefs act as buffer zones providing vital shoreline protection from storms and tsunami. The Bahamas occasionally gets struck by tropical storms and the shallow water above a reef forces waves to break early before reaching the islands. This reduces coastal erosion and the risk of flooding.
- **Fish breeding grounds** – Corals provide sheltered conditions for the growth of mangrove forests, which themselves are important breeding grounds for fish. Fish are important commercially and for tourism, as well as being vital elements in the reef ecosystem. In the Bahamas, local and export markets for snapper, grouper, lobster and conch generate millions of dollars.

▲ Figure 5 The Andros Barrier Reef

- **Tourism** – The reefs in the Bahamas are the base for commercial and recreational activities like fishing, sport fishing, cruising, snorkelling and scuba diving (see Figure 6). These industries bring in over US$150 million per year. The vertical wall and sunlight penetration due to its east-facing aspect makes Andros Barrier Reef one of the most spectacular diving experiences in the region.
- **Healthy coral reef** – The Andros Barrier Reef is recognised as being one of the healthiest reefs in the world. As such it is superb outdoor laboratory for scientific research in the face of serious problems faced by coral reefs elsewhere.

On a larger scale, coral reefs are important to humans and the planet. They provide jobs, livelihoods, food, shelter, and protection for coastal communities in the tropics.

▲ **Figure 6** Scuba diving at the Andros Barrier Reef

The global value of the world's coral reefs has been estimated at almost US$30 billion each year! In Hawaii alone, the benefits associated with tourism, fishing and biodiversity amount to US$360 million a year.

They provide a home to over 25 per cent of all known marine fish. One hectare of reef off South East Asia was found to support over 2000 species of fish!

Coral reefs are extremely popular tourist destinations, providing a huge source of income and employment for thousands of people. For example, millions of people visit the Caribbean each year to enjoy its tropical beaches and coral reefs.

Coral Reefs

Coral reefs are extremely important commercial fishing grounds providing some 25 per cent of the LIC's total fish catch. It is estimated that coral reef fisheries in East Asia feed over 1 billion people.

Coral reefs are increasingly valued for medicinal purposes. Scientists believe that some of the chemicals released by coral species for self-protection could have applications for the treatment of some viruses and cancers.

▲ **Figure 7** How coral reefs are important

Activities

1. Use Figures 4 and 5 to help you describe the location, extent and characteristics of the Andros Barrier Reef. Explain why it is called a 'barrier' reef.
2. Produce an information poster describing some of the main characteristics of the Andros Barrier Reef ecosystem. Consider the climate, ecology, and human uses. What makes the Andros Barrier Reef special?
3. How does the coral reef benefit the economy of the Bahamas?

What are the threats to the Andros Barrier Reef?

In many parts of the world, coral reefs are under threat from natural causes – primarily climate change – and the actions of people. They are considered by scientists to be one of the most endangered ecosystems on the planet.

The Andros Barrier Reef – in common with many reefs elsewhere in the world – faces among threats to its biodiversity.

▲ **Figure 8** Coral bleaching

Over-fishing – Commercial fishing and intensive tourism can cause immense harm to the ecosystem, causing it to become unbalanced. Corals can be killed by physical contact with anchors, boat hulls and even people's feet. The harvesting of sponges (see Figure 9) is an important local industry but can also have a harmful impact on the reef ecosystem.

Pollution – This can involve agricultural chemicals, sewage and silt, eroded from hillslopes and discharges by rivers. Silt causes the water to become cloudy restricting the penetration of sunlight used by zooxanthellae to photosynthesise.

Climate change and global warming – Higher water temperatures trigger a stress reaction in corals causing them to expel the zooxanthellae. This has a huge effect on nutrient flows and causes the coral to become bleached, turning white (see Figure 8). Eventually the coral dies. Projections from climate models suggest that reefs in the Bahamas will annually experience thermal stress severe enough to cause bleaching after 2040.

Marine-based pollution – This results from oil and chemical discharges from boats and ships. The Andros Barrier Reef is very popular for deep sea fishing and such discharges can be harmful to both corals and fish.

▲ **Figure 9** Harvesting sponges from the Andros Barrier Reef

How is the Andros Barrier Reef managed?

Management of coral reefs in the Bahamas is shared by the Department of Marine Resources (DMR) and the Bahamas National Trust (BNT). The government is committed to protect 20 per cent of its near-shore habitat by 2020. There are several National Parks and Reserves established to help preserve parts of the valuable reef ecosystem. Some are shown on Figure 10.

- The Andros West Side National Park, includes Andros Island and part of the coral reef. The National Park was designated by the government in 2002 to balance long-standing traditions of the island, such as fishing and sponging, while also promoting resource conservation, recreational fishing and ecotourism. Developments in the National Park are strictly controlled.

- The North Marine Park and South Marine Park were established in 2002 on the eastern side of the island. These are areas of conservation where some activities are regulated or prohibited, such as fishing and collecting wildlife, mining, vessel anchoring, scuba diving and the discharging of materials.

- The Crab Replenishment Reserve has been identified as the best land crab habitat in central Andros. This area was set aside to ensure a sustainable crab population for future generations.

- In the Exuma Cays Land and Sea Park, a coral nursery has been established. Here, threatened species are conserved and monitored-prior to being planted back in the coral reef.

- There are plans to establish a new National Park to the north of Andros Island at Joulter Cays. This part of the reef is prized for its fishing and for its varied and extensive shallow water ecosystem. It is under pressure from excessive fishing, damage from boats and marine discards.

Several organisations monitor the environmental quality of the reef ecosystem to assess coral bleaching and to identify any harmful impacts from human activity. Fortunately, the Andros Barrier Reef remains one of the healthiest reefs in the world.

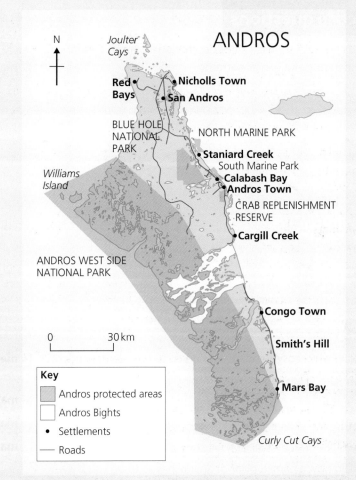

▲ **Figure 10** Reef management and conservation at Andros Island, the Bahamas

Activities

1. What are the main natural and human threats to the Andros Barrier Reef?

2. Study Figure 10.
   a. Describe the location and extent of West Side National Park.
   b. Where is the Crab Replenishment Reserve?
   c. Why is it important to have preserves acting as research laboratories and nurseries?
   d. How can the reef be managed sustainably?

→ Take it further

3. Should Joulter Cays become a National Park? Use the internet to help you investigate this part of the Andros Barrier Reef.

Practice questions

1. Study Figure A showing a hot desert climate graph. Describe the yearly temperature and rainfall patterns. **[2 marks]**

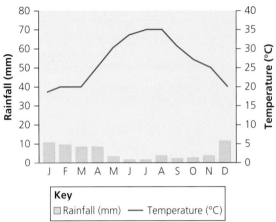

▲ Figure A

Look at question 1. You need to make sure that you describe (say what you see) for both temperature *and* rainfall. Remember, for this type of question you do not need to give reasons for the pattern you notice.

Tip

2. Explain why ecosystems are considered to be 'interdependent'. **[4 marks]**

3. Compare two canopies of the tropical rainforest with the forest floor. **[4 marks]**

4. State two species of animal found in coral reefs. **[2 marks]**

5. Describe the climate of tropical grasslands. **[3 marks]**

6. Explain how a named plant or animal has adapted to survive in the hot desert. **[3 marks]**

7. What is the term for the process by which water is lost from the pores in leaves and evaporated by heat?

   a) Convectional rainfall

   b) Condensation

   c) Evapotranspiration

   d) Microclimate **[1 mark]**

8. Which **two** statements below best explain why the nutrient cycle of tropical rainforests is rapid?

   a) Heavy rainfall washes away dead plant material.

   b) Nutrients are in high demand from the fast-growing plants.

   c) The forest floor conditions allow for the quick decomposition of dead plant material.

   d) There is great biodiversity in tropical rainforests. **[1 mark]**

9. Study Figure 2 on page 134 which shows the distribution of tropical rainforests. Describe the global distribution of tropical rainforests. **[4 marks]**

10. Study Figure 3 on page 135 which shows the tropical rainforest nutrient cycle. Explain why biomass is the most important nutrient store. **[4 marks]**

Tip

Describe the overall pattern using supporting information from the map and refer to any anomalies.

11. Study Figure 4 on page 135 which shows the water cycle in the tropical rainforest.

    a) What is 'transpiration'? **[1 mark]**

    b) Explain why 'evaporation of water from rainforest soil' is 0.0%. **[2 marks]**

    c) Discuss the implications of deforestation on the components of the water cycle illustrated in Figure 4. **[6 marks]**

> **Tip**
>
> Make sure that you refer to your chosen case study in detail.

12. With reference to a case study, describe the interdependence that exists between plant and animal species in a tropical rainforest. **[6 marks]**

13. Evaluate the threats to biodiversity in rainforests. **[6 marks]**

14. Assess the extent to which rainforests can be managed sustainably. **[6 marks]**

> **Tip**
>
> Make sure that in evaluating you weigh up the importance of the different threats.

15. Study Figure 1 (below) which shows the global distribution of coral reefs. **[1 mark]**

Which of the following statements is correct?

    a) The Red Sea Coral Reef is located in the Southern Hemisphere.

    b) Most coral reefs are located within the Tropics, between 30N and 30S.

    c) The Florida Reef is located to the south of the Andros Coral Reef.

    d) The Great Barrier Reef is located to the east of the New Caledonia Barrier Reef.

16. Outline two environmental conditions necessary for the growth and development of coral reefs. **[4 marks]**

17. Describe the characteristics of the coral reef ecosystem. **[4 marks]**

18. With reference to a case study, outline the threats to coral reef ecosystems. **[6 marks]**

19. With reference to a case study, evaluate the strategies for managing coral reefs. **[6 marks]**

> **Tip**
>
> Make sure that in evaluating you weigh up the different strategies in relation to your chosen case study.

People of the Planet

Historically, the world has developed unevenly. This theme explores the causes of this uneven development and the differences between countries. The case study on Ethiopia focuses on interrelated factors that affect its economic development. The causes and consequences of growth in urban areas are explored, particularly relating to the process of rapid urbanisation. The case study on Rosario in Argentina (an EDC) examines its people and culture and looks at the influence they have on shaping the city and its distinct ways of life and challenges.

Chapter 18: Global development

Key idea: The world is developing unevenly.

In this chapter you will study:

➡ the social, economic and environmental definitions of development, including the concept of sustainable development

➡ different development indicators, including GNI per capita, Human Development Index and Internet Users, and the advantages and disadvantages of these indicators

➡ how development indicators illustrate the consequences of uneven development

➡ the current patterns of advanced countries (ACs), emerging and developing countries (EDCs) and low-income developing countries (LIDCs).

Chapter 19: Uneven development

Key idea: There are many causes of uneven development.

In this chapter you will study:

➡ the reasons for uneven development, including the impact of colonialism on trade and the exploitation of natural resources

➡ the different types of aid and their role in both promoting and hindering development.

Chapter 20: **Ethiopia**: changing economic development

Key idea: Many factors contribute to a country's economic development.

In this chapter you will study

➡ a case study of Ethiopia (an LIDC), to explore:

— the country's geographical location, and environmental context (landscape, climate, ecosystems, availability and type of natural resources)

— the country's political development and relationships with other states

— principal imports and exports and the relative importance of trade

— the role of international investment

— population and employment structure changes over time social factors, including access to education and healthcare provision

— technological developments, such as communications technology

— one aid project.

➡ Rostow's model to determine the country's path of economic development.

Chapter 21: Global urbanisation

Key idea: The majority of the world's population now live in urban areas.

In this chapter you will study:

→ the definition of city, megacity and world city

→ the distribution of megacities and how this has changed over time

→ how urban growth rates vary in parts of the world with contrasting levels of development.

Chapter 22: Rapid urbanisation in LIDCs

Key idea: There are causes and consequences of rapid urbanisation in LIDCs.

In this chapter you will study:

→ an overview of the causes of rapid urbanisation in LIDCs including push and pull migration factors, and natural growth

→ an outline of the social, economic and environmental consequences of rapid urbanisation in LIDCs.

Chapter 23: Rosario: a major city in an EDC

Key idea: Cities have distinct challenges and ways of life, influenced by their people and culture.

In this chapter you will study

→ the case study of Rosario in Argentina (an EDC) including the influences of:

— the city within its region, the country, and the wider world

— migration (national and international) and its impact on the city's growth and character

— the ways of life within the city, such as culture, ethnicity, housing, leisure and consumption

— contemporary challenges that affect urban change, including housing availability, transport provision and waste management

→ sustainable strategies to overcome one of the city's challenges.

CHAPTER

18

Global development

Key idea: The world is developing unevenly.

➡ In this chapter you will study:

- ➡ the social, economic and environmental definitions of development, including the concept of sustainable development
- ➡ different development indicators, including GNI per capita, Human Development Index and Internet Users, and the advantages and disadvantages of these indicators
- ➡ how development indicators illustrate the consequences of uneven development
- ➡ the current patterns of advanced countries (ACs), emerging and developing countries (EDCs) and low-income developing countries (LIDCs).

Definitions of development

Development can be defined in various ways. For example:

'The act or process of change, evolution, maturity, progress' (dictionary.com)

'A state of growth or advancement' (*Oxford Dictionary*)

Everything develops over time: humans develop from tiny babies to adults, villages develop into small towns, seeds develop into forests, valleys develop into gorges. In general, development is seen as a positive process. The dictionary suggests its opposite counterpart is 'deterioration, disintegration'.

In a geographical sense, we think of development as being about improving people's lives. It is often associated with wealth but it is much more complicated than that. For example, you might consider human and environmental health as more important than wealth. The international economist Hans Rosling said, 'You move much faster if you are healthy first than if you are wealthy first.' Or perhaps being able to feel safe in your country and have a democratic, fair government with your human rights protected might be just as important as money. Figure 1 shows some of the many different features of development.

Development can happen on a small scale or a large scale, affecting either small groups of people or whole nations. It can be a slow process or more rapid. It is greatly influenced by the actions of humans and the decisions that influential people, governments or companies make.

▲ **Figure 1** How can we describe development?

What is social development?

Social development is to do with people and society. It is about the improvement that has been made by a country in improving the quality of life of people who live there. This could include improving literacy levels through access to education, housing conditions, healthcare, reducing infant mortality and increasing life expectancy. Social measures of development are shown on page 154.

What is economic development?

Economic development is about the improvement that has been made by a country in terms of wealth. This could include the value of goods and services that the country is producing, or the proportion of the population working in primary, secondary, tertiary or quaternary jobs.

What is environmental development?

Environmental development recognises the importance of the natural world and includes looking at how countries are monitoring the emissions of greenhouse gases, or what they are doing to improve water quality. The Environmental Performance Index uses 22 indicators to determine the health of people and the environment, including policies on air pollution, climate change and water quality.

What is sustainable development?

Sustainable development means that the needs of the present will be met (socially, economically and environmentally) while protecting the needs of the future. Resources cannot be exhausted and environments need to be protected. It is a balance (see Figure 2). It could include countries looking at using their resources to benefit the population but ensuring that they are sustainable, for example looking at using renewable energy sources rather than depleting stocks of gas and oil.

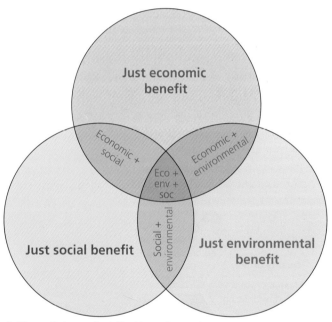

▲ **Figure 2** A sustainability Venn diagram

Activities

1. Write your own definitions of 'social development', 'economic development' and 'environmental development'.
2. Explain the concept of sustainable development.

→ Take it further

3. Use the internet to research examples of sustainable development in different countries.

Development indicators

Geographers find it useful to be able to measure how developed places are, and to compare them and see how they change over time. To do this they use different development indicators, which will be explored in this section. Some of these are social indicators (to do with people and society) and some are economic indicators (to do with money), and some, such as the Human Development Index, can measure both social and economic development.

Social measures of development

Social measures are to do with individual people and what it would be like for them living in that place. Sometimes social and economic indicators do not match: for example, some countries have excellent healthcare but a low income per person. Figure 3 illustrates some of the many social indicators we can use to measure development.

There are lots of other social indicators, including **population density** (the number of people per square km) or the food intake per person.

Economic measures of development

Economic measures tend to focus upon money and the features of a country's economy, such as employment and trade. These indicators are entwined with social measures, since without money it would be impossible to improve features like healthcare and education. Traditionally countries were evaluated and classified as more or less developed based upon the economic value of the **gross domestic product (GDP)** (the yearly value of goods and services produced within the country). It is now considered more accurate to combine multiple sources of information such as those in Figure 4.

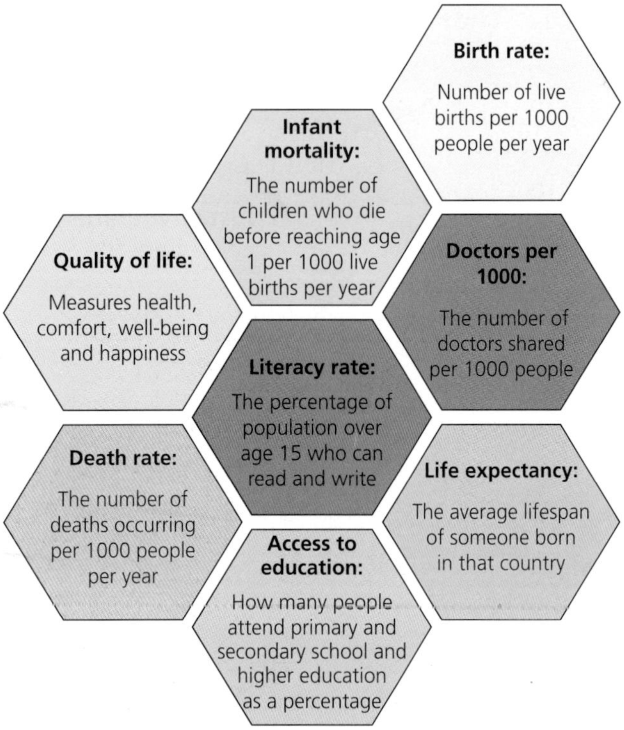

Birth rate:
Number of live births per 1000 people per year

Infant mortality:
The number of children who die before reaching age 1 per 1000 live births per year

Quality of life:
Measures health, comfort, well-being and happiness

Doctors per 1000:
The number of doctors shared per 1000 people

Literacy rate:
The percentage of population over age 15 who can read and write

Death rate:
The number of deaths occurring per 1000 people per year

Life expectancy:
The average lifespan of someone born in that country

Access to education:
How many people attend primary and secondary school and higher education as a percentage

▲ **Figure 3** Social development indicators

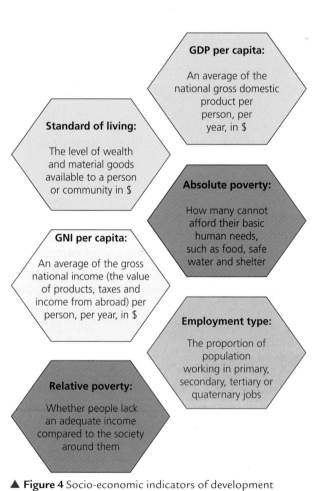

GDP per capita:
An average of the national gross domestic product per person, per year, in $

Standard of living:
The level of wealth and material goods available to a person or community in $

Absolute poverty:
How many cannot afford their basic human needs, such as food, safe water and shelter

GNI per capita:
An average of the gross national income (the value of products, taxes and income from abroad) per person, per year, in $

Employment type:
The proportion of population working in primary, secondary, tertiary or quaternary jobs

Relative poverty:
Whether people lack an adequate income compared to the society around them

▲ **Figure 4** Socio-economic indicators of development

Absolute poverty and relative poverty

Poverty is not always a clear-cut term; there are two forms. You might be considered to be in a state of **relative poverty** if you are living in an area where those around you have more wealth than you so that you cannot maintain the same lifestyle as them, even though you might have enough money to live. In the modern UK, 13 million people are living in relative poverty; 4 million of these are children (source: Joseph Rowntree Foundation). **Absolute poverty** measures your ability to meet your basic human needs of minimal food, water, safe shelter, sanitation, health and education. Someone living in absolute poverty may spend over 30 minutes a day walking to collect water or drinking from streams. They generally live on less than US$1 a day.

Employment type

As a country becomes more developed, employment structure will change. This is illustrated graphically in Figure 5.

The changes can be seen as useful indicators of development because they show how society changes; modern workers prefer tertiary jobs that have improved conditions and pay. This model is useful when geographers wish to classify a country.

United Nations

The United Nations also assesses development by considering the value of infrastructure (roads, buildings, machinery, etc.), 'human capital' (the skills and health of the people) and 'natural capital' (resources such as forests, fuel and water). Considering more varied criteria produces a more detailed picture of a country.

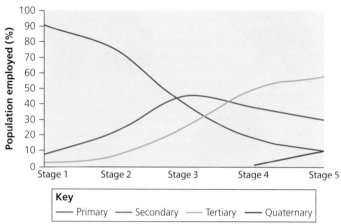

▲ **Figure 5** Employment structure changes over time compared with the Rostow model (see pages 176 and 177)

GNI per capita

Gross national income (GNI) is the value of all products, taxes and income from abroad that a country has per year, in US dollars. Per capita means that the figure is divided by the population of that country to give an average amount per person (see Figure 6).

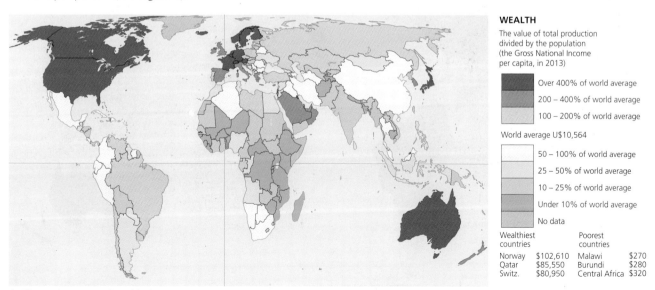

WEALTH

The value of total production divided by the population (the Gross National Income per capita, in 2013)

- Over 400% of world average
- 200 – 400% of world average
- 100 – 200% of world average

World average U$10,564

- 50 – 100% of world average
- 25 – 50% of world average
- 10 – 25% of world average
- Under 10% of world average
- No data

Wealthiest countries		Poorest countries	
Norway	$102,610	Malawi	$270
Qatar	$85,550	Burundi	$280
Switz.	$80,950	Central Africa	$320

▲ **Figure 6** Gross national income per capita, 2013

Human Development Index (HDI)

The **Human Development Index (HDI)** measures life expectancy, education and income per capita to give countries a ranking and a score from 0 to 1 (with 1 being the highest) (see Figure 7). For example, Norway has an HDI of 0.944 whereas the Democratic Republic of Congo has an HDI of just 0.344.

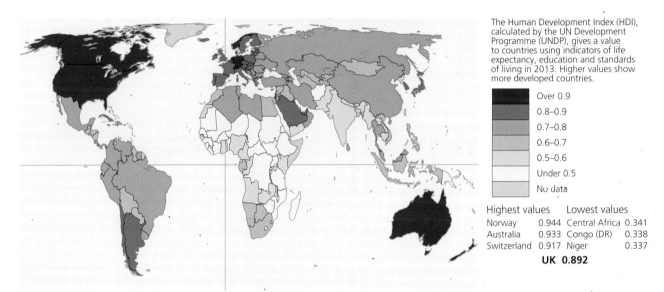

The Human Development Index (HDI), calculated by the UN Development Programme (UNDP), gives a value to countries using indicators of life expectancy, education and standards of living in 2013. Higher values show more developed countries.

- Over 0.9
- 0.8–0.9
- 0.7–0.8
- 0.6–0.7
- 0.5–0.6
- Under 0.5
- No data

Highest values		Lowest values	
Norway	0.944	Central Africa	0.341
Australia	0.933	Congo (DR)	0.338
Switzerland	0.917	Niger	0.337

UK 0.892

▲ **Figure 7** Human Development Index patterns worldwide

Internet users

Internet users is an indicator showing the percentage of the population who have access to the internet.

Why might this be a useful indication of how developed a country is?

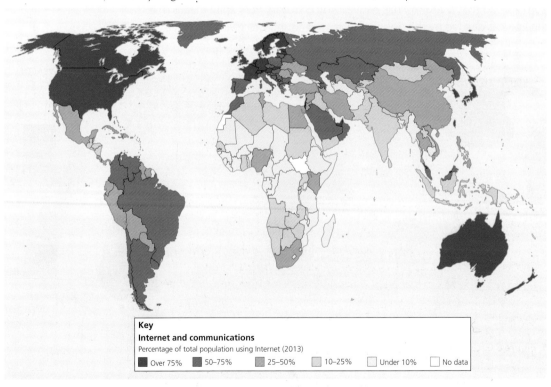

Key
Internet and communications
Percentage of total population using Internet (2013)

- Over 75%
- 50–75%
- 25–50%
- 10–25%
- Under 10%
- No data

▲ **Figure 8** Internet users, 2013

Advantages and disadvantages of different development indicators

Development indicator	Advantages	Disadvantages
GNI per capita	Looking at GNI can be used effectively to show the differences between countries and show global patterns. It can be used to prioritise aid payments. Easy to calculate using official government figures.	As an economic development indicator, it which focuses just on the wealth within a country, so does not measure welfare or quality of life. It does not reflect some of the more informal, subsistence economies which are very important in LEDCs. Economic growth can lead to negative impacts on the environment. Does not take into consideration variations in wealth within countries and hides inequalities. Data from some LEDCs can be unreliable.
HDI	HDI can be used effectively to show the differences between countries and show global patterns. Looking at HDI can be seen as more useful than GNI per capita as it helps to consider the wider factors and influences on development other than wealth. It shows how wealth within countries has been used to increase social welfare and can indicate how successful the impact of the government has been on the population of the country.	It only focuses on basic measurements and doesn't take into account other important factors. Does not take into consideration variations in life expectancy, education and standards of living within countries and hides inequalities. Data from some LEDCs can be unreliable.
Internet Users	Useful as it relies upon other infrastructure to be in place. Having a high proportion of the population with internet access relies upon access to electricity, service engineers, satellite access, disposable income, etc., so it is an interlinked indicator.	Does not take into consideration variations in access to the internet within countries and hides inequalities.

Activities

1. Which development indicator do you think is most useful? Why?
2. Why might a country such as the UK have a low birth rate?
3. Suggest a range of factors that might lead to high death rates in less developed places.
4. Suggest how access to education might be able to influence other social and economic measures.
5. Why might $GNI *per capita* be more useful than gross domestic product?
6. Which parts of the world have the lowest HDI rates? Why might this be?

The consequences of uneven development

Now that we understand development and how it is measured, it is useful to compare the development of nations across the world.

Wealth

Figures 9a and 9b are distorted proportional maps that show the wealth of nations and GNI per capita, respectively. Countries are represented as either larger or smaller than their actual area dependent upon wealth. For example, Japan is much larger than usual because it has a high national wealth and a high income per person. On the other hand, while Figure 9a shows that China's national wealth is large, Figure 9b shows that the GNI per capita is very low.

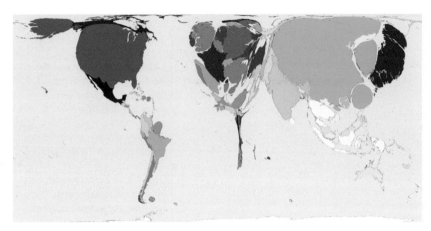

▲ **Figure 9a:** A proportional map showing the wealth of nations

Activity

Describe the pattern of wealth given in Figure 9b.

✚ Geographical skills

When analysing maps, begin with the overall pattern and then focus on specific places using direction and specific place names or regions (continent, country, cities, tropics, etc.). Practise this by comparing Figures 9a and 9b.

▲ **Figure 9b:** A proportional map showing $GNI per capita across the world. How does it compare with Figure 9a?

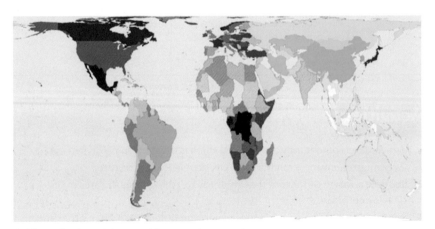

▲ **Figure 9c:** A world map with normal proportions

1. The richest 62 people in the world (53 men and 9 women) own as much wealth as the poorest half of the world.
2. One per cent of the world own more wealth than the rest of the world combined.

▶ **Figure 10** Unequal world

Number of people whose wealth is equal to that of poorest half of world

Year	Number of people
2010	388
2011	177
2012	159
2013	92
2014	80
2015	62

The development gap

According to Oxfam (see Figure 10), 48 per cent of all of the world's wealth is owned by just one per cent of the population. It is estimated that these wealthy people will own more than half the world's wealth by the end of 2016. In fact, the top 62 billionaires own more wealth than *half* of the world's poorest people (over 3.5 billion)!

Over time nations should become more developed and move out of the LIDC group. Figure 11 shows that the growth of wealth has been highest in LIDCs and EDCs since 2000, even during the global recession. However, in the last 50 years, only nine countries have graduated to the emerging economies category. So what is holding development back?

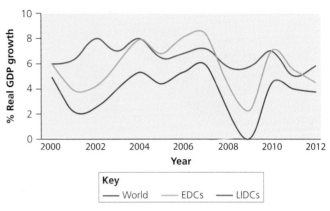

▲ **Figure 11** How has wealth grown in different parts of the world?

Health

Many LIDCs have high levels of infant mortality, high birth rates and low life expectancy levels. These indicators can show low levels of investment in health care, education, water supply, food supply and sanitation. The lower the number of doctors shared per 1000 people, the lower the development levels in a country.

As a country develops, the levels of infant mortality decrease, life expectancy levels increase, and birth rates go down. The number of doctors goes up as there are higher levels of education. In the UK, the birth rate is 11 per 1000, however in Ethiopia it is 33.5 per 1000.

Education

Literacy rates indicate levels of how many people can read and write. Low literacy levels as well as low numbers of people attending schools suggest money for investment in education is low. In the UK, the literacy level is 99 per cent, whereas in Ethiopia this is just 36%.

Standards of living

In LIDCs, a large number of people live in areas where there is poor infrastructure such as lack of running water and sanitation, and lack of decent housing. In ACs, people live in houses with fresh water supply and sanitation.

Did you know?

It would cost US$10 billion to provide clean water for everyone in the world, yet in Europe we spend US$11 billion each year on ice cream.

Activity

➜ Take it further

1. Use the internet to find updated statistics for at least two contrasting countries. Try using The CIA World Factbook and the website of the United Nations Development Programme. How has the situation changed since this textbook was written?

How are countries classified in terms of development?

The International Monetary Fund (IMF) classifies nations into three categories of development:

- **Advanced countries (ACs)**
- **Emerging developing countries (EDCs)**
- **Low-income developing countries (LIDCs).**

Countries are categorised according to wealth per person, trade and links with other nations. Only 16 per cent of world nations are classed as ACs, with 45 per cent as EDCs and 38 per cent as LIDCs (see Figure 12). However the pattern is not evenly spread.

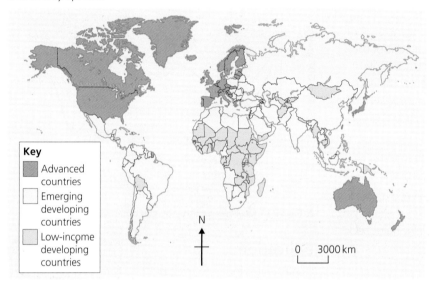

Key
- Advanced countries
- Emerging developing countries
- Low-income developing countries

N

0   3000 km

▲ **Figure 12** IMF country classifications

LIDCs account for one-fifth of the whole world's population yet have a tiny fraction of the wealth, with people living on an income of just US$370 to US$2500 a year.

Advanced countries (ACs) share a number of important economic development characteristics including well-developed financial markets, high levels of financial links with other nations and diversified economic structures with rapidly growing service sectors. An example of an AC is the UK.

Emerging developing countries (EDCs) do not share all the economic development characteristics required to be advanced but are not eligible for the Poverty Reduction and Growth Trust. An example of an EDC is South Africa.

Low-income developing countries (LIDCs) are eligible for the Poverty Reduction and Growth Trust from the IMF. An example of an LIDC is Ethiopia.

Activities

1. Write your own definition for 'development'.
2. Where are the world's emerging developing countries located?
3. Name three low-income developing countries.
4. How are the countries in Figures 13 to 16 classified and what proof do you have?

▼ **Figure 13** The Hoover Dam, United States

▼ **Figure 14** Spain

▲ **Figure 15** Morocco

▲ **Figure 16** London, UK

CHAPTER 19

Uneven development

Key idea: There are many cause of uneven development.

→ **In this chapter you will study:**

→ the reasons for uneven development, including the impact of colonialism on trade and the exploitations of natural resources

→ the different types of aid and their role in promoting and hindering development.

The reasons for uneven development

National development is a long, slow process. It is influenced by a variety of factors that can either increase or hold back the speed of change. These factors can be caused by humans or nature.

Physical factors affecting development

Figure 1 shows a selection of natural (physical) factors that influence development. These are features that are present, or not present, in an area that are perhaps uncontrollable.

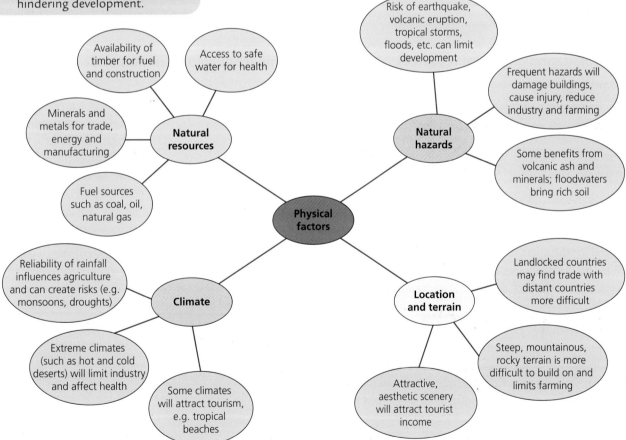

▲ **Figure 1** Physical factors affecting development

Human factors affecting development

A selection of human factors can be seen in Figure 2. They are often interlinked: for example, politics links to trade, healthcare, culture and even technology.

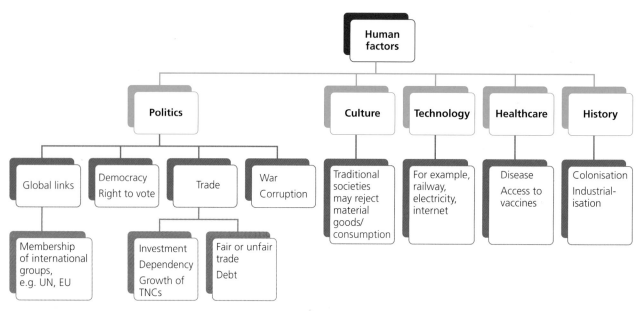

▲ **Figure 2** Human factors influencing development

The exploitation of natural resources

Humans have been shaping and moulding their environment since they first appeared in order to make living conditions comfortable and to find ways to improve their lives. We manipulate natural environments in order to extract the resources we need for fuel, for construction and for industry.

In the nineteenth century, the UK discovered large quantities of coal which was used in early industries and generated wealth for the country. This wealth was then invested in education, to create a skilled workforce, as well as spending money on exploring other countries and colonising them, in turn exploiting new raw materials in those places.

Exploiting resources can lead to damage to the environment and ecosystems (see Chapter 12). Sometimes this manipulation crosses national borders, like when Transnational Corporations (TNCs) work in multiple countries or when resources are imported from elsewhere.

The impact of colonialism on trade

Colonialism is where one country goes into another country and claims they are in power. This happened from the sixteenth century to the mid-twentieth century where European powers colonised much of Africa in order to exploit their raw materials by use of force through organised armies and fire power. Raw materials were taken from Africa and transported to countries in Europe which meant that African countries could not take advantage of their own resources to generate their own development.

There were restrictions on trade whereby colonies were only allowed to trade with the 'mother country' who had colonised them. However, by the mid-nineteenth century, the British Empire introduced the principle of free trade which had fewer restrictions, and trade was easier through the links that had already been made. However, these links are not always beneficial to all concerned; colonies have often suffered and host nations are sometimes exploited by TNCs. Historical influences can be felt for centuries, for good or bad.

Activities

1. Which factor do you think will have the most influence on development? Why?
2. How can political stability have an influence on national wealth?
3. Norway has an HDI of 0.944 compared with 0.33 for Niger. Which specific factors will have had an influence on these different countries?
4. What advantages and disadvantages has the UK had that could explain how it became an advanced country?

5. How might trans-national companies help to improve national development?

→ Take it further

6. Choose one country in the world and find its HDI and $GDP/GNI per capita. Research the country and suggest which factors, physical and human, have most influenced its development, and why.

How can aid promote and hinder development

Aid is when a country, organisation or individual gives resources to another country. These resources could be money, products, training or technology and may be delivered on a short-term or long-term basis. Short-term aid helps in an emergency, such as a disaster, and usually involves food, shelter, search and rescue, bottled water and clothing. Long-term aid is sustainable if it brings benefit to the economy, society and the environment. For example, digging wells for water is more sustainable than bottled water; planting seeds and building irrigation schemes for local farmers is more sustainable than offering bags of food.

Aid may be given in different ways, as shown in Figure 3.

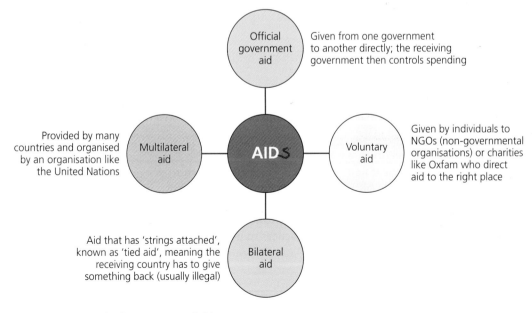

Official government aid — Given from one government to another directly; the receiving government then controls spending

Multilateral aid — Provided by many countries and organised by an organisation like the United Nations

AIDS

Voluntary aid — Given by individuals to NGOs (non-governmental organisations) or charities like Oxfam who direct aid to the right place

Bilateral aid — Aid that has 'strings attached', known as 'tied aid', meaning the receiving country has to give something back (usually illegal)

▲ **Figure 3** Types of aid

Two successful examples of sustainable aid are Goat Aid and Water Aid. In these schemes, local communities take control of resources, such as a pair of goats or a well, and then use them to bring long-term benefits. Goat Aid involves giving a pair of goats to a community, particularly to young girls, in order for them to breed the goats and use their milk to produce surplus for sale. The proceeds from the sale of the milk can be reinvested in more goats or fertiliser or clothing, or to pay for school.

'Goat cycle'

The UK-based charity Oxfam's Unwrapped scheme offers people the chance to choose a 'gift' of a goat. A goat gift from Oxfam costs £25. The donation supports their Livelihoods projects, which include giving out livestock such as goats to communities in the developing world, as well as activities like business and agricultural training for farmers. The goats that Oxfam distribute are vaccinated and locally sourced. Goats can provide their owners with manure and milk, and can give birth to other goats over time, which can be sold. This means that agriculture is supported as well as the family that receives the goat.

As a goat can continue to provide milk, manure and other baby goats over time, it is a sustainable gift. It is also a fairly hardy animal that can survive in most locations. Oxfam only provides livestock where keeping them is a traditional or essential part of people's way of life. They don't introduce the practice of animal husbandry, release animals into the wild or import animals.

▲ **Figure 4** The Oxfam Unwrapped scheme

Some criticism of such schemes suggests that animals are being provided in areas that are already suffering from water shortages and desertification, which will add to the demands for water. They also suggest that the scheme is designed to ease the conscience of people in the UK rather than being truly helpful in the long term. Andrew Tyler of Animal Aid has said that: 'All farmed animals require proper nourishment, large quantities of water, shelter from extremes of weather and veterinary care. Such resources are in critically short supply in much of Africa.'

Oxfam are clear that the provision of livestock is always part of a larger sustainable livelihoods programme, and they are concerned with long-term environmental sustainability because it is an essential requirement for human development and well-being – especially relevant to poor people, whose lives and livelihoods are more closely linked with the natural environment. Local staff, partners and local communities have detailed knowledge of the grazing patterns and feeding practice needed to decide if and where animals should be provided. Communities are also supported in adopting environmentally friendly farming practices to help them use land and water resources more efficiently, protect and even restore natural resources.

Activities

1. Why might Goat Aid be considered sustainable?

→ Take it further

2. Research an example of an aid scheme that has been used in a particular country. Decide how sustainable this method is and explain why and how it impacts different stakeholders.

Ethiopia: changing economic development

Ethiopia has been called the 'Cradle of Humankind' with evidence of the earliest known modern human bones found in the south west at Omo. It is the tenth largest African nation by area and the second largest by population size after Nigeria.

Ethiopia's economic development

Ethiopia is categorised as an LIDC and in 2015 had a GNI per capita of just US$505, compared with a world average of US$10,858 and a UK GNI per capita of US$40,967. Compared with other Sub-Saharan nations, Ethiopia is significantly less wealthy per person and is also below the average level for other LIDCs across the world.

Figure 1 shows how the level of wealth per person has changed over recent years. Its changing economic development has been influenced by many factors, which will be investigated in this chapter.

Key idea: Many factors contribute to a country's economic development.

→ **In this chapter you will study:**

→ a case study of Ethiopia (an LIDC), to explore:

- the country's geographical location, and environmental context (landscape, climate, ecosystems, availability and type of natural resources)
- the country's political development and relationships with other states
- principal imports and exports and the relative importance of trade
- the role of international investment
- population and employment structure changes over time social factors, including access to education and healthcare provision
- technological developments, such as communications technology
- one aid project.

→ Rostow's model to determine the country's path of economic development.

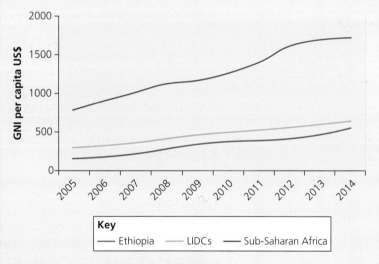

Key
— Ethiopia   — LIDCs   — Sub-Saharan Africa

▲ **Figure 1** Ethiopia's wealth over time

Ethiopia factfile

→ Population: 94 million

→ Land area: 1.1 million km²

→ Language: Amharic

→ Capital: Addis Ababa

→ Currency: Ethiopian birr (ETB)

Ethiopia's location and environmental context

Location

Ethiopia is a country located in the continent of Africa. It is landlocked and shares land borders with five countries: Sudan, Somalia, Djibouti, Eritrea and Kenya. Its capital, and largest city, is Addis Ababa.

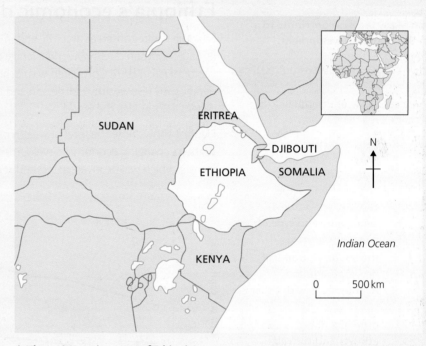

▲ **Figure 2** Location map of Ethiopia

Landscape

The landscape of Ethiopia varies dramatically. The Ethiopian Highlands has mountains that are over 4500 m high as well as deep canyons. There are lowlands where there are areas of land that are fertile enough for agriculture and grazing animals, as well as semi-arid regions where it is difficult to grow crops.

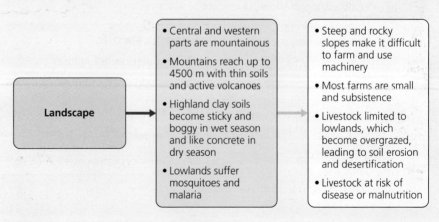

▲ **Figure 3** Landscape influences development

Climate

Ethiopia is divided into different zones, which experience a range of different climates. Figure 4 shows how the country can be simplified into three zones: Western Highlands, Central Zone and Eastern Lowlands.

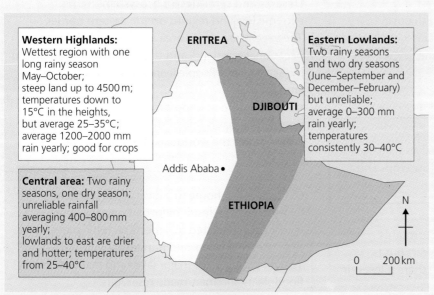

Western Highlands:
Wettest region with one long rainy season May–October; steep land up to 4500 m; temperatures down to 15°C in the heights, but average 25–35°C; average 1200–2000 mm rain yearly; good for crops

Eastern Lowlands:
Two rainy seasons and two dry seasons (June–September and December–February) but unreliable; average 0–300 mm rain yearly; temperatures consistently 30–40°C

Central area: Two rainy seasons, one dry season; unreliable rainfall averaging 400–800 mm yearly; lowlands to east are drier and hotter; temperatures from 25–40°C

ERITREA, DJIBOUTI, ETHIOPIA, Addis Ababa

▲ **Figure 4** Ethiopia has a varied physical environment.

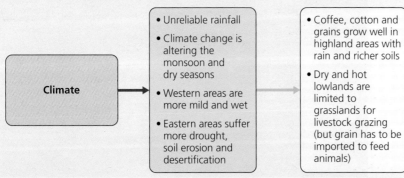

Climate

- Unreliable rainfall
- Climate change is altering the monsoon and dry seasons
- Western areas are more mild and wet
- Eastern areas suffer more drought, soil erosion and desertification

- Coffee, cotton and grains grow well in highland areas with rain and richer soils
- Dry and hot lowlands are limited to grasslands for livestock grazing (but grain has to be imported to feed animals)

▲ **Figure 5** Climate and relief influence development

Activities

1. What is malaria and how can it affect people?
2. Why is it important for a nation to have access to food and water to become developed?
3. Describe why desertification can be such a devastating problem.

Landscapes and climate both exert an influence on how successful agriculture can be, and since access to safe drinking water and food are essential in order to improve a nation's health and wealth, this is a key factor influencing Ethiopia's development.

One of the key issues with climate is the unpredictable and unreliable nature of rainfall. In the mid-1980s, Ethiopia suffered severe drought and famine as they did not have enough rain to grow crops. Ethiopia is close to the Equator yet due to the relief and to winds, temperatures can vary wildly (lowland desert areas can reach up to 60 °C) and the monsoon season can often fail. This makes agriculture very difficult to manage.

In many places, inaccessibility, water shortages and infestations of disease-carrying insects such as mosquitoes and tsetse flies prevent the use of potentially valuable land. As a result, agriculture has remained subsistence level until recently. Eastern areas particularly suffer from drought when rainfall is limited and unreliable, and this has led to farmers over-farming or over-grazing the remaining land leading to soil erosion and desertification (where areas become dry and desert-like; a problem which is a cycle of decline).

Ironically for a nation suffering repeated drought and famine, Ethiopia is one of the world's main producers of food; but food for export, not for locals. In recent years, the more productive land has been bought up by nations such as Saudi Arabia who import food from Ethiopia and are setting up their own farms leading to Ethiopian farmers losing out.

Ecosystems

Owing to its varied landscape and climate, Ethiopia has a diverse range of ecosystems from forests to deserts to wetlands:

Mountainous regions in the northwest and southeast. In the highest areas of the Ethiopian Highlands, there are chains of mountains which have a cold climate near to 0°C all year round, sometimes even with snow cover.

Woodland forests grow on the lower areas of the highlands which have good, fertile soil and are now mostly used for agricultural use to grow crops and graze animals.

Tropical savannahs and **grassland** surrounds the highlands. This is fertile in good years but is vulnerable to drought in years where there is less rain.

Deserts and semi-desert ecosystems in the extreme lowland regions on the eastern border. The vegetation in this area is mainly shrubs, with occasional grassland, and the landscape is dominated by Acacia trees. People living in this area farm the land for their own use, but large-scale agriculture is starting to gain in importance. In the northeast is a desert area that is one of the world's hottest places and contains the world's inhabited location, a place called Dallol.

Ethiopia is also home to a diversity of **wetland ecosystems** as a result of formation of diverse landscapes subjected to various tectonic movements, processes of erosion, and human activities. There are 12 river basins, eight major lakes and many swamps, floodplains and man-made reservoirs.

There are between 6500 and 7000 species of plants, around 15 per cent of which can only be found in Ethiopia. There is also a great variety of different animals and birds found in Ethiopia, including lions, zebras, gorillas and flamingos. It also has a large number of vulnerable and endangered species including lions, cheetahs, the black rhinoceros and the African elephant. Many are facing a high risk of extinction in the future due to habitat destruction from deforestation.

▲ **Figure 6** Subsistence agriculture dominates (source: Darren Thompson)

Natural resources

Ethiopia has small reserves of mineral resources such as gold, platinum and copper, as well as reserves of natural gas. However, the development of its oil, gas and mineral resources has not been a key driver in the country's economic growth.

There is currently only one large-scale gold mine in operation, but there are plans to develop more mines and to explore the potential of oil and natural gas reserves. Although this industry is only in its early stages, mining already contributes to the country's exports – in 2012, more than 19% of the total value of exports was from the mining sector (mainly from gold). However, the industry needs to be developed and manageably sustained in order to have a positive impact on the economic and social development of Ethiopia.

Activities

1. Draw a table that compares the different physical influences upon Ethiopia's development: location, landscape, climate, ecosystems and availability of natural resources.
2. Which influence do you think is the most significant in terms of development? Why? How does it link to other factors?

Ethiopia's political development

Ethiopia has been influenced by its relationships with other states.

▼ **Figure 7** A timeline of recent Ethiopian history.

Date	What was happening?
Pre-1935	Ethiopia was once known as Abyssinia and was one of only two African countries (with Liberia) that avoided European control in the colonial era.
1935–41	During the build up to the Second World War, Italy colonised Ethiopia and had control from 1935 until 1941, when rebels and British troops claimed back independence.
1941–74	Although the Italians had invested in highways, rail and power, the nation was set back after the Second World War, due to the conflict and the loss of life and instability that followed.
	Years of unrest, coupled with drought and famine and the growth of Communism, led to a successful military coup in 1974. The Soviet Union (now known as Russia) and Cuba financed this rebellion, and the military evicted the government leading to many arrests, banishments and deaths.
1974–87	At least 1.4 million people died in the civil war and the Derg government remained in power until 1987. The monarchy was abolished and the land was declared a new republic state.
	The period 1977–78 became known as the Ethiopian 'Red Terror'. During this time, the government grabbed tracts of land and evicted owners leading to migration, refugees and economic decline. There were up to 50,000 people killed during the Derg era; a further 1.5 million were forcibly relocated.
1984–85	The Derg government pursued a strict policy on agriculture, but productivity declined. From the mid-1980s onwards Ethiopia suffered severe drought and eventual famine.
	The 1984–85 famine (the inspiration for the original Live Aid *Do They Know It's Christmas* charity song) killed a million people in just one year due to drought and high food prices. International agencies became involved and over US$2000 million in food aid was delivered from NGOs. Ethiopia has remained food deficient since this time, made worse by continued population growth.
1991–2001	With the collapse of the Soviet Union, and the international spotlight on famine, support from other nations helped to stabilise the nation and remove Derg control and from 1991 it became the Federal Democratic Republic. The new government allowed free trade, lifted price controls and provided farmers with cheaper access to imported fertilisers and machinery without paying tax.
2001 to now	Following the events of 11 September 2001 and the Middle East conflicts, the USA gave more support to Ethiopia and agricultural production and the economy have been rising gradually since then.
	The Growth and Transformation Plan is the government's ambitious plan to end poverty following on from the Millennium Development Goals. Since 2012, new training programmes and investment have enabled farmers to learn new skills (such as mixing crop types with beans to help soils stay fertile) and increase yields.
	The government is stable, although there are some claims that free speech is limited, but more trust is now being shared with local authorities and the people themselves.

Tip

Physical, political and social influences on development are interlimited. Try to make links between multiple factors, for example, between rainfall and politics.

Ethiopia's imports and exports

Currently Ethiopia has a trade deficit since exports value US$3 billion but imports value US$11 billion. This means debt remains, and there is less government income to support development.

Figure 9 shows the major Ethiopian exports: 80 per cent of exports and 46 per cent of the national GDP is from agriculture. Ethiopia is one of the world's largest producers of food and flowers, although this economy is vulnerable to climate change and global price changes.

▲ **Figure 8** Ethiopa's trade and economy

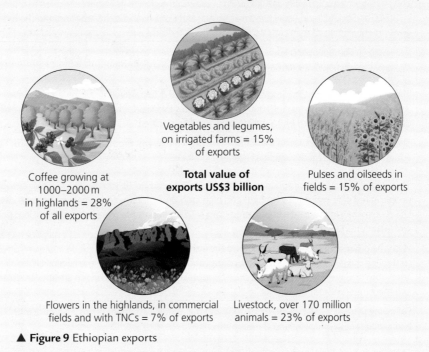

Coffee growing at 1000–2000 m in highlands = 28% of all exports

Vegetables and legumes, on irrigated farms = 15% of exports

Total value of exports US$3 billion

Pulses and oilseeds in fields = 15% of exports

Flowers in the highlands, in commercial fields and with TNCs = 7% of exports

Livestock, over 170 million animals = 23% of exports

▲ **Figure 9** Ethiopian exports

The economy has been growing at an average of 11 per cent per year (see Figure 10), which is considerably faster than the rest of the world. At the same time, per person income has grown from a GNI per capita of US$203 in 1990 to US$505 in 2015. This means that fewer people now live in poverty.

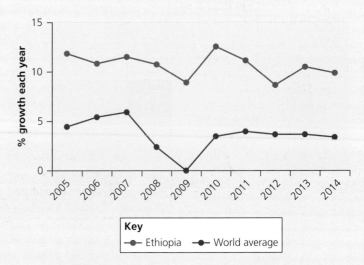

▲ **Figure 10** GDP annual growth (%) (Data source: World Bank)

Figure 11 shows that Ethiopia has links with other nations. The increase in international trade is evidence that the government and the economy are becoming more stable. Interestingly, the imports shown in Figure 12 include the products expected for a developing nation with refined petroleum (needed for manufacturing industries particularly) and construction materials showing an investment in improving infrastructure and building quality.

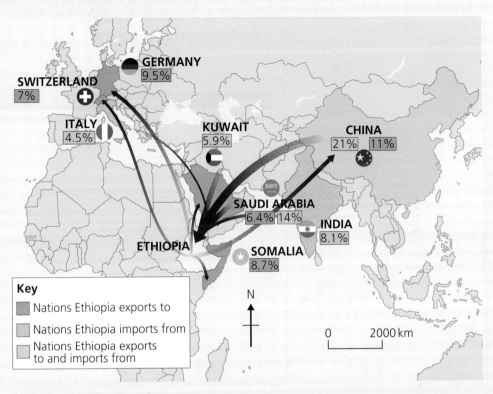

▲ **Figure 11** Ethiopia's trading partners

Activities

1. Why is trade important to aiding development?
2. What is a trade deficit?
3. Analyse Figure 10. Compare Ethiopia's trend against the rest of the world.
4. What might be the cause of the dips in growth shown in Figure 10?
5. Describe the pattern of countries which Ethiopia trades with.

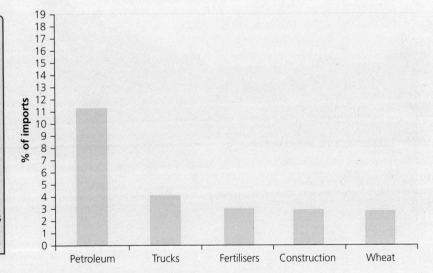

▲ **Figure 12** Ethiopia's top five imports

International investment

Ethiopia has increasingly strong global links, as seen through trade and through politics. As part of the UN strategy, there is also global support from other nations to assist Ethiopia and other LIDCs to meet their development goals. Support can be from one government to another, from organisations such as the UN, from NGOs and charities, or from businesses.

Trans-national corporations: help or harm?

A range of TNCs have begun operating in Ethiopia, in primary, secondary and some tertiary industries.

Company	What do they do in Ethiopia?
Hilton Hotels	Leisure and recreation services, hotel creation
Siemens	Manufacturing of telecommunications, electrical items, medical technology
General Electric (GE)	Aviation manufacturing, delivering rail links
Afriflora	Flower growing, the world's largest producer of fair trade roses
Dow Chemicals	Manufacturing chemicals, plastics and agricultural products
H&M	Textiles manufacturing, university education in textiles

▲ **Figure 13** TNC investment in Ethiopia

TNCs can bring both advantages and disadvantages. Investment in hotel infrastructure can increase tourism. Workers in hotels are often paid a fair wage and may have access to the facilities out of hours. However this is not always the case. Although TNCs bring employment and therefore income, workers in LIDCs are often paid a low salary and working conditions can be difficult. The companies wish to make a profit and the reason they locate to LIDCs like Ethiopia is because regulations on wages and working conditions are less strict than in more developed locations. For example, workers in factories in Ethiopia may get US$50 a month while workers in an EDC might receive US$175 for the same job.

Activities

1. Draw up a table that compares the advantages and disadvantages of TNCs for the host country.
2. How can the growth of tourism be beneficial for national development?

▲ **Figure 14** Tourism is a growing economy in Ethiopia (Source: Darren Thompson)

Population and employment structure

Ethiopia has a large population of over 94 million, making it the thirteenth most populous nation in the world. In comparison, the population of the UK is 64 million.

The high birth rate and a slowly falling death rate means that natural increase is occurring and the population is growing by 2.6 per cent per year. As healthcare improves, life expectancy is gradually increasing and death rates decline which means the population will continue to grow.

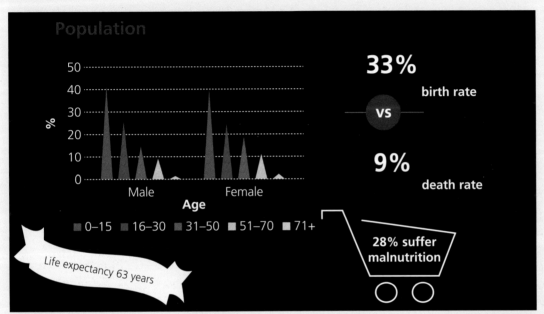

▲ **Figure 15** Ethiopia's population in numbers

Owing to a history of famine, drought, poor healthcare, disease, poverty and conflict, Ethiopia has one of the lowest levels of development in the world with an HDI of 0.435 and although life expectancy is increasing, at 63 years it is still lower than the world average of 72.

Economically, the country is reliant on agriculture with 89 per cent of all exports and 80 per cent of all jobs. The landscape is largely rural and large-scale agriculture has only recently begun to develop.

For Ethiopia to continue to develop, other sources of income other than primary industry are required. Secondary manufacturing is taking off, and TNCs are being encouraged to invest. A country with higher levels of development would have more employment in tertiary jobs, such as customer service and leisure, and recently the tourism and travel trade has begun to take off in Ethiopia. There are over 2.5 million workers involved in tertiary service jobs in tourism, contributing four times as much to the national economy in just ten years. In a land full of adventure, mountains, desert, volcanoes and historical sites (including nine World Heritage Sites), there is plenty of potential for tourism to take off and numbers have been growing. There is still a lack of hotels and services for tourists, but investment is increasing. Simien Lodge is the highest hotel in Africa and was built by a British entrepreneur.

Activities

1. The total world population is 7.3 billion. What percentage of the world's population does Ethiopia have compared to the UK?
2. What is 'natural increase' and why is it occurring in Ethiopia?

Social factors – education and health

In Ethiopia, massive government investment has seen improvements in access to education and healthcare provision.

Access to education

- A national Education Development Plan has ensured that 96 per cent of children enrol in primary school, which has risen from 50 per cent in 1990.
- The Education gap is closing now, as 93 per cent of girls are in primary schools (compared to 43 per cent in 2000).
- However, the quality of education provision varies, and the adult literacy rate is still just 36 per cent.
- There are more males than females in primary education, and very few females in secondary education.

Healthcare provision

- Maternal mortality has dropped 23 per cent due to better before and after care.
- 55 per cent of women now receive access to contraception.
- Child mortality has been reduced successfully from 97/1000 to 45/1000 since 1900, following investment in maternal health and child health, although rural areas lag behind and there is a rural-urban divide.
- 65 per cent of children now receive vaccinations for preventable illnesses.
- Diarrhoea and malaria are still the biggest killers of children year – diarrhoea accounts for 20 per cent of all child deaths and malaria accounts for another 20 per cent
- The HIV/AIDS pandemic has stabilised and new cases have declined since new treatment centres and education were established. However, there are still 1.1 million adults living with HIV
- Malaria was the leading cause of death among adults but now 100 per cent of the population can access a malaria net.
- Eighty-nine per cent of the population live within 10 km of a doctor, however every doctor is shared by 3333 people.

Technological developments

Ethiopia is still behind other African countries in terms of technology and innovation. Ethiopia is one of the last African countries to have a state-owned monopoly, operated by Ethio Telecom (ETC), on all telecoms: fixed-line, mobile, internet and data. This lack of competition has led to slow technological developments and even though the market for mobile phones may be growing, the network coverage is poor. There are no credit cards and no international banking systems which makes online purchasing inaccessible. In 2015, less than 4 per cent of Ethiopia's population were connected to the internet, and only 12 per cent of the population used mobile phones. This means it is difficult for small technology start-ups to develop.

Things may be changing now, as there has been success in countries such as South Africa or Morocco, where developments in communications technology has improved their country's economies and social developments. In 2013, technology developed so that mobile phones could be used to send money to people instantly, to pay for goods in shops or to pay bills, see www.m-birr.com. There has also been a change in the last few years where Chinese companies have invested in ETC, which has led to mobile costs being cut, fixed-line broadband becoming cheaper and the mobile network has been expanded. Because of this, we expect to see strong growth in internet and mobile phone usage in the future, which is likely to contribute to the growth of the economy.

Activities

1. Diarrhoea is preventable, so why are 20 per cent of deaths still due to this?

➜ Take it further

2. Use the internet to research current information about the percentage of the Ethiopia's population who are now using the internet or own mobile phones. How has this changed since 2015? How has it affected economic development?

Aid

Ethiopia has benefited from international development support through aid and debt relief. Five million people receive food aid each year. Charities such as Oxfam, Farm Africa and Mission Aviation Fellowship (MAF) have been working to support Ethiopians for over 30 years. In fact aid from MAF was so successful that it led to the local creation of Abyssinian Flight Services who have now taken on the responsibility of flying aid to those in need, as a sustainable aid example.

Oxfam has operated to provide 'Goat Aid' in Ethiopia (see Figure 16 and page 164), which is a particularly sustainable form of aid especially when targeted at young women. The 'Girl Effect' is the idea that if young girls can be supported to receive education, income, status and security then they will be able to avoid potential issues such as early/forced marriage, prostitution, unplanned pregnancies, disease and poverty, and can then be equal members of society. This, in turn, improves development. Providing a pair of goats through Goat Aid to young girls can encourage this Girl Effect and so support equality and reduce birth rates.

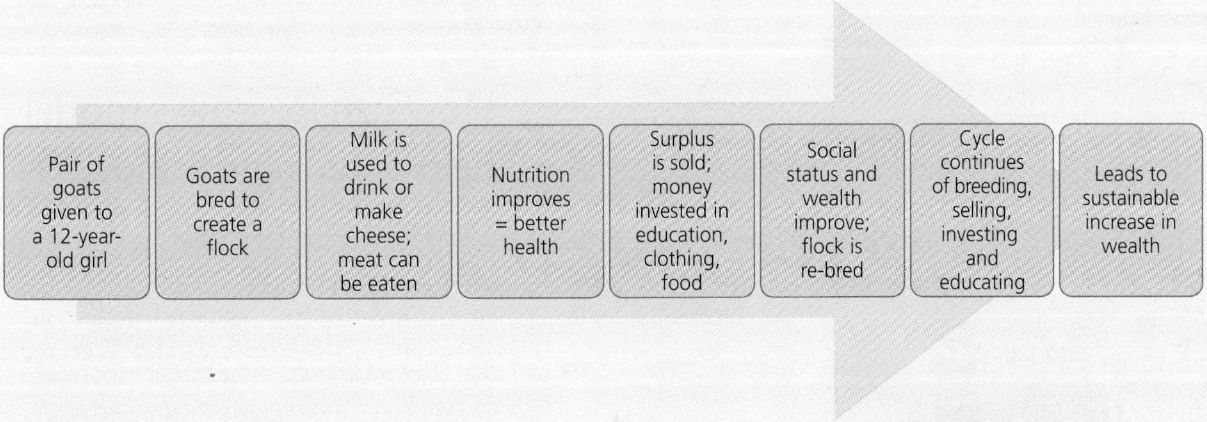

Pair of goats given to a 12-year-old girl → Goats are bred to create a flock → Milk is used to drink or make cheese; meat can be eaten → Nutrition improves = better health → Surplus is sold; money invested in education, clothing, food → Social status and wealth improve; flock is re-bred → Cycle continues of breeding, selling, investing and educating → Leads to sustainable increase in wealth

▲ **Figure 16** Sustainable Goat Aid

Support from the international community meant that in 2006 Ethiopia benefited from debt relief. In 1995, the national economy was in debt by 155 per cent (US$10 billion). As a result of debt relief, by 2012 the debt had declined to 21 per cent of the national economy (US$7 billion). These debt payment savings meant that the government could invest more in local services. However, Ethiopia does still depend upon international aid of over US $550 million each year.

Activities

1. Why is it important for Ethiopia to have received debt relief?
2. Describe the benefits of aid. Think back to the previous chapter.
3. Why is it important to invest in young girls through aid?
4. What negative issues can be associated with aid?

Ethiopia's path of economic development

Modelling development

It can be useful to think of development as a process that occurs over time. In 1960 an American economist named Rostow created a model to show the stages that countries are likely to pass through on their way to being more developed. There are various development models but Rostow suggested that all countries have the potential to break out of the cycle of poverty and develop through five linear stages and ultimately reach what he called 'economic maturity'. This can be considered similar to the way in which a child develops into an adult. The model has been criticised for being too simplistic and perhaps outdated, however, it can provide a useful guide as seen in Figure 18.

There are five stages of progression shown in the model and outlined in Figure 17.

So according to the Rostow model, as countries become more mature you will see employment patterns change from mainly primary to secondary, then tertiary and finally some quaternary jobs. This links to improving levels of technology, education and social aspiration as the population moves away from working the land to working in more comfortable and better-paid conditions. However, this model does rely on countries starting from the same point and having similar access to resources before take off. Many countries might actually skip stages and progress more rapidly.

More people are employed in primary jobs such as agriculture in LIDCs, with such countries typically in Stage 1 or 2 of the Rostow model. ACs use considerably more energy and spend more years in education, reflecting that such nations are in Stage 4 or 5 of the Rostow model.

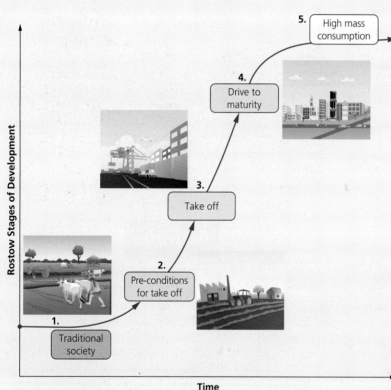

▲ **Figure 17** Rostow's model of development

How can Rostow's model help determine Ethiopia's path of economic development?

With a negative balance of trade meaning that Ethiopia imports more than it exports, and with primary employment dominating the population, it could appear that Ethiopia is in Stage 1 of the Rostow model. However, government spending has led to improvements in healthcare and education and with the arrival of TNCs and improving infrastructure, it seems Stage 2 is more appropriate. While traditional practices such as nomadic livestock farming and water collection still happen, these are now being modified by newer technologies to improve efficiency and quality of life. So the pre-conditions for take off are emerging.

Activities

1. If development means 'change', it might have varying consequences. Draw a mindmap or table to suggest the positive and negative consequences of development on people and place.
2. Draw a flow chart or diagram of your own to explain how a country can develop through the stages of the Rostow model.
3. Using information in this chapter, explain which stage you think Ethiopia is in now.

➔ Take it further

4. Research a trans-national company (TNC) such as BP and Nestlé and find out where it is based around the world. At what stage of the Rostow model are these places?

Stage 1: Traditional society

This is what we might have expected in the UK before the Industrial Revolution. Economies are based upon subsistence which relies on collecting natural resources to meet an individual's basic needs for survival, with very little extra for trade. Primary industries, such as farming, mining and logging, dominate employment. Agriculture is the most important industry with the most employment; you cannot become developed without first having secure access to food and water. Farming here is mostly small-scale and labour intensive. It often involves shifting cultivation (where farmers move regularly), 'slash and burn' techniques and nomadic lifestyles. During Stage 1, the economy is very vulnerable to uncontrollable influences such as the weather, disease, war, pests and famine.

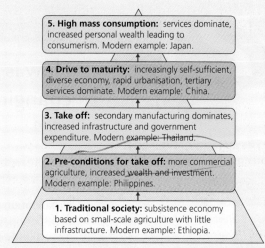

▲ **Figure 18** Development is a progression

Stage 2: Pre-conditions for take off

By this stage, people are beginning to have surplus produce that they can trade, and infrastructure (particularly roads and communications) has improved so that trade is easier. Agriculture still dominates but now becomes more commercial and large-scale, using machinery and fewer workers. Because productivity increases, resources can be processed more efficiently and some more profit is made. This leads to investment and an increase in wealth. Secondary industries such as manufacturing start to take off, particularly in textiles and processing raw materials extracted by primary workers. Governments start to encourage **TNCs** to invest; for example, an international clothing company may set up factories here. As a result, the economy begins to experience globalisation: countries become interconnected by trade and culture with other places.

Stage 3: Take off

During this stage, secondary manufacturing dominates the economy as industrialisation occurs and more factories are built and machinery is introduced. The increase in wealth means that governments can invest in social schemes like education and health, as well as general infrastructure. TNCs often dominate the economy, which can lead to dependency as the country relies upon these international companies to provide investment and jobs. This may lead to problems such as workers being exploited or environmental damage. As workers increasingly switch from primary to secondary jobs, this leads to rural–urban migration and urbanisation as towns and cities grow. There might be some inequality of wealth; a rural–urban divide can exist between places that have more wealth and services and those which do not. Increasingly the nation becomes more modernised with new airports, roads, railways, public services, education and healthcare as well as access to electricity and the internet. This continues to encourage international investment and can lead to a 'spiral of prosperity', or the multiplier effect, whereby investment leads to wealth, which leads to more investment.

Stage 4: Drive to maturity

The country is becoming more self-sufficient as the economy diversifies and does not have to rely upon foreign investment so much. A snowballing of government investment leads to rapid urbanisation and a depopulation of rural areas. This can cause issues of urban congestion and rural decline. As education and aspirations improve, employment changes again so that more are involved in tertiary 'service' jobs, such as customer care, sales, nursing, teaching, IT support, etc. Very few people now work in primary jobs, as resources can often be imported cheaply from somewhere else. Universities and easy school access mean that high-tech industry and the beginnings of quaternary jobs (such as research and development) start to appear.

Stage 5: High mass consumerism

This is seen as the ultimate point to reach. Tertiary service jobs now dominate the economy and secondary manufacturing shifts to smaller factories with less environmental impact. As the population becomes wealthier, **consumption** (buying or using resources) increasingly focuses on high-value goods such as cars, electronics, leisure activities and designer goods.

CHAPTER

21

Global urbanisation

Key idea: The majority of the world's population now live in urban areas.

→ In this chapter you will study:

→ the definition of a city, megacity and world city

→ the distribution of megacities and now this has changed over time

→ how urban growth rates vary in parts of the world with contrasting levels of development.

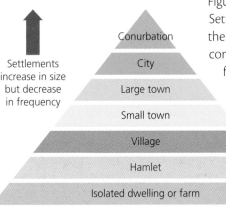

Settlements increase in size but decrease in frequency

Conurbation
City
Large town
Small town
Village
Hamlet
Isolated dwelling or farm

▲ **Figure 1** Settlement hierarchy

How is the global pattern of urbanisation changing?

In 2007, the UN announced that for the first time more than 50 per cent of the world's population lived in **urban** areas. The number of urban dwellers rises by an estimated 180,000 every day. By 2050, 75 per cent of the world's population could live in towns and cities.

Urbanisation is an increase in the amount of people living in urban areas, such as towns or cities, compared with those living in rural areas, such as the countryside. This could be because of **migration** from rural to urban areas, or a natural increase if there is a high birth rate and low death rate within these urban areas (**internal growth**). The world is more urbanised than ever – a trend which will continue.

What is a city?

Figure 1 shows that cities are nearer the top of the settlement hierarchy. Settlements move up through the hierarchy as more people live in them; they develop more **functions** and provide more **services** as a consequence. The hierarchy starts at the bottom with isolated dwellings and farms where single families live, moving through hamlets, villages, towns and cities to **conurbations**. A conurbation is made up of a major city and its suburban areas, housing tens of millions of people and performing a large number of functions. An example of a conurbation is the Pearl River Delta area in China (see Figure 2). These can then merge with other cities to form sprawling **urban belts**, such as the Taiheiyō Belt which follows the *shinkansen* (bullet train) routes on the main Japanese island of Honshu. It runs for over 700 miles and houses around half of the country's total population.

The actual point which determines when a settlement passes the threshold from town to city varies from country to country. In Sweden, a population of around 50,000 is needed for a settlement to be called a city. In contrast, the Welsh city of St David's had a population of less than 2000 at the 2011 census. It also lacks many of the functions that one would expect a city to have.

▲ **Figure 2** The Pearl River Delta, China; an example of a conurbation

City locations

The first cities to flourish were found along major river valleys which allowed residents to settle and feed themselves. The first real cities are thought to have started after the Stone Age, around 10,000 years BP, in what is now Iraq, followed by cities in the Mediterranean. Agriculture was at the heart of the development of early settlements, as hunter-gatherers stopped their nomadic lifestyle. Specialist occupations and trades served the population.

Major city growth took place during the development of the Greek and Roman empires. More recently, one of the greatest stimuli for growth was the Industrial Revolution of the late eighteenth century. The growth of colonial powers, and the British Empire, led to more international trade, which boosted the importance of port cities such as Liverpool and Southampton. Today's major cities grow for similar reasons. Industrial development and raw materials still draw people to the major cities, but there are other factors now, such as global outsourcing and cities planned for a specific purpose such as Canberra and Brasilia.

Why is water an important factor for settlements?

Water is still an important site factor, providing communication and opportunities for trade, along with water supply and waste disposal. Many of the world's major cities are situated on a major river, sometimes close to its mouth, such as Rio de Janeiro. They are often built on the flat land created by the river, which sometimes floods the same area. The major floods that occurred in Brisbane, Australia, in 2011 were a reminder that many of the world's major cities may be vulnerable to sea level rise because of their location. Many cities were originally located on islands, for the added benefit of defence, even though they may have grown beyond those original locations and this factor is no longer relevant, for example New York and Paris.

Activities

1. Study Figure 1.
   a. Where does the settlement where you live sit on the settlement hierarchy?
   b. What do you think were the functions which led to it being settled in the first place?
   c. What have been the major phases of growth in its history?

→ Take it further

2. Access the most recent census results to find out what the population of your home settlement is. What else can you discover from the census data? Use a tool such as http://datashine.org.uk/ and enter your postcode to find out more about the settlement you live in.
3. Produce an annotated map of your chosen settlement, adding details of the site, functions and nearby resources that may have contributed to its current status on the hierarchy.

Cities, megacities and world cities and their changing distribution since 1950

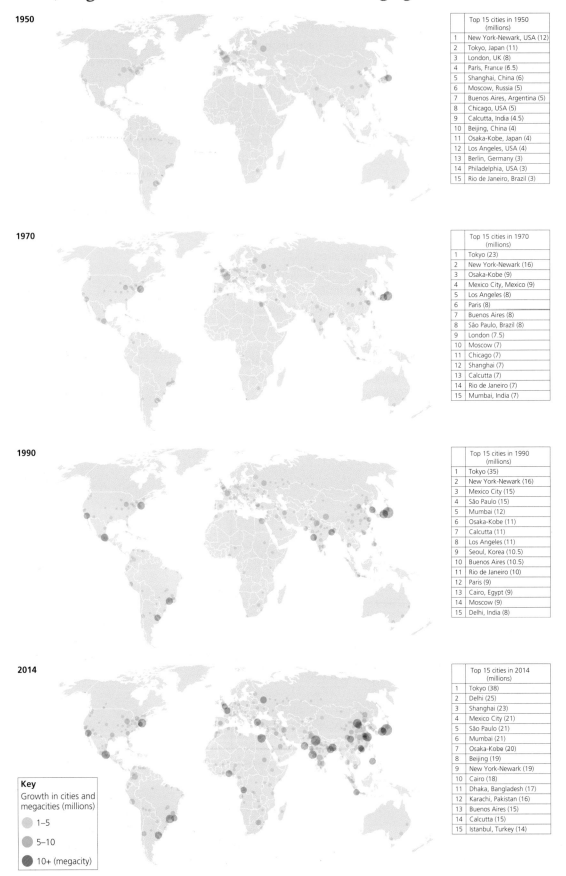

1950

	Top 15 cities in 1950 (millions)
1	New York-Newark, USA (12)
2	Tokyo, Japan (11)
3	London, UK (8)
4	Paris, France (6.5)
5	Shanghai, China (6)
6	Moscow, Russia (5)
7	Buenos Aires, Argentina (5)
8	Chicago, USA (5)
9	Calcutta, India (4.5)
10	Beijing, China (4)
11	Osaka-Kobe, Japan (4)
12	Los Angeles, USA (4)
13	Berlin, Germany (3)
14	Philadelphia, USA (3)
15	Rio de Janeiro, Brazil (3)

1970

	Top 15 cities in 1970 (millions)
1	Tokyo (23)
2	New York-Newark (16)
3	Osaka-Kobe (9)
4	Mexico City, Mexico (9)
5	Los Angeles (8)
6	Paris (8)
7	Buenos Aires (8)
8	São Paulo, Brazil (8)
9	London (7.5)
10	Moscow (7)
11	Chicago (7)
12	Shanghai (7)
13	Calcutta (7)
14	Rio de Janeiro (7)
15	Mumbai, India (7)

1990

	Top 15 cities in 1990 (millions)
1	Tokyo (35)
2	New York-Newark (16)
3	Mexico City (15)
4	São Paulo (15)
5	Mumbai (12)
6	Osaka-Kobe (11)
7	Calcutta (11)
8	Los Angeles (11)
9	Seoul, Korea (10.5)
10	Buenos Aires (10.5)
11	Rio de Janeiro (10)
12	Paris (9)
13	Cairo, Egypt (9)
14	Moscow (9)
15	Delhi, India (8)

2014

	Top 15 cities in 2014 (millions)
1	Tokyo (38)
2	Delhi (25)
3	Shanghai (23)
4	Mexico City (21)
5	São Paulo (21)
6	Mumbai (21)
7	Osaka-Kobe (20)
8	Beijing (19)
9	New York-Newark (19)
10	Cairo (18)
11	Dhaka, Bangladesh (17)
12	Karachi, Pakistan (16)
13	Buenos Aires (15)
14	Calcutta (15)
15	Istanbul, Turkey (14)

Key
Growth in cities and megacities (millions)

- 1–5
- 5–10
- 10+ (megacity)

▲ **Figure 3** Growth in cities and megacities

What are the characteristics of megacities?

In early 2015, a World Bank report suggested that the Pearl River Delta area of China (see Figure 2 on page 178) had overtaken Tokyo as the world's largest urban area, both in terms of area and total population. It is thought to house over 40 million people. Cities of such size would have been unheard of in the past, but are now becoming increasingly the norm.

The rapid rate of growth which has taken place in ACs (and more recently in LIDCs) has led to the creation of a number of cities with a population over ten million. Cities with a population of this size are called **megacities**. These are often, but not exclusively, capital cities. In 1950 there were only two megacities, but there are now thought to be over 30 and the number is growing. This is a dramatic rate of growth in just 65 years and the number continues to grow. Some of the most recent megacities have developed as a result of industrialisation and outward investment from ACs and are found in Africa and Southeast Asia. Although the number of megacities is growing, they still only house five per cent of the world's population at present. Some cities now have populations of over 20 million people, and these are continuing to grow, drawing in surrounding populations as well as growing internally.

Why are megacities important?

> **The risks relating to megacities**
>
> *'Megacities are major global risk areas. Due to highest concentration of people and extreme dynamics, they are particularly prone to supply crises, social disorganisation, political conflicts and natural disasters. Their vulnerability can be high.'*
>
> (Source: www.megacities.uni-koeln.de/index.htm)

As cities grow, their demographic pattern changes. People who move in are often of working age or younger, and are looking to support their families and offer them better life chances. Greater financial stability often gives couples the confidence to raise larger families, increasing the rate of growth still further, even without a rapid rate of immigration.

Many urban areas also get denser as they grow. This could potentially bring environmental benefits in the longer term, as people are concentrated in a small area rather than causing urban sprawl. It is important to plan for growth, or the urban form that develops in the early stages of a city's development tends to persist for decades.

Singapore is an example of a city that was planned carefully, initially under the leadership of Lee Kuan Yew, to cope with future development. Infrastructure was considered at the beginning as part of the planning process and there were long-term plans for its growth. During Mr Lee's time as prime minister, the city grew from a small settlement on a marshy island to a global hub for trade and a popular stopover destination for international travellers.

The megacity can offer some of the benefits of 'economies of scale' so that the impact of people is concentrated in one area, rather than sprawling over a larger area. There can also be a better 'civic identity' with the city, which fosters pride, rather than resentment at those in charge. Megacities may be more stable, and offer better public services, but internal divisions need to be tackled. The 'spread cities' of the USA are not a good model for this, as they involve too much internal movement, which is inefficient. Solar energy generation, recycled materials and careful integration of techn ology could help these cities become more efficient.

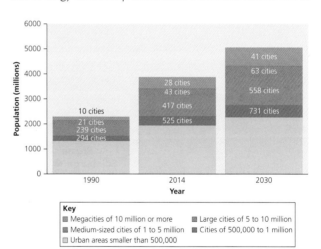

▲ **Figure 5** Urban population growth is propelled by the growth of cities of all sizes

Year	Number of megacities
1950	2
1975	3
2007	19
2025	27 (estimated)

▲ **Figure 4** The growth in number of megacities (population over 10 million)

Activities

1. Study Figure 3.
   a. Identify the locations of the largest cities in each year.
   b. Describe the major changes that have taken place in the locations of the largest cities.
   c. What is likely to happen in the future?
2. Explain why there was a decline in the growth of cities in the ACs during the period from 1950 to 2014.

▲ **Figure 6** Shipping docks in Singapore, a world city

What is a world city?

A **world city** (also known as a global or alpha city) is one which is considered to be an important hub in the global economic system. As with many urban definitions, there is some variation as to what qualifies a city to become a 'world city', but they tend to have some or all of the characteristics detailed in the following box.

Characteristics of world cities

- Headquarters of multinational companies based in the city
- A centre for innovation in business
- A centre for media and communications: broadcasting and technology
- Integration into the global economy
- A major centre for manufacturing
- Important port facilities capable of handling bulk carriers (see Figure 6)
- Financial services: home of an important stock exchange or major banks
- Regional importance compared with other cities
- Highly rated universities, often specialising in research, which links to a high quality of healthcare provision
- Cultural opportunities including opera and ballet as well as cinema and live music

World cities are found in all continents. There are clusters in North America and western Europe. Figure 7 shows those cities which are generally thought of as being world cities.

▲ **Figure 7** World cities

▲ **Figure 8** Canary Wharf, the financial district in London, a world city

Although it is not a megacity, London is a world city. Its status as a world city comes from its financial importance (see Figure 8) with the London Stock Exchange, the scientific research from its many universities, the cultural importance of the city's theatres and the commercial power of the many companies located there. It also has iconic buildings which are familiar to people all over the world, some of them relatively new. Decisions made here influence people around the world. For many overseas visitors it is the only part of the UK which they visit, so comes to 'represent' the UK to them.

World cities need to continue to grow if they are to keep their status; they also face competition from other cities hope to be classed as 'world cities' in their place. The nature of this growth needs to be managed if the cities are to remain competitive.

👣 Fieldwork ideas

For those learning in a rural location, it is worth investigating the possibility of immersing yourself in a busy city, so that you can remember what it was like when discussing cities during this part of the course.

Activities

1. What are the main differences between a megacity and a world city?
2. Create a table to show the strengths and opportunities provided by megacities for the people who inhabit them.
3. Explore the megacities that already exist using this interactive map: www.megacities.uni-koeln.de/documentation. Do they have any common characteristics?

→ Take it further

4. Look at Figure 7. Using the list of characteristics of world cities, suggest why at least three of these cities have been given world city status. You may want to use www.urbanobservatory.org to help with this activity.
5. Do you think it is possible for a world city to lose its status? What factors might lead to this happening?

✛ Geographical skills

One of the issues that face large cities is air quality. This is seen by the World Health Organization (WHO) as one of the greatest global threats to health, and large cities are the worst culprits.

Investigate the air quality around the world using the Plume Labs map: https://air.plumelabs.com

In which country is air quality particularly bad?

What is the global pattern of urban growth?

The pattern of growth in urban areas has not been the same across the world. Cities in Europe and North America reached the peak of their growth in the 1950s or earlier. The most sustained period of urban growth in these **advanced countries (ACs)** took place during the Industrial Revolution of the late 1700s and early 1800s. Increase in population, driven by the 'baby boom' and the building of new houses, led to urban sprawl and the growth of the 'suburbs'. London and Paris were the first 'millionaire' cities (those with a population of more than 1 million people), but they have long since slipped down the league tables of the world's largest. Urbanisation is currently much more rapid in **emerging and developing countries (EDCs)** and **low-income developing countries (LIDCs)**. Cities in Asia and Africa have now overtaken these earlier cities in Europe and North America in terms of population size. EDCs and LIDCs tend to have towns and cities with youthful populations, as the younger people in the rural areas move to urban areas to get jobs. As many of the people are of child-bearing age, there is a high birth rate in these areas, which leads to a rapid natural growth. This trend will continue to cause growth for decades to come.

Growth in Chinese cities is driven by the huge rural–urban migration caused by the economic development of these urban areas and the demand for a large workforce. Almost 200 million people moved to urban areas in East Asia between 2000 and 2010. Measurement of this change is important, as managing new growth requires reasonable accuracy in the number of people involved. Infrastructure development has to keep pace with the growing population. Cities in China have grown despite the adoption of the 'one-child' policy. This policy was in place for 35 years and was only dropped by the government in 2015.

In cities such as Lagos in Nigeria the rate of growth has been particularly rapid. In the 1950s, the city had a population of around 300,000 people. Today, it is Africa's second largest city (after Cairo) with an estimated population of around 18 million people.

Most ACs have populations that are more than 70 per cent urban, but LIDCs have more potential for growth, with around two million people a week moving into cities in Africa and Asia. About 40 per cent of Africans lived in cities in 2015, but this is expected to rise to well over 50 per cent by 2050.

Classification of countries

For more information on the classification and distribution of ACs, EDCs and LIDCs, look at Chapter 18, page 160.

▼ **Figure 9** Population growth per hour in some of the fastest growing cities

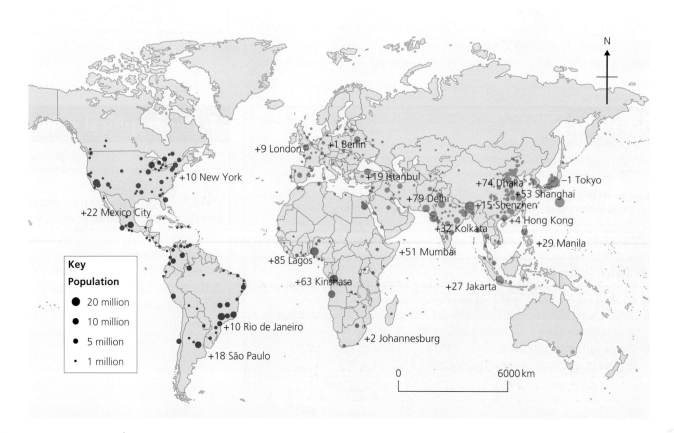

Key
Population
● 20 million
● 10 million
● 5 million
· 1 million

+9 London +1 Berlin
+10 New York
+19 Istanbul +74 Dhaka −1 Tokyo
+79 Delhi +53 Shanghai
+22 Mexico City +15 Shenzhen
+4 Hong Kong
+32 Kolkata
+29 Manila
+51 Mumbai
+85 Lagos
+63 Kinshasa +27 Jakarta
+10 Rio de Janeiro
+2 Johannesburg
+18 São Paulo

0   6000 km

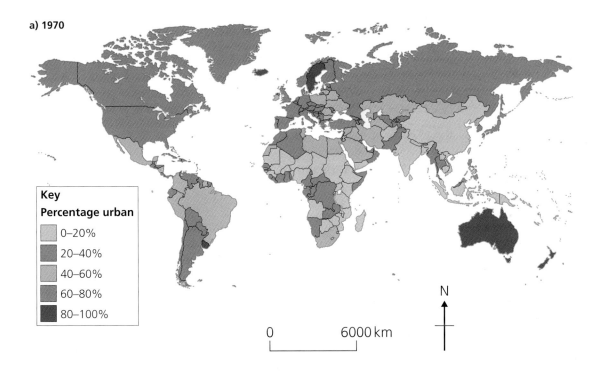

a) 1970

Key
Percentage urban
- 0–20%
- 20–40%
- 40–60%
- 60–80%
- 80–100%

0   6000 km

N

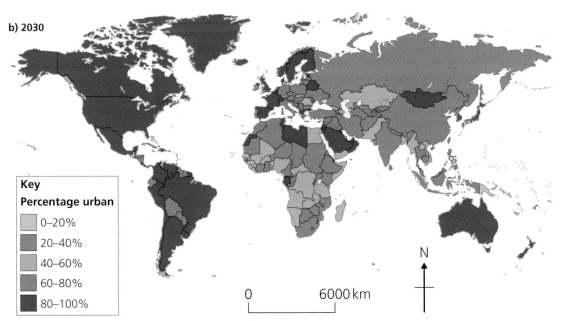

b) 2030

Key
Percentage urban
- 0–20%
- 20–40%
- 40–60%
- 60–80%
- 80–100%

0   6000 km

N

▲ **Figure 10** How urban areas across the world are changing. These maps compare the percentage urban by size for (a) 1970 and (b) 2030

Activities

1. Compare the percentage urbanisation shown in Figure 10 and how it has changed in:
   a. the Americas
   b. Africa
   c. South East Asia
2. Which parts of the world have undergone the greatest change in urbanisation over time?

Rapid urbanisation in LIDCs

Key idea: There are causes and consequences of rapid urbanisation in LIDCs.

➜ **In this chapter you will study:**

➜ an overview of the causes of rapid urbanisation in LIDCs, including the push and pull migration, factors and natural growth

➜ an outline of the social, economic and environmental consequences of rapid urbanisation in LIDCs.

What does rapid urbanisation mean for cities?

What are the causes of rapid urbanisation in LIDCs?

The rate of growth of LIDC cities is now the fastest in the world. The highest population growth rate is in the continent of Africa; urban populations there are expected to triple in size by 2050. There is still less than 40 per cent urban population in Africa, with plenty of potential to grow further. Cities such as Yamoussoukro, Côte d'Ivoire, may grow by over 40 per cent in the next five years.

City dwellers are predicted to double in number by 2050, rising to over 6 billion people, which will lead to further urban sprawl or increased density of occupation. There has been particular growth in the Pearl River Delta in China, including cities such as Shenzhen and Guangzhou. Some cities have specialised in manufacturing particular products, and this has drawn people into them from surrounding rural areas, looking to improve their quality of life.

Urbanisation is driven by:

● rural–urban migration – people being drawn from the rural areas to live in cities
● internal growth – when people who have moved into the cities have lots of children.

Rural–urban migration

The factors which draw people to cities are referred to as **pull factors**. These work in combination with **push factors** which tend to drive people away from rural areas.

Push factors	Pull factors
● Opportunities for employment other than agricultural work are limited and wages in rural areas are at poverty levels in many countries. ● Rural areas often have fewer services (including access to education and healthcare) and poorer infrastructure.	● There are more opportunities for employment than in rural areas and wages are often better. ● There are often better healthcare systems and schools in urban areas. ● There is the draw of stories which may filter back from people who left the village and who are now apparently doing better in the city. ● Cities become transport hubs, with road, rail, canal and air networks meeting there or passing through them. This encourages new arrivals to travel there and in turn this creates benefits for industrial location, drawing in a workforce from the surrounding area. ● Prestige comes from a city location, which drives up the cost of property and office space through demand.

Internal growth

Once people arrive in cities and find employment and housing, they will tend to have children. This increase in population due to higher birth rates is called internal growth and it can result in a rapid rate of population growth, particularly in LIDCs where cities have a large youthful population. By contrast, many cities in ACs are facing ageing populations and declining numbers.

It is not just cities and megacities that are experiencing an increase in population. Towns great and small are seeing rapid growth in many parts of the world. Are LIDCs going to repeat the pattern of the United States, where rural areas are often neglected as a consequence?

Jing-Jin-Ji

The Chinese government is currently pushing forward a plan to develop a city region centred on Beijing which may eventually house 130 million people. It is known as Jing-Jin-Ji (see Figure 1). The idea is that integrating existing urban areas into one supercity may lead to further innovation and environmental protection. The settlement could spread over 207,200 km² and would require significant investment in transport, including high-speed rail, as well as services such as schools and hospitals. This is an extreme example of the planning decisions that are needed to cope with the increase in urban growth.

▲ **Figure 1** Jing-Jin-Ji, a planned supercity which will connect Beijing, Tianjin, and Hebei

What are the consequences of rapid urban growth in LIDCs?

LIDC towns and cities are facing rapid rates of growth and may not always be able to cope with it very well. Investment needs to continue or the growth may slow. Infrastructure issues such as traffic congestion, poor air quality and inadequate housing may begin to restrict further economic growth.

In Africa, the last two decades have seen cities growing at their fastest ever rate. Urbanisation has not always resulted in improvements in the quality of life for those who live there, although the perception that leads them to move to the cities is that they will improve their life chances. As slums have grown, air quality has deteriorated and some cities are facing severe water shortages.

Infrastructure improvements such as paved highways and new bridges, sometimes as a result of World Bank funding, have enabled easier access to some LIDC cities. New arrivals to the city have some key priorities. They need to find somewhere to live and secure employment or a source of income. They have food, water and sanitation needs and their children will require education. The whole family may need healthcare. For some new arrivals, most of these needs are only partially met and their situation is precarious.

Informal growth of cities

Cities often grow in a planned way, but many cities, particularly those in LIDCs, attract people in such large numbers that the city's infrastructure cannot keep pace with that of the arrivals. Available land, even that which is unsuitable for development, is soon used, expanding along transport routes such as main roads and railways. This informal growth is characterised by the absence of services, particularly sanitation and healthcare, high population densities and criminal activities. Many people are employed in the **informal sector**, where they do not pay tax and have no legal working rights, for example working for cash on a building site or as a domestic cleaner. These jobs may be less reliable than formal employment.

Urban trends

The United Nation's Department of Economic and Social Affairs publishes a regular report on urban trends. The 2015 edition features a wealth of data, statistics and analysis of recent global urban trends. A PDF of the report can be downloaded from: http://esa.un.org/unpd/wup/Highlights/WUP2014-Highlights.pdf.

Lagos: a better life for new arrivals?

Lagos is a port which lies on the coast of Nigeria, guarding a swampy lagoon (see Figure 2). The city flourished during the slave trade. More recently, Lagos has experienced a rapid population increase with numbers growing by 3.4 million people between 2000 and 2010. As a consequence, the city has effectively run out of room and now extends along bridges, leading to traffic congestion and sprawls up to 24 km inland. The lack of space is not slowing growth; in fact the city is expected to double in size in the next 10 years. Lagos is Nigeria's most important city, and is the economic centre for West Africa, but many people live in one of hundreds of slum areas.

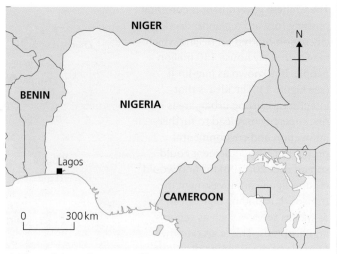

▲ **Figure 2** Location map of Lagos

Many residents live without access to electricity or sanitation, and are threatened by flooding and disease; human waste flows through people's homes when it rains. Outbreaks of typhoid, yellow fever and the virus H5N1, among others, have occurred. Rates of HIV/AIDS infection are high. Life expectancy has dropped below 50. Near catastrophe was averted when a traveller infected with Ebola arrived in the city in late 2014, but the disease was contained. Many residents are also affected by corruption and the need to pay bribes to officials, and crime rates are high. There has been investment in high-profile developments such as a sport stadium and convention centre, but most residents don't benefit from this investment.

One particular area attracting attention is the slum area called Makoko (see Figures 3 and 4). Unlike many slums which are built on land which has been left unused for some reason, Makoko extends out over the water, with buildings on stilts over a lagoon that is polluted and full of rubbish. The marshy ground used to swallow houses built of materials such as breeze blocks. It has been given the ironic nickname 'the Venice of Africa', but it is not a romantic place.

The area has become a floating city, extending out to the point where the water gets too deep. Canoes called *okos* transport residents around and act as floating shops for food, domestic fuel and also drinking water. It is thought that as many as 250,000 people may be living in the area. The slum at Makoko has not appeared overnight; it has been growing for at least one hundred years. Smoke from fires used for cooking and heating hangs over the houses.

In 2006, the World Bank identified nine of Lagos' largest slums for upgrading. These included Makoko. A loan of US$200 million will be used to help improve drainage and the management of solid waste.

In July 2012, the authorities removed many dwellings in Makoko to try to slow down its growth. Machetes and chainsaws were used to cut through the piles, however many people are still living in boats and refusing to leave as they have nowhere to go to. A fire in 2013 also destroyed many houses. There are some interesting plans in place to redevelop the area. Some involve communities of floating homes along with a floating school. However, it is unlikely that slum dwellers could afford these homes.

▲ **Figure 3** Makoko, Lagos

▲ **Figure 4** Makoko, Lagos

Activities

1. Draw a table with three columns headed 'Economic' 'Social' and 'Environmental'. Read through the information on page 188 about the consequences of rapid urban growth for Lagos and add notes to the correct column in your table.

2. Name a different type of graph or chart that could be used to represent the data in Figure 5.

What is informal housing?

Informal housing is built on land which does not belong to those who are building it. This is often land which may not be suitable for the purpose: river beds which may fill with water after rains, land close to industrial activity which may be bad for people's health, or land on steep and unstable slopes. These properties are sometimes affected by landslides and flooding.

Children may have to leave education and go to work to support their families. This may include informal work such as street trading. There have been some projects focusing on improving the lives of young people as a way of leading new growth and reducing the numbers being drawn into criminal activity. In areas of informal housing, infrastructure is poor and there are problems with the reliability of electricity supplied and other utilities. Over time, areas are improved and self-help communities develop.

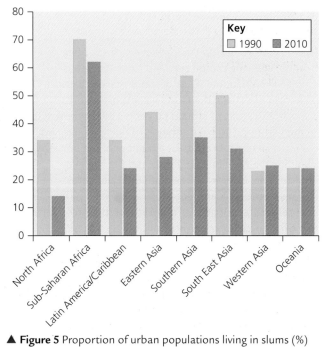

▲ **Figure 5** Proportion of urban populations living in slums (%)

CHAPTER

Rosario: a major city in an EDC

23

Key idea: Cities have district challenges and ways of life, influenced by its people and culture their.

➜ In this chapter you will study:

➜ the case study of Rosario in Argentina (an EDC) including the influences of:

- the city within its region, the country, and the wider world

- migration (national and international) and its impact on the city's growth and character

- the ways of life within the city, such as culture, ethnicity, housing, leisure and consumption

- contemporary challenges that affect urban change, including housing availability, transport provision and waste management

➜ sustainable strategies to overcome one of the city's challenges.

What is the city's location and importance?

▲ **Figure 1:** Location map for Rosario, Argentina

Rosario is the largest city in the southern part of the Argentinian province of Santa Fe.

It is the third most populous city in Argentina after Buenos Aires (the capital city) and Cordoba. It has an estimated population of just over one million, based on information from the most recent census, and a population density of around 50 people per hectare. It is located around 300 km northwest of Buenos Aires and is a regional transport hub for a number of major roads, including the Aramburu Highway and the Highway Ernesto 'Che' Guevara, named after the city's most famous former resident. Rosario is also served by an international airport, called *Islas Malvinas*: the Argentinian name for the disputed territory of the Falkland Islands.

It lies on the Paraná River, which eventually flows into the Atlantic and is the second longest river in South America after the Amazon. The city is low lying; it is only around 40 m above sea level, which moderates its climate compared with other cities.

The city is made up of six districts, each of which has its own characteristics.

Rosario has rail, river and air transport links which have helped it develop as an important industrial centre within the region. The city's location on the *costanera*, the bank of the Paraná River which connects to the Plata Basin, places it on one of the largest and busiest waterways in the world and a major artery for communications throughout the region. The associated dockside development meant that it was a key point for the import and export of agricultural products. The fortunes of these industries have changed over the decades, but many remain profitable and the city is prosperous as a result. Its industrial importance means that it attracts investment.

How did Rosario develop?

Rosario was founded in the late seventeenth century when land was gifted to a soldier called Luis Romero de Pineda for services to the crown. A small settlement grew on his land, close to the River Paraná, as settlers drawn from across Santa Fe mixed with indigenous people. Livestock were farmed and the city developed through farming in the immediate area and trade.

In the late nineteenth century, the city became Argentina's first port to export goods and this drew in migrant workers. The importance of grain led to the city being called 'Argentina's Chicago', which developed alongside gang and Mafia activity after Italian migrants arrived.

Some industries fared less well and parts of the river bank became derelict with empty warehouses. These areas have recently started to undergo renovation as part of the redevelopments aimed at attracting tourism and further new investment. Around the year 2000, many of the city's chemical and steel plants had closed and unemployment was high. The city's fortunes have improved dramatically since that time.

The city's architecture, such as French renaissance buildings and the impressive Stock Exchange, are a sign of the city's wealth and importance over the last few centuries.

Alongside its port facilities, the city has developed as a milling and meat-packing centre for the region. A large complex run by Swift produces products such as corned beef for export. This has attracted people from across Argentina. In the last century, there have also been dramatic increases in the growth of soybeans, which are in demand for foodstuffs, vegetable oil and other products.

Patterns of national and international migration

- Rosario has attracted people from across Argentina. It is estimated that the country is second only to the USA in the number of immigrants it has received, and these have enriched the culture of cities such as Rosario.
- Arrivals included the Spanish in the sixteenth century and migrants from Europe in the nineteenth century. More recently, there has been an influx of migrants from other countries within South America and even from as far away as Korea, China and Taiwan.
- Italian immigration has been a key element in the growth of the city and has influenced hugely the culture (including the food) and the architecture. Italians formed the majority of immigrants into Rosario over the last century. One famous Italian Argentine is Jorge Mario Bergoglio, also known as Pope Francis.

The city has a relatively young demographic, as do many Argentinian cities given the country as a whole has a youthful population with a relatively high birth rate (see Figure 2). There are, however, signs of some ageing across the city; this is part of a general trend with all cities.

✝ Geographical skills

A population pyramid is a type of graph which shows the number of people in a range of cohorts (age groups). It shows the population structure of a country and allows for long-term planning as the relative sizes of each cohort will reduce over time, unless there are significant changes in birth and death rate.

Tip

It is important that you don't fall into the trap of thinking that people living in cities like Rosario are less well off than those in Leeds or other cities in ACs. All cities provide benefits for their residents and not everyone can share in the wealth that they generate. Avoid seeing cities as places which only have problems; they also provide a range of opportunities for the people who live there and as these chapters have shown, they may well be our future salvation. Remember to be critical of images and text you may be shown out of context. What images of Rosario are presented if you carry out an image search online?

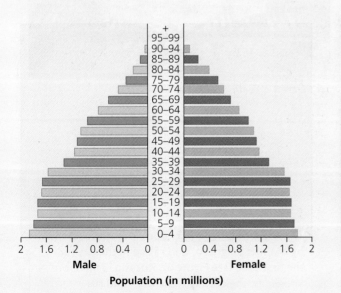

▲ **Figure 2** A population pyramid for Argentina, 2009

What are the ways of life for people in Rosario?

A socialist city

Rosario has been described as the socialist and liberal hub of the country. It has a history of socialist activity. Ernesto (Che) Guevara, who later gained notoriety for his political involvement across South America, was born in the city. The city also has close links with the trade unions because of its industrial heritage.

▲ **Figure 3** Che Guevara

▲ **Figure 4:** El Centro, Rosario

Shopping in Rosario

Residents and visitors have good opportunities for shopping in *El Centro*: the central mall area. This is an area which has undergone investment and now attracts young people and families alike.

The importance of meat

Argentina as a country has a close cultural connection to meat. It is an important part of the diet (see Figure 5). In fact, Argentinians eat far more meat than other nations. There is a close link with the production of beef too. Cattle graze the large grassland areas called pampas and the gauchos, or 'cowboys', are still important. The *asado*, or grill, is an important feature of many restaurants, particularly in *La Florida* – the beach at the river's edge. Argentina is the third largest exporter of meat products.

▲ **Figure 5** Argentina is famous for its steak

▲ **Figure 6** The Argentinian flag

Raising the flag

The Argentinian flag was born in Rosario, created by Manuel Belgrano, and raised in the city for the first time (see Figure 6). Rosario is therefore known as 'the cradle of the flag', and the impressive National Flag Memorial is sited on the bank of the Paraná.

What are the challenges facing Rosario?

Like any city of comparable size, Rosario has some issues that those in charge of the city have to deal with.

Unemployment

As recently as 2001 there were riots in the city, with high unemployment and economic problems leading to looting of supermarkets. There are still some crime problems facing the city, but there has been some improvement in the employment situation.

Crime

In some parts of the city, slum districts known locally as *villas miserias* are beset by high levels of poverty and crime. Drug use has grown among the city's population and spawned a violent drug war in some districts. Sicilian mobsters have been active in the city.

Criminals have allegedly infiltrated the police in the past and football in the city (and indeed in the country as a whole) is controlled by violent groups known as *barras bravas*. The two football teams in Rosario are Rosario Central and Newell's Old Boys. The city's reputation has been damaged by its association with crime.

Barrios are the neighbourhoods where people live.

Social inequality and divisions

Not everyone who lives in Rosario shares in the success of the city. There are many irregular settlements, or slums, which house over 100,000 people and occupy around 10 per cent of the space in the city.

Cities often grow in a planned way, but many (particularly in LIDCs) attract people in such large numbers that the city's infrastructure cannot keep pace with that of the arrivals. Available land, even that which is unsuitable for development, is soon used and settlements expand along transport routes such as main roads and railways. This informal growth is characterised by the absence of services, particularly sanitation and healthcare, high population densities, structural deficiencies and a low quality of life.

What is being done about these challenges?

Initiatives such as the Rosario Habitat Program are part of a wider regeneration of areas of Rosario. Regeneration can include one or more of the following options:

- complete replacement – demolition followed by rebuilding to meet the architectural styles of the present day and the ambition of the developers

The Rosario Habitat Programme

The Rosario Habitat Programme has been set up to reduce the inequalities in the city. The programme is led by the Public Housing Service, which has been in existence for over 80 years. Since it started in 2000, the scheme has helped over 5000 people to upgrade their houses. The programme involves comprehensive improvements, including:

→ new urban planning – new roads and basic infrastructure including sewerage, storm drains and community facilities

→ adding toilet facilities to houses

→ legal ownership rather than the previous uncertainty over the status of tenure

→ education programme for young people regarding risky behaviour

→ employment and income generation for residents; training and work experience for 16–25 year olds

→ money invested in social enterprises

→ targeted support for women in the community.

The project has achieved financial sustainability. It has generated over 150 construction and professional jobs, and trained almost 1000 people in business and entrepreneurial skills.

- regeneration – improvements to the fabric of the building, which might include changes internally or externally
- increasing height – the addition of new floors or replacing low-rise with high-rise development
- infill – additions to the area which may be out of keeping with the area they are slotted into.

One trend is the arrival of gated communities, known locally as *barrios privados* or *barrios cerrados*. These are designed to provide residents with a feeling of safety, with security guards and fences. Rosario has tried to limit these in order to keep the community spirit within the city and prevent the rich from becoming isolated from the poor. It is the first city in the country to have taken this step. Such gated communities are a common feature of other South American cities, where wealthy individuals often have a perception that they are at risk of crime. Footballer Lionel Messi was born in Rosario and he has a property in the area as his family has close ties with the city.

Empty land close to the city centre is prime development land and high-rise developments often locate in these places. In recent years, young people have returned to the city centres. These single and well-educated 'millennials' are joined in some cities by a large student population.

Does the city have a sustainable future?

Rosario has a plan to become more sustainable in its food production. Cities are hungry places and require a lot of resources each day. Food supply is one resource which needs careful thought, as cities are not naturally producers of food.

Rosario: a green city

One key development in Rosario has been the growth of **urban forestry** and agriculture. The city is gaining a reputation as a world leader in this aspect of urban design. Rosario promotes the development of urban forestry as a way of reducing the impacts of climate change within the city (see Figure 7). This programme is called *Pro Huerta* (literally, Pro Garden).

▲ **Figure 7** Trees within the city of Rosario

Trees are planted among all new housing developments to reduce the ambient temperature in the area. Flood risk zones and peri-urban land have been planted up with food crops; this improves the diet of some low-income families, as well as providing them with some additional income from the sales of their produce. Community groups were given tools and seeds, and vacant land was turned over to the urban farmers some years ago. The production of food locally also reduces the need to transport crops into the city from nearby regions; this reduces CO_2. Local hotels and restaurants support this campaign by using these vegetables and fruits and promoting the value of local food and reduced food miles.

There are now over 800 community gardens in the city, supporting over 40,000 people. The city won a UN-Habitat award for its work in this area. Importantly, the majority of gardeners are women, who now earn income from their involvement, as well as gaining further skills. This is a scheme which other cities have also looked at copying, because of its many benefits.

▶ **Figure 8** Rosario lies on the Paraná River

Sustainable tourism

Rosario, along with Argentina as a whole, is a growing tourist destination and attracts people from a wide area. The city is making the most of its many attractions and adding tourism as one of its functions and main sources of income. Rosario is also attracting those who wish to learn Spanish, with a growing range of colleges and courses for overseas students who can study in the city. The city has a range of physical attractions, including the waterfront and some of the buildings which have been built over the years.

Activities

1. Create a table with two columns headed 'Physical attractions' and 'Human attractions'. Put these tourist attractions into the correct column in the table.
   - The River Paraná and its *costanera*
   - The National Flag monument: *Monumento Nacional a La Bandera*
   - Tree-lined parks
   - Art galleries
   - Cafés and restaurants
   - The temperate climate, with warm summer temperatures
   - French renaissance architecture
   - A local cuisine based on meat, cooked on an *asado* (barbecue)
   - Paraná Gorge with its sandy beaches
   - Local musicians
   - Salsa and tango clubs for dancing
   - Nightclubs

→ Take it further

2. Visit the website for tourism in the city of Rosario (www.rosarioturismo.com/en/city/) and identify additional attractions that the city might have for visitors from within the country and overseas.
3. Find out more about the green cities scheme and the city farms in Rosario. What are the economic, social and environmental benefits of the scheme for Rosario and its inhabitants? The city's website has some useful additional information: www.rosario.gov.ar.

▲ **Figure 9** Rosario Station

Practice questions

1. Study the image in Figure 1 on page 152. Describe what is meant by 'development'. **[1 mark]**

2. Name one social measure of development. Describe how it shows how developed a country is. **[3 marks]**

3. Complete the following table. **[3 marks]**

Country classification	Example nation
Advanced countries (ACs)	
Emerging developing countries (EDCs)	
	Somalia

4. Study Figure A. The Rostow Model demonstrates how countries can develop over time from being traditional to becoming more developed. Describe what is meant by Stage 3 'take off'. **[4 marks]**

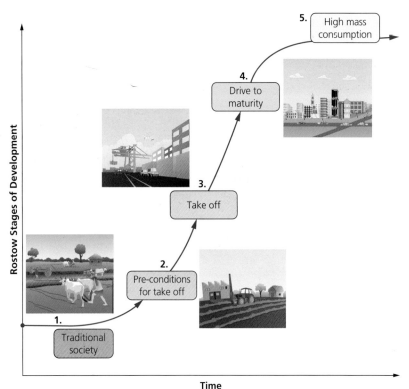

▲ **Figure A** Rostow's model of development

5. Name one economic measure of development. Describe how it shows how developed a country is. **[3 marks]**

6. Study Figure 9b on page 158, which shows wealth per person. Which of the following statements is incorrect?

   a) Wealth is evenly spread across the world.

   b) The northern parts of the world have more wealth per person.

   c) North America and Europe have more wealth per person.

   d) Africa has the least wealth per person. **[1 mark]**

Tip

For question 6, work out which statements are definitely correct to select the incorrect statement by a process of elimination.

7. How can physical factors, such as natural resources, affect how developed a place can become? **[3 marks]**

8. Study Figure B. How has Ethiopia's wealth changed over time? **[2 marks]**

Tip

Refer to stimulus information to support your answer.

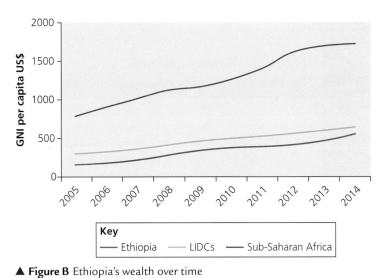

▲ **Figure B** Ethiopia's wealth over time

9. Evaluate the impact that a trans-national company can have on a location. Suggest some possible advantages and disadvantages for the host nation. **[4 marks]**

10. Describe how aid can bring benefit to an area. **[3 marks]**

11. Define the following terms:
    a) Urbanisation **[1 mark]**
    b) Megacity **[1 mark]**
    c) World city **[1 mark]**

Tip

To evaluate, as in question 9, make sure that you weigh up both the advantages and disadvantages and ensure that your answer is balanced.

12. How has the global location of megacities changed since the 1950s? **[3 marks]**

13. Suggest some advantages and disadvantages of megacities for the people who live in them. **[3 marks]**

14. With reference to London, or another world city you have studied, explain why it has gained its status. **[3 marks]**

15. With reference to a city you have studied, outline the negative consequences of rapid urban growth in LIDCs. **[5 marks]**

16. How have some LIDC cities attempted to improve the quality of life for people who live in them. Evaluate the success of these schemes. **[5 marks]**

17. Define the term 'social inequality'. **[1 mark]**

18. Suggest how cities in advanced countries can be classed as divided cities as a result of social inequality, with reference to a named city. **[4 marks]**

19. Sustainability involves three elements. What are those three elements? **[2 marks]**

20. With reference to a city that you have studied, outline one scheme for improving the sustainability of a particular area. **[4 marks]**

Tip

For question 20, make sure you provide some detailed information about the scheme you have studied.

THEME 3

Environmental Threats to Our Planet

Climate change and extreme weather conditions cause many threats to both people and the environment. This theme helps you to understand these key environmental threats that afffect countries and the world as a whole.

Chapter 24: Climate change from the start of the Quaternary period

Key idea: The climate has changed from the start of the Quaternary period.

In this chapter you will study:

→ an overview of how the climate has changed from the beginning of the Quaternary period to the present day, including ice ages

→ the key periods of warming and cooling since AD 1000, including the medieval warming, Little Ice Age and modern warming

→ the evidence for climate change over different time periods, including global temperature data, ice cores, tree rings, paintings and diaries.

Chapter 25: Causes of climate change

Key idea: There are a number of possible causes of climate change.

In this chapter you will study:

→ the theories of natural causes of climate change including variations in energy from the sun, changes in the Earth's orbit and volcanic activity

→ how human activity is responsible for the enhanced greenhouse effect which contributes to global warming.

Chapter 26: Consequences of climate change

Key idea: Climate change has consequences.

In this chapter you will study:

→ a range of consequences of climate change currently being experienced across the planet.

Chapter 27: Global circulation of the atmosphere

Key idea: The global circulation of the atmosphere controls weather and climate.

In this chapter you will study:

→ the distribution of the main climatic regions of the world

→ an outline how the global circulation of the atmosphere is controlled by the movement of air between the poles and the Equator

→ how the global circulation of the atmosphere leads to extreme weather conditions (wind, temperature, precipitation) in different parts of the world.

Chapter 28: Extreme weather: tropical storms and drought

Key idea: Extreme weather conditions cause different natural weather hazards.

Key idea: Drought can be devastating for people and the environment.

In this chapter you will study:

→ an outline the causes of the extreme weather conditions that are associated with the hazards of tropical storms and drought

→ the distribution and frequency of tropical storms and drought, and whether these have changed over time

→ a case study of `The Big Dry' in Australia, a drought event caused by El Niño/La Niña including:

— how the extreme weather conditions of El Niño/La Niña develop and can lead to drought

— effects of the drought event on people and the environment

→ ways in which people have adapted to drought in the case study area.

Climate change from the start of the Quaternary period

Key idea: The climate has changed from the start of the Quaternary period.

➜ In this chapter you will study:

➜ an overview of how the climate has changed from the beginning of the Quaternary period to the present day, including ice ages

➜ the key periods of warming and cooling since AD 1000, including the medieval warming, Little Ice Age and modern warming

➜ the evidence for climate change over different time periods, including global temperature data, ice cores, tree rings, paintings and diaries.

Activities

1. Study Figure 1. Which of the following statements are true?
   a. The Quaternary period started 2.6 million years ago.
   b. Before the Quaternary period, global temperatures were mostly higher than today's average temperature.
   c. The lowest temperature occurred about 0.5 million years ago.
   d. The highest temperature was +2°C.

2. Study Figure 2.
   a. We are currently in a relatively warm period. Roughly how long has this lasted?
   b. The last warm (inter-glacial) period occurred about 125,000 years ago. How high did temperatures reach during this period compared with today's average?

How has climate changed during the Quaternary geological period?

Climate change is nothing new. Over geological time, measured in hundreds of millions of years, climate has changed constantly, affecting the distribution and development of life on Earth. Look at Figure 1. It shows the pattern of global temperatures for the last 5.5 million years using evidence from deep ocean sediments. The graph shows how temperature has changed over time compared with today's average temperature (shown by the dashed line at 0°C).

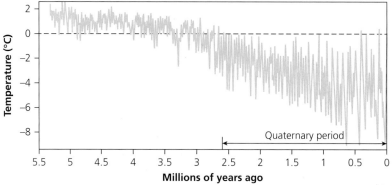

▲ **Figure 1** Average global temperatures for the last 5.5 million years

Notice that the last 2.6 million years is known as the **Quaternary geological period**. During this period of time, temperatures have fluctuated wildly, although there has been a gradual overall cooling. The cold 'spikes' in the graph are **glacial periods** when ice advanced over parts of Europe and North America. In between are warmer **inter-glacial periods**. Notice that today's average temperature is higher than almost all of the Quaternary period. The current warm period that began some 10,000 years ago may turn out to be another inter-glacial period, with ice returning at some point in the future.

Now look at Figure 2 which shows temperature changes during the last 400,000 years. The temperature values on the graph are in comparison to today's global average temperature placed at 0°C. To help you appreciate this time scale, the human species evolved about 200,000 years ago.

The graph shows clearly how the cold glacial periods have alternated with warm inter-glacial periods.

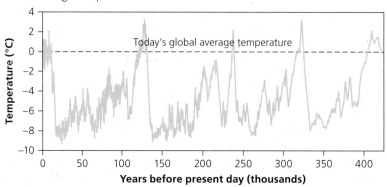

▲ **Figure 2** Trends in average global temperatures (400,000 years ago to the present day)

Figure 3 shows the most recent changes in average global temperatures from 1880 to 2013. It suggests clearly that in the last few decades, average global temperatures have increased relative to the 1901–2000 average. It is this current warming trend that has become known by the term **global warming**.

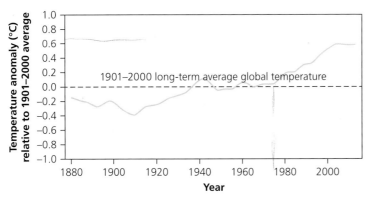

▲ **Figure 3** Average global temperatures, 1880–2013

Since AD 1000 there have been several key periods of warming. The Medieval Warm Period (MWP) lasted from about 950 to 1250 and was a time of warm climate in the North Atlantic region. Temperatures in some regions of the world were the same or higher than recent temperatures, but on average, the global temperature was cooler than it is now. This warm period was followed by a cooler period called the Little Ice Age (see below) from 1300 to 1870. Over the last 100 years, we have seen modern global warming as the Earth's average surface air temperature has increased by around 1°C. The ocean temperatures are the warmest they have been since 1850.

Activities

1. Study Figure 3.
   a. Describe the average global temperature trend from 1880 to 1940.
   b. From what date did the average global temperature start to rise rapidly above the long-term average?
   c. Describe the trend in average global temperature since 2000.
   d. What is the difference in average global temperature between 1880 and 2013?
   e. Do you think this graph provides strong evidence for global warming?

2. Look at Figure 4. It shows a typical winter scene during the Little Ice Age.
   a. What is the evidence in the painting that this is a sever winter?
   b. What are the daily problems facing the people?
   c. Can you suggest any advantages of this severe winter weather for the people in the painting?

The Little Ice Age (1300–1870)

The Little Ice Age is the name given to a period of time when parts of Europe and North America experienced much colder winters than today. The coldest periods were in the fifteenth and seventeenth centuries.

- The price of grain increased and vineyards in much of Europe became unproductive.
- Sea ice engulfed Iceland, preventing ships from landing. As crops failed many people decided to emigrate. Iceland lost half its population during the Little Ice Age.
- The sea froze around parts of the UK and regular winter 'Frost Fairs' were held on the frozen River Thames.
- Throughout Northern Europe, rivers froze and people suffered from intensely cold winters when food supplies were limited.

Despite these harsh climatic conditions European culture and technology flourished. Huge innovations occurred in

▲ **Figure 4** *Winterlandschaft mit Vogelfalle* ('Winter Landscape with Skaters and Bird Trap') by Pieter Brueghel the Elder (1601)

agriculture, land was reclaimed in the Netherlands and the UK and sea trading expanded. Did the Little Ice Age perhaps trigger these human responses in the face of the harsh climatic conditions?

Evidence for climate change

The reliable measurement of temperature using thermometers goes back about a hundred years. In the UK, for example, reliable weather records began in 1910.

Informed judgements about ancient climates can be made using evidence from tree rings. Scientists can also use data that have accumulated over long time periods and been trapped and stored within ice or deep-sea sediments.

1. Global temperature data

Look at Figure 5. It shows temperature anomalies (variations from the long-term average) for the period 2008–12. This map was produced by NASA (National Aeronautics and Space Administration) using data collected from over 1000 ground weather stations together with satellite information.

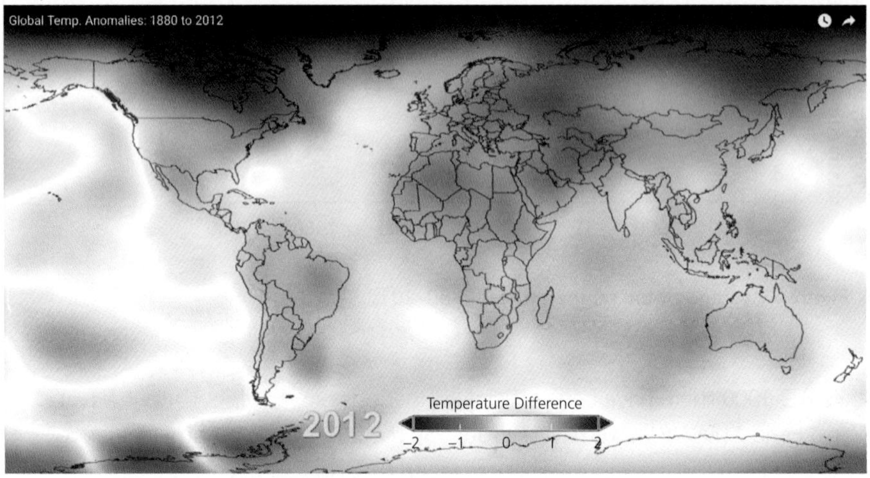

If you study the colour key, you should notice that there is a warming trend for most of the world. This is consistent with earlier maps produced over several decades. NASA suggests that average global temperatures have increased by 0.6°C since 1950 and 0.85°C since 1880.

Global Temp. Anomalies: 1880 to 2012

Temperature Difference

2012

-2   -1   0   1   2

▲ **Figure 5:** Global temperature anomalies, averaged 2008–12

Weather stations are not evenly distributed across the world and some regions, especially in Africa, have a fairly sparse network. Computer programmes have been used to produce global maps such as Figure 5 but this does not make them absolutely accurate and reliable.

2. Ice cores

Ice cores extracted from the Antarctic and Greenland ice sheets have proved to be an important source of information about past global temperatures. When snow falls in cold polar environments it gradually builds up layer upon layer, year upon year. The buried layers of snow are compressed and gradually turn to ice. The Antarctic ice sheet is nearly 5 km thick in places and the oldest ice – at its base – is thought to be 800,000 years old.

Scientists are able to drill deep into the ice to extract cylindrical cores (see Figure 6) from ice that is many thousands of years old. The layers of ice within a core can be dated accurately. By analysing the trapped water molecules, scientists can calculate the temperature of the atmosphere when the snow fell.

▲ **Figure 6** An ice core extracted from the Antarctic ice sheet

This information about accurate dates and temperatures has enabled scientists to create graphs of temperature changes over the last 400,000 years. The results of this research show the fluctuating temperatures that indicate past glacial and inter-glacial periods (see Figure 2, page 200).

3. Tree rings

Every year, the growth of a tree is shown by a single ring. If the ring is narrow it indicates a cooler drier year. If it is thicker it means the temperature was warmer and wetter. These patterns of growth are used to produce tree ring timescales, which give accurate climate information.

▲ **Figure 7** Section of tree trunk showing growth rings

4. Paintings and diaries

Historical records, such as paintings and diaries, can provide additional evidence of climate change.

- Ancient cave paintings of animals in France and Spain depict nature as it was between 40,000 and 11,000 years ago, a period of time when the climate changed significantly. The problem with cave paintings is dating accurately when they were drawn.

- Much of the evidence of the Little Ice Age (see page 201) comes from diaries and written observations made at the time.

- Several painters at the time of the Little Ice Age captured the winter landscapes (see Figure 4, page 201), including paintings and drawings of ice fairs and markets on the River Thames when it froze.

- Diaries and written observations can also provide evidence of climate change, although personal accounts can lack objective accuracy.

Activities

1. Study Figure 5.
    a. Which areas of the world recorded the highest temperature anomalies?
    b. Which areas of the world recorded the lowest temperature anomalies?
    c. How does this map provide evidence supporting the idea of global warming?

2. Study Figure 6.
    a. What do you think the scientist is doing in the photo?
    b. What are the challenges of working in such a hostile environment?
    c. Describe briefly how ice cores provide scientists with data about past temperatures.

3. Suggest advantages and disadvantages of paintings and diaries in providing reliable evidence for climate change.

CHAPTER

25

Causes of climate change

Key idea: There are a number of possible causes of climate change.

→ In this chapter you will study:

→ the theories of natural causes of climate change including variations in energy from the sun, changes in the Earth's orbit and volcanic activity

→ how human activity is responsible for the enhanced greenhouse effect which contributes to global warming.

Activities

1. Study Figure 1.
   a. What are the Milankovitch cycles?
   b. Briefly describe each of the three cycles. Include the time periods involved.
   c. What is the evidence that the Milankovitch cycles may have affected the Earth's climate in the past?

Is climate change a natural process?

Climate change is often in the news. The question is, how much of the measured increase in global temperature is due to natural causes and how much is related to the actions of people?

● **Natural causes:** some changes in climate can be explained by natural factors such as variations in energy from the Sun, volcanic activity and changes in the Earth's orbit.

● **Human activities:** scientists consider that the rapid rise in temperatures since the 1970s can be linked to human activities, such as burning fossil fuels, deforestation and waste disposal.

What are the natural causes of climate change?

1. Changes in the Earth's orbit

You have already seen how there have been regular patterns of cold (glacial) and warm (inter-glacial) periods throughout the Quaternary period (see Figure 2, page 200). But how were these caused?

The **Milankovitch cycles** are cyclical time periods that relate to the Earth's orbit around the Sun (see Figure 1). Scientists believe that these cycles affect the timings and seasonality of the Earth's climate. In particular, the 100,000 year eccentricity cycle coincides closely with the alternating cold (glacial) and warm (inter-glacial periods) in the Quaternary period. Look back to Figure 2 on page 200 to see how the spacing between warm inter-glacial periods was about 100,000 years.

◀ **Figure 1** The Milankovitch cycles

Precession
26,000 years

Precession: this describes a natural 'wobble' that occurs with the Earth rather like a spinning top. A complete wobble cycle takes about 26,000 years. The Earth's wobble accounts for some regions of the world experiencing very long days and very long nights at certain times of the year, such as northern Norway.

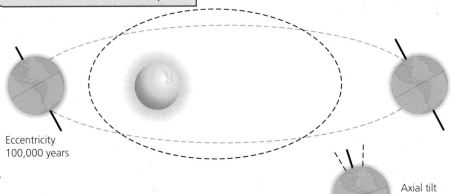

Eccentricity
100,000 years

Axial tilt
41,000 years

Eccentricity: this describes the path of the Earth as it orbits the Sun. The Earth's orbit is not fixed; it changes over time from being almost circular to being mildly elliptical. A complete cycle from circular to elliptical and back to circular again occurs about every 100,000 years. It appears that colder periods occur when the Earth's orbit is more circular and warmer periods when it is more elliptical.

Axial tilt: the Earth spins on its axis, causing night and day. The Earth's axis is currently tilted at an angle of 23.5 degrees. However, over a period of about 41,000 years, the axial tilt of the Earth moves back and forth between two extremes: 21.5 degrees and 24.5 degrees. A greater degree of tilt is associated with the world having a higher average temperature.

2. Volcanic activity

Violent volcanic eruptions blast huge quantities of ash, gases and liquids into the atmosphere. Fine particles of ash can block out the Sun, leading to a reduction in surface temperatures. This is called a **volcanic winter**. Ash can be carried by winds across the globe, transferring these cooling conditions to many regions far beyond the location of the volcano.

Ash does not usually stay in the atmosphere for more than a few weeks so is unlikely to have a long-term impact on climate. Sulfur dioxide, however, can lead to longer-term cooling. The fine aerosols that result from the conversion of sulfur dioxide to sulfuric acid act like tiny mirrors reflecting radiation from the Sun. This results in the cooling of the lower atmosphere.

The eruption of Mount Pinatubo in the Philippines on 15 June 1991 was one of the largest eruptions of the twentieth century.

An enormous cloud of ash and gases, including sulfur dioxide, was ejected more than 32 km into the stratosphere.

Satellites recorded the highest concentration of sulfur dioxide since observations began in 1978.

The aerosols cooled the world's climate for a period of three years by up to 1.3°C.

▲ **Figure 2** The eruption of Mount Pinatubo, Philippines, 1991

3. Variations in energy from the Sun

Variations in the amount of heat energy that comes from the sun are very small and difficult to detect. Sunspots on the Sun's surface do seem to have an impact on the heat energy of the Sun, and therefore the climate of the Earth (see Figure 3).

Very few sunspots were observed between 1645 and 1715, a period known as the Maunder Minimum. This coincided with the coldest period during the Little Ice Age (see page 201). So, despite the fact that sunspots are dark areas on the Sun, it seems that the more sunspots there are, the more effective the Sun is at giving off heat.

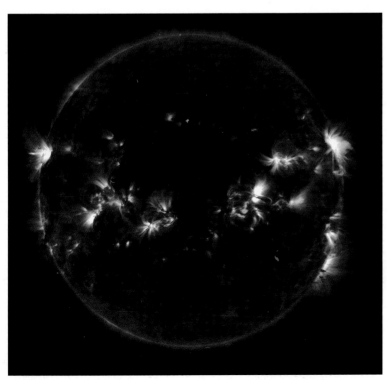

▲ **Figure 3** Sunspots and solar flares on the surface of the Sun, 2014

Activities

1. How do variations in energy from the Sun affect the Earth's climate?
2. What is a 'volcanic winter' and how is it caused?

→ Take it further

3. Use the internet to find out more about the eruption of Mount Pinatubo and how it affected global climates. Present your work in the form of an information poster. They should be captioned or annotated. Your poster should also include:
   - the location of Mount Pinatubo
   - brief details of the eruption
   - a description of how the eruption affected the world's climate.

Human activity and the enhanced greenhouse effect

Many scientists believe that human activities are at least partly to blame for the rapid rise in temperatures (global warming) since the 1970s. To understand how this is possible we need to consider a natural feature of the atmosphere called the **greenhouse effect**.

What is the greenhouse effect?

A greenhouse is a 'house' made of glass. If you have been inside a greenhouse you will know that it is warm at night and even during the winter. This is why people often grow vegetables and fruit such as tomatoes in greenhouses. The reason why a greenhouse is warm is because it retains the heat from the Sun. Look at Figure 4. Notice that heat from the Sun passes through the glass into the greenhouse but does not escape.

The Earth's atmosphere behaves in a similar way (see Figure 5).

- Heat in the form of short-wave solar radiation travels some 150 million km to reach the Earth's outer atmosphere.
- As it passes through the atmosphere some is absorbed by gases and liquids and some is reflected off the tops of the clouds.

- Radiation that reaches the Earth warms up the surface.
- This warmth is then released in the form of long-wave infrared radiation (like heat given off by a radiator).
- The heat is easily absorbed by liquids and so-called 'greenhouse gases' in the atmosphere, particularly carbon dioxide, methane and nitrous oxides (see Figure 6).
- Some heat escapes to space.

The warm atmosphere acts like a blanket over the Earth, keeping us warm. Without the greenhouse effect, it would be too cold for life to exist on Earth.

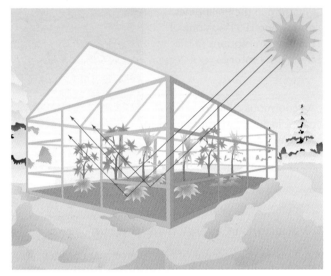

▲ **Figure 4** The greenhouse effect ... in a greenhouse!

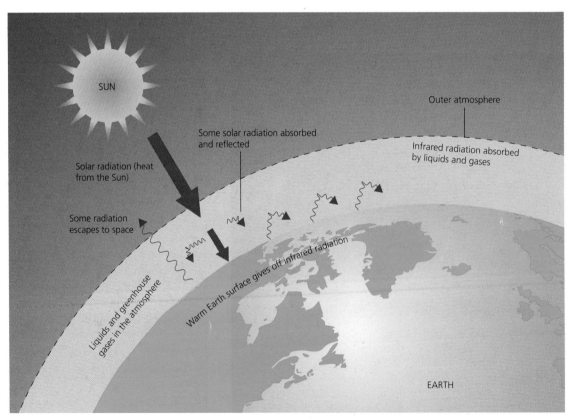

▲ **Figure 5** The natural greenhouse effect

What is the enhanced greenhouse effect?

Many scientists believe that in recent decades the natural greenhouse effect has become more effective at retaining infrared heat given off from the Earth. The 'blanket' around the Earth has in effect become warmer.

The main reason why this has happened is because human activities such as burning fossil fuels, deforestation and emissions from vehicles have increased the concentration of the greenhouse gases in the atmosphere (see Figure 6). Scientists name this the **enhanced greenhouse effect.**

Gas	Sources
Carbon dioxide (CO_2)	• Burning of fossil fuels (coal, gas and oil) • Deforestation (burning wood) • Industrial processes (e.g. making cement)
Methane (CH_4)	• Emitted from livestock and rice cultivation • Decay of organic waste in landfill sites
Nitrous oxides (NO_x)	• Vehicle exhausts • Agriculture and industrial processes

▲ **Figure 6** The main greenhouse gases

Gas	Percentage
Carbon dioxide (burning fossil fuels)	57%
Carbon dioxide (deforestation, decay of vegetation)	17%
Carbon dioxide (other)	3%
Methane	14%
Nitrous oxide	8%
Fluorinated gases	1%
TOTAL	**100%**

▲ **Figure 7** Global greenhouse gas emissions

Tip

When drawing a pie chart start with a vertical line and work clockwise around the 'pie' (circle.)

⊥ Geographical Skills

Use the data in Figure 7 to draw a pie chart to show global greenhouse gas emissions.

● Remember that you will need to multiply each percentage figure by 3.6 to convert it to degrees.
● Check that your total adds up to 360 degrees.
● If it doesn't add up, round the largest figure up or down.
● What is the total percentage for carbon dioxide?

Activities

1. Draw your own diagram based on Figure 5 to show the enhanced greenhouse effect.
   a. Consider the following points before starting:
      • Think about the various sources of greenhouse gases (see Figure 6); you could use simple sketches or thumbnail photos to show these causes on your diagram.
      • Consider using arrows of different thicknesses to indicate how more heat is retained in the atmosphere.
      • Draw a rough diagram to try out your ideas.
   b. Add text boxes to your diagram in the form of a sequence (1, 2, 3, etc.) to describe how the enhanced greenhouse effect works.

2. Many people blame global warming on carbon dioxide emissions. Is this an accurate judgement?
3. Methane is a very effective greenhouse gas. What are the sources of methane gas emissions?
4. How could methane gas emissions be reduced in the future?

→ Take it further

5. Use the internet to investigate fluorinated gases. What are they and what causes them to be emitted? Are they important greenhouse gases?

26

Consequences of climate change

Key idea: Climate change has consequences.

→ **In this chapter you will study:**

→ a range of consequences of climate change currently being experienced across the planet.

Intergovernmental Panel on Climate Change (IPCC)

- Concentrations of greenhouse gases are at their highest levels for at least 800,000 years
- Sea level has risen by 20cm since 1900
- Average global temperatures have increased by 0.85°C since 1880
- By 2100 the sea level will rise by another 26-82cm
- By 2100 average global temperatures will increase by 0.3-4.8°C

▲ **Figure 1** Selected findings from the IPCC report, 2013

Worldwide impacts of climate change

Climate change is having, and will continue to have, significant impacts on people and human activities. It is possible to consider three types of impact:

- **Social:** these are the impacts on our lives and our lifestyles.
- **Economic:** these impacts are to do with money and the increasing costs of coping with climate change.
- **Environmental:** these impacts involve changes to natural ecosystems.

In 2013 the Intergovernmental Panel on Climate Change (IPCC) reported that it is 'virtually certain that humans are responsible for global warming'. Some of the report's findings are listed in Figure 1.

Sea level rise

An average rise in sea level of 20 cm since 1900 may not sound very much but it has already had a significant impact on natural and human systems. It has been suggested that the sea level may rise by up to 1 m by the end of the century.

Rising sea levels threaten low-lying coastal areas with flooding and more frequent damage from storms and tropical cyclones. Figure 2 lists some social, economic and environmental effects of sea level rise.

Social	Economic	Environmental
600 million people live in coastal areas that are less than 10 m above sea level.	Many important world cities including New York, Venice and London could be affected by flooding.	Fresh water sources such as wells could be polluted by salty seawater; this is called salinisation.
People living in vulnerable areas may have to move home or even move to different countries. Some small island states such as Tuvalu and Vanuatu are particularly at risk.	Valuable agricultural land (e.g. in Bangladesh, Vietnam, India and China) may be lost to the sea or polluted by seawater. Harbours and ports may be affected, which will have an impact on fishing and trade.	Damage could occur to coastal ecosystems such as mangrove swamps, which form natural barriers to storms.
People may suffer increased frequency of flooding and storm damage.	Transport systems, such as railways, roads and airports may be damaged or destroyed.	Damage to coral reefs by storms and powerful waves will affect fish breeding grounds and ecosystems.
People may lose their jobs, for example in fishing or tourism, and have to learn new skills.	Valuable land and property will need expensive measures of coastal defence.	The IPCC estimates that up to 33% of coastal land and wetlands could be lost in the next 100 years.
The numbers of environmental refugees – people who have lost their homes due to flooding – will increase.	Many countries depend on coastal tourism as their main source of income. Beaches may be eroded or flooded, forcing hotels to close. People may decide not to visit.	Harbours may become blocked by sediment due to increased rates of coastal erosion.

▲ **Figure 2** Social, economic and environmental impacts of sea level rise

Tuvalu

Where is Tuvalu?

Tuvalu is a group of nine tiny islands in the South Pacific. Figure 3 shows the location of Tuvalu in relation to Australia.

What is Tuvalu like?

Most of the islands of Tuvalu are low-lying. In fact, the highest point on the islands is only 4.5 m above sea level (see Figure 4). Around 11,000 people live on Tuvalu and the economy is based on the export of copra (dried coconut kernel used to extract coconut oil), the sale of fishing licences for tuna and the sale of its colourful postage stamps!

What are the issues facing Tuvalu?

Along with Vanuatu and the Maldives, Tuvalu is threatened by sea level rise, which could swamp the entire islands.

- Increased level of salinisation (pollution by saltwater) is affecting the soils, which is having an impact on agricultural productivity.
- There are no rivers on Tuvalu, as rainwater soaks into the coral rock. Water comes from wells but these are increasingly becoming polluted by seawater. At times, seawater actually bubbles up to the surface through the porous coral.
- Water supply is a key issue, with droughts becoming more common due to climate change.
- Coastal erosion has affected some of the islands, eroding away productive land.
- During king tides (highest tides of the year) the islands are battered by powerful waves, threatening homes and flooding roads (see Figure 5).
- The main runway is under threat from flooding.

How are the people in Tuvalu responding?

The Tuvalu government has been campaigning for the international community to tackle global warming by reducing carbon emissions. Some people have already decided to leave the islands for nearby New Zealand, fearing that their homes will become uninhabitable. They are a new wave of 'environmental refugees'.

Some low seawalls have been constructed but they themselves are now suffering from erosion. Seawalls are not the long-term solution.

Japan is supporting a coral reef restoration programme to reintroduce species to damaged reefs. This could provide some protection from storms as sea levels continue to rise.

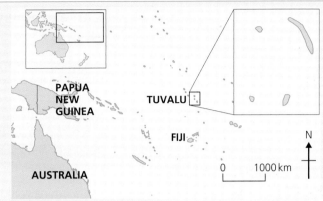

▲ **Figure 3** Location of Tuvalu

▲ **Figure 4** Tuvalu

▲ **Figure 5** The impacts of a king tide in Tuvalu

Activities

1. Study the information on Tuvalu.
   a. What are the arguments for and against building a sea wall at the back of the beach?
   b. Should future developments be allowed to take place here?
2. Outline the social, economic and environmental impacts of sea level change.
3. Suggest the alternative futures for the people who live in Tuvalu.

Can extreme weather events be linked to climate change?

A single extreme weather event, such as a thunderstorm or a heavy snowfall, cannot be linked to long-term changes in the climate. Extreme weather events such as these have always occurred from time to time. However, scientists have noticed that there have been an exceptional number of these extreme events in recent decades. In 2013 the IPCC reported a clear increase in the number, frequency and intensity of heatwaves and heavy rainfall events. If this trend continues, then the link with long-term climate change may become stronger.

In a warming world, there is more energy in the atmosphere. Greater rates of evaporation from the world's oceans result in more water vapour that can in turn lead to more rainfall or snow. Climate patterns may shift, so that some areas become much drier and others much wetter.

The atmosphere is extremely complex and it is impossible to make accurate predictions into the future. But it does seem that we are now living in a world with more extreme weather events (see Figure 6).

▼ **Figure 6** Weather extremes of the early twenty-first century

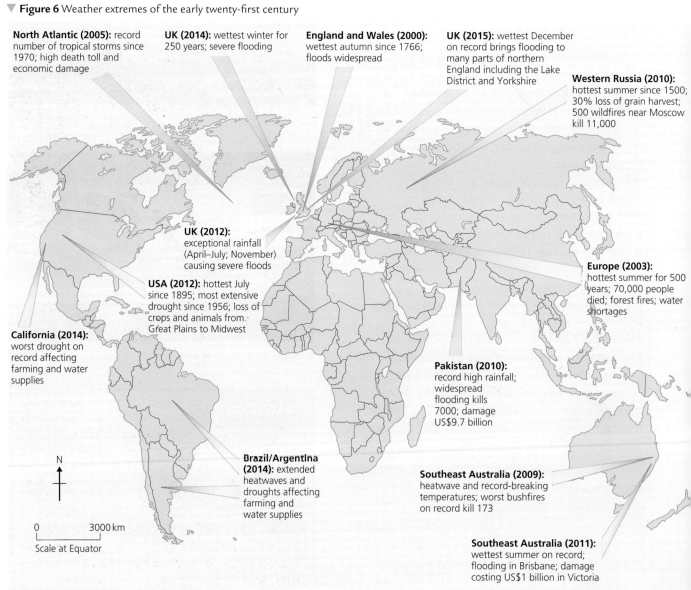

North Atlantic (2005): record number of tropical storms since 1970; high death toll and economic damage

UK (2014): wettest winter for 250 years; severe flooding

England and Wales (2000): wettest autumn since 1766; floods widespread

UK (2015): wettest December on record brings flooding to many parts of northern England including the Lake District and Yorkshire

Western Russia (2010): hottest summer since 1500; 30% loss of grain harvest; 500 wildfires near Moscow kill 11,000

UK (2012): exceptional rainfall (April–July; November) causing severe floods

USA (2012): hottest July since 1895; most extensive drought since 1956; loss of crops and animals from Great Plains to Midwest

California (2014): worst drought on record affecting farming and water supplies

Europe (2003): hottest summer for 500 years; 70,000 people died; forest fires; water shortages

Pakistan (2010): record high rainfall; widespread flooding kills 7000; damage US$9.7 billion

Brazil/Argentina (2014): extended heatwaves and droughts affecting farming and water supplies

Southeast Australia (2009): heatwave and record-breaking temperatures; worst bushfires on record kill 173

Southeast Australia (2011): wettest summer on record; flooding in Brisbane; damage costing US$1 billion in Victoria

N

0   3000 km

Scale at Equator

Brazilian drought 2014

In 2014 Brazil faced a record-breaking dry season resulting in drought conditions across parts of the country. As water levels fell in reservoirs (see Figure 7), some of Brazil's major cities including Sao Paulo faced water shortages. Many people had to collect water from water bowsers or had to endure water rationing in their homes.

Shortages of water affected industrial production (e.g. aluminium) and farming, due to the lack of water for irrigation. The exceptionally dry weather also affected the coffee industry in Brazil with beans shrivelling on the bushes in January and February due to lack of rainfall (see Figure 8). Coffee production dropped significantly due to the drought.

The drought also led to a reduction in the production of hydroelectric power (HEP), due to falling water levels in reservoirs. In parts of the southeast, HEP reservoirs were operating at 30 per cent of their capacity. Alternative forms of energy such as liquefied natural gas (LNG) had to be used to maintain Brazil's energy supply.

As reservoir levels dropped to 10 per cent of their capacity and rivers dried up, levels of pollution increased, damaging natural ecosystems and killing fish.

Useful weblinks

Extreme weather in the USA:
www.ncdc.noaa.gov/billions/overview

Weather events in the UK:
www.metoffice.gov.uk/climate/uk/interesting

▲ **Figure 7** The Cantareira reservoir that supplies much of Sao Paulo's water

▲ **Figure 8** Coffee beans in Brazil shrivelling due to the intense heat and drought

Activities

1. Study Figure 7 which shows the Cantareira reservoir at the height of the 2014 drought.
   a. What is the evidence of drought shown in the photo?
   b. Suggest some possible environmental impacts in the reservoir.
   c. What were the economic impacts of the drought?
   d. How were the lives of ordinary people affected by the water shortages?

➡ Take it further

2. Study Figure 6 which shows a selection of recent extreme weather events. Select an extreme weather event that interests you and use the internet to write a short report. Aim for a similar length to the information on the Brazilian drought. Make sure that you examine the social, economic and environmental impacts of your chosen event. Include a couple of captioned or annotated photos.

3. Use the internet to research other recent extreme weather events. You could use this information to draw a map similar to Figure 6 or to write additional reports. You could use the useful weblinks provided in the box above to help you.

CHAPTER 27

Global circulation of the atmosphere

Key idea: The global circulation of the atmosphere controls weather and climate.

→ In this chapter you will study:

- the distribution of the main climatic regions of the world
- an outline of how the global circulation of the atmosphere is controlled by movement of air between the poles and the Equator
- how the global circulation of the atmosphere needs to extreme weather condition in different parts of the world.

The major climate zones of the world

A number of climate zones, or belts, can be traced between the Equator and the pole in each hemisphere as a result of the global movements of air and the atmospheric pressure that this generates.

TEMPERATE CLIMATE

In the mid-latitudes, 50°–60° north and south of the Equator, two air types meet, one warm from the Ferrel cell and one cold from the Polar cell. Low pressure is created from the rising of the warm, sub-tropical winds over the cold, polar winds at a front. As this air rises and cools, it condenses to form clouds and ultimately frequent rainfall. This is typical of the UK (see Figure 1).

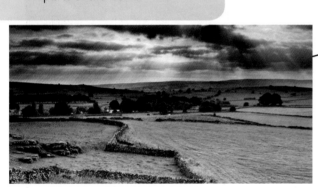

▲ **Figure 1** Peak District, Derbyshire, England

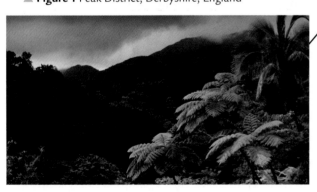

▲ **Figure 2** Windward Islands, Dominica, Caribbean

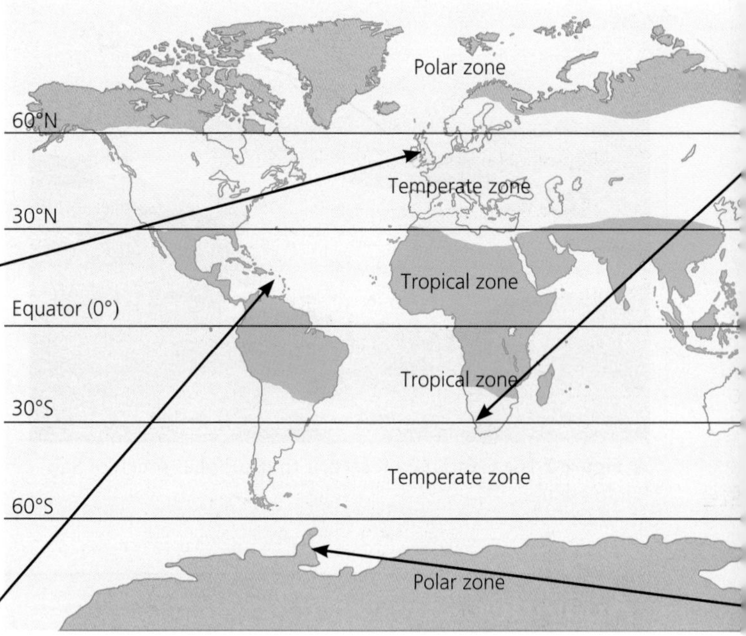

▲ **Figure 3** Map of the three common climate zones

TROPICAL CLIMATE

This is a belt of relatively low pressure, heavy rainfall and thunderstorms as a result of rising air in the Hadley cell. Places such as northern Brazil in South America and Malaysia in South East Asia experience this climate.

	Jan	Feb	Mar	Apr	May	Jun	July	Aug	Sept	Oct	Nov	Dec
Average temp (°C)	12.4	15.4	19.3	25.1	29.0	31.7	31.5	30.8	29.0	23.8	17.7	13.1
Rainfall (mm)	3.2	2.9	2.2	1.6	2.5	1.1	0.0	0.7	2.1	1.4	1.8	1.6

▲ **Figure 4** Climate data for Djanet, Algeria

SUB-TROPICAL (DESERT) CLIMATE

At 30° north and south of the Equator there is high pressure as a result of sinking, dry air as the Hadley and Ferrel cells meet. This creates a belt of desert regions. These include the Sahara in northern Africa and the Namib desert in Namibia, southern Africa (see Figure 5). Daytime temperatures can exceed 40° C, while at night, due to a lack of cloud cover, temperatures can fall to below freezing.

▲ **Figure 5** Namib desert, Namibia, Africa

▼ **Figure 6** Antarctic Peninsula

POLAR CLIMATE

At the highest latitudes, cold air from the Polar cell sinks, producing high pressure. This is characterised by dry, icy winds caused by the spin of the Earth. In some places in Antarctica (see Figure 6), the average annual wind speed is nearly 50 miles per hour!

Activities

1. Use the climate data in Figure 4 to draw a climate graph for Djanet, Algeria.
2. In which climate zone is Djanet located? How do you know this?

→ **Take it further**

3. Why is the **average** daytime temperature for a high pressure region misleading?

✛ Geographical skills

A climate graph (see Figure 7) shows the average temperature and rainfall for a place during a year. It is measured using months of the year on the *x* axis and both *y* axes are used to plot the rainfall in bars and the temperature as a line.

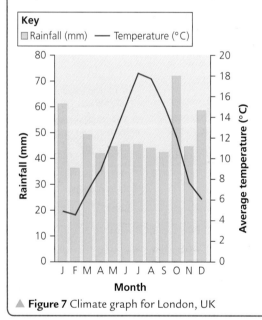

▲ **Figure 7** Climate graph for London, UK

The global pattern of air circulation

There are large-scale circular movements of air all over the Earth's surface. These circulations of air transport heat from the tropical regions at the Equator, where the Earth gets more heat from the Sun, to the polar regions at the poles.

The imaginary lines that surround the Earth are known as lines of **latitude**. The Equator is at the 0° latitude line and the region spanning it is known as the 'low' latitudes. The polar regions are towards 90° north and south of the Equator line and are known as the 'high' latitudes.

The world is divided into two at the Equator line to create the northern and southern **hemispheres**. In each hemisphere there are three specific 'cells' of air called Hadley, Ferrel and Polar (see Figures 8 and 9). Within these cells, air circulates within the **troposphere**, an area of the atmosphere from the Earth's surface up to 10–15 km high. The troposphere is the part of the atmosphere where the Earth's weather takes place. The three cells of air play an important role in creating the distinct **climate zones** that we experience on Earth.

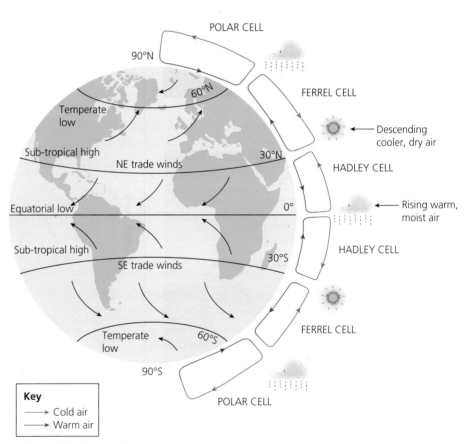

▲ **Figure 8** Global circulation system

	Where is it?	What happens?
Hadley cell	The largest cell which extends from the Equator to between 30° and 40° north and south.	• **Trade winds** are winds that blow from the tropical regions towards the Equator. They usually travel from an easterly direction. • Near the Equator, the trade winds meet and the warm air rises and forms thunderstorms. • From the top of these storms air flows towards higher latitudes where it becomes cooler and sinks over sub-tropical regions.
Ferrel cell	The middle cell, which generally occurs from the edge of the Hadley cell to between 60° and 70°.	• This is the most complicated cell as it moves in the opposite direction from the Hadley and Polar cells, similar to a cog in a machine. • Air in this cell joins the sinking air of the Hadley cell and travels at low heights to mid-latitudes where it rises along the border with the cold air of the Polar cell. • This occurs around the latitude of the UK and accounts for the frequently unsettled weather. • Air then flows back towards the low latitudes, in the direction of the Equator.
Polar cell	The smallest and weakest cell, which extends from the edge of the Ferrel cell to the poles at 90°.	• Air in this cell sinks over the highest latitudes, at the poles, and flows out towards the lower latitudes.

▲ **Figure 9** Differences between the three circulatory cells

What happens in areas of high pressure and low pressure?

What we know as wind is air moving from high to low pressure. **Atmospheric air pressure** is the force exerted on the Earth's surface by the weight of the air. It is measured in millibars. The normal range of air pressure is 980 millibars (**low pressure**) to 1050 millibars (**high pressure**). Where the air in the Hadley cells rises at the Equator, low pressure is created. However, where the Hadley and Ferrel cells meet at 30° north and south of the Equator, air descends, creating high pressure on the ground below (see Figure 10). The contrasts in air pressure associated with the different cells, combined with distance from the Equator, creates regions with distinctive average temperature and rainfall patterns.

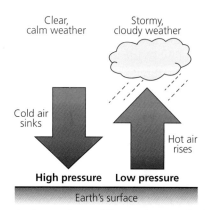

▲ **Figure 10** The difference between high and low pressure

What happens in areas of low pressure?

A low-pressure system occurs when the atmospheric pressure is lower than that of the surrounding area. It is usually associated with high winds and warm, rising air. As the warm air cools and condenses as it rises, it forms clouds. **Condensation** is the process whereby this rising vapour turns into a liquid. Eventually, moisture falls from the atmosphere as rain, sleet, snow or hail, collectively known as **precipitation**. Daytime ranges of temperatures are unlikely to be large, as the cloud cover reflects solar radiation during the day and traps heat during the night.

What happens in areas of high pressure?

When air cools it becomes denser and starts to fall towards the ground, increasing the air pressure. This cool air is subjected to warming, which causes any clouds to evaporate. Also, heavy rain at the Equator means that most of the moisture in the atmosphere is removed before the air reaches the sub-tropics. At 30° north and south of the equator high pressure systems are usually associated with clear skies and dry (possibly hot), calm weather.

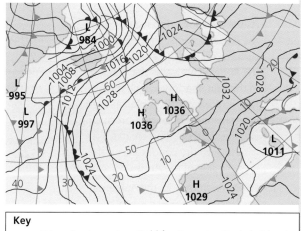

▲ **Figure 11** A synoptic weather chart showing an area of high pressure over the UK recording 1036 millibars

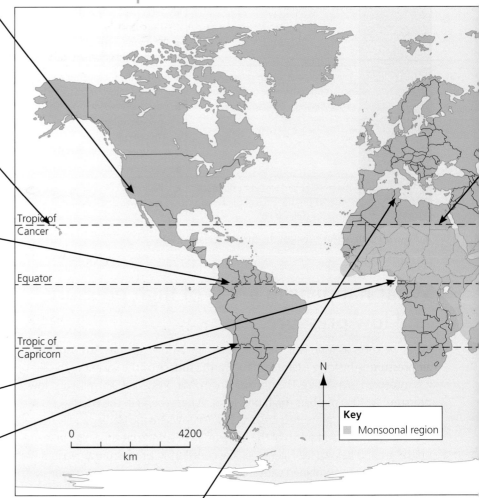

Weather extremes: where are the coldest, hottest, driest, wettest and windiest places in the world?

DEATH VALLEY: Driest place in North America with an average rainfall of 500 mm. Storms coming from the Pacific Ocean must travel over a series of mountain ranges on their journey eastwards. This means that many of the clouds have already cooled, condensed and fallen as rain before they reach Death Valley.

MOUNT WAIALEALE: Located on the island of Kauai in Hawaii, this is the wettest place in America with an annual average rainfall of 9763 mm.

PUERTO LÓPEZ: A small fishing village in Colombia is one of the wettest places on Earth. It has an annual rainfall of 12,892 mm. In the mid-1980s, it rained every single day for two years!

URECA: Located on the southern tip of Bioko Island in Equatorial Guinea, this is the wettest location in Africa with an average annual rainfall of 10,450 mm.

ATACAMA DESERT: Coastal mountains to the west block moist air from the Pacific and the Andes block rain from the Amazon in the east (see Figure 13). The prevailing wind (most frequent wind direction) comes from the southeast and carries moist air from the Atlantic.

As the air is forced to rise to cross the Andes it cools, condenses and turns to rain on the eastern side of the Andes. This leaves the Atacama in the rain shadow, which means that it receives little rainfall as high land shelters it from rain-producing weather systems. This creates a 'shadow' of dry conditions on the western side of the Andes.

On its western side, the Atacama lies close to the ocean where a cold current flows northwards along the coastline. As it is cold, onshore winds do not have enough warmth to pick up moisture from the ocean surface. This lack of rising air prevents precipitation from forming.

Key
▨ Monsoonal region

▲ **Figure 12** Location of the world's weather extremes

AL–AZIZIYAH, LIBYA: The hottest place on Earth is Al-Aziziyah in Libya. 40 km south of Tripoli, Al-Aziziyah is where, on 13 September 1922, the world experienced its hottest air temperature ever recorded at 57.8 °C.

VOSTOK, ANTARCTICA: The coldest place on Earth is Vostok in Antarctica. At a height of around 3500 m above sea level, the Russian research station at Vostok is always cold. On 21 July 1983, the coldest air temperature on the planet was recorded here at −89.2 °C.

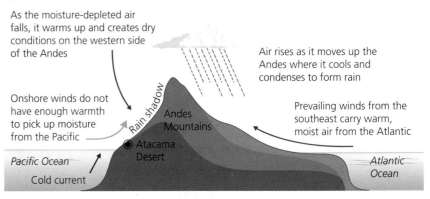

As the moisture-depleted air falls, it warms up and creates dry conditions on the western side of the Andes

Air rises as it moves up the Andes where it cools and condenses to form rain

Onshore winds do not have enough warmth to pick up moisture from the Pacific

Prevailing winds from the southeast carry warm, moist air from the Atlantic

Rain shadow

Andes Mountains

Atacama Desert

Pacific Ocean

Cold current

Atlantic Ocean

▲ **Figure 13** Why is the Atacama Desert so dry?

ASWAN: Located in the driest region of Egypt, it has a rainfall of only 0.861 mm per year! Its proximity to the Tropic of Cancer contributes to the high temperatures and dry weather.

MAWSYNRAM: The 10,000 villagers of Mawsynram cope with 11 m of rain per year. That's 20 times the average rainfall for London! eighty per cent of all of India's rain arrives in the seasonal monsoon deluge from June to September. During this time, more heat from the Sun (solar radiation) is hitting the northern hemisphere. The monsoon is powered by the difference between land and sea and the ways that they respond to the Sun. The sea is cooler than the land as there is both more of it to be heated and it is always on the move due to the winds. The land therefore heats quicker than the sea. As the Sun bakes the land in India, the warm air above it rises and draws in cooler air from the sea. With the triangular shape of India and the long coastline, there is a powerful and sustained current of air moving northwards through India, which bring rains known as the monsoon.

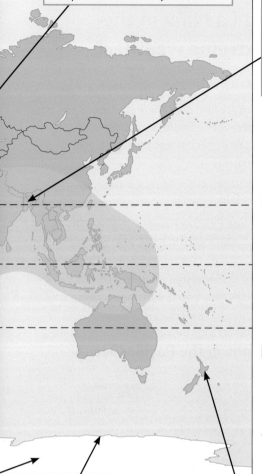

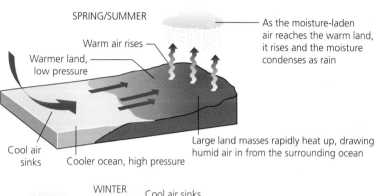

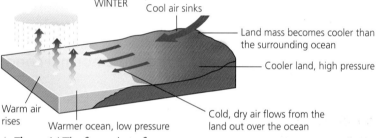

▲ **Figure 14** The formation of monsoons

	Location	Rainfall (mm per year)
	London, UK	558
1	Mawsynram, India	11,871
2	Cherrapunji, India	11,777
3	Tutendo, Columbia	11,770
4	River Cropp waterfall, New Zealand	11,516
5	Ureca, Bioko Island in Equatorial Guinea, Africa	10,450
6	Debundscha, Cameroon, Africa	10,229
7	Big Bog in Maui, Hawaii	10,272
8	Mt Waialeale in Kauai, Hawaii	9,763
9	Kukui in Maui, Hawaii	9,293
10	Mount Emei, Sichuan Province in China	8,169

▲ **Figure 15:** Top ten wettest places in the world

COMMONWEALTH BAY, ANTARCTICA: This is the windiest place on Earth with winds regularly exceeding 240 km/h, with an average annual wind speed of 80 km/h. Storms are causes by katabatic winds, which are winds that carry air from high ground down a slope due to gravity.

WELLINGTON, NEW ZEALAND: The highest gust of wind ever recorded in Wellington was 248 km/h and the average annual wind speed is 29 km/h. Gusts of wind exceed gale force (75 km/h) on 175 days of the year. The mountainous landscape either side of Wellington acts as a funnel for the winds, increasing their speed.

Activities

1. Choose three of the locations of weather extremes in the world. **Analyse** the reasons why the weather is so extreme. Use the information from other areas of this chapter to help you, including Figure 1.

→ Take it further

2. To what extent would you agree that Antarctica is the 'most extreme' place in the world? Use evidence from these pages.

✝ Geographical skills

Create a bar graph of the data in Figure 15. Colour code the bars according to the continent. Label the axes and give your graph a title.

Extreme weather: tropical storms and drought

Key idea: Extreme weather conditions cause different natural weather.

Key idea: Drought can be devastating for people and the environment.

→ **In this chapter you will study:**

- → an outline the causes of the extreme weather conditions that are associated with the hazards of tropical storms and drought
- → the distribution and frequency of tropical storms and drought, and whether these have changed over time
- → a case study of 'The Big Dry' in Australia, a drought event caused by El Niño/La Niña including:
  - how the extreme weather conditions of El Niño/La Niña develop and can lead to drought
  - effects of the drought event on people and the environment
- → ways in which people have adapted to drought in the case study area.

What is El Niño?

El Niño was the term first used for the appearance of warm surface water around the coast of Peru and Ecuador. It was originally spotted by a group of Peruvian fishermen who relied on the usually colder waters swelling up from beneath the sea surface to bring up nutrient-rich waters from the deep ocean. This in turn improved their catch of small fish called anchovies. They noticed the unusually high sea surface temperatures occurring about every two or three years around Christmas.

Activity

1. Summarise the conditions in the Pacific Ocean in 50 words for each of the following; a normal year, El Niño and La Niña

How does El Niño and La Niña in the Pacific Ocean cause extreme weather?

What causes El Niño?

Scientists continue to study the exact causes of El Niño. There is a strong interaction between ocean and atmosphere in the Pacific, so even small changes can be enough to have a large-scale impact across the region and cause global changes to weather and climate.

For a brief time, seafloor heating as a result of volcanic activity became a popular theory. It was noted that two separate eruptions in the region were followed closely by El Niño events. For example, Mount Pinatubo erupted in 1991, the same year in which an El Niño event began. However, this is not a likely theory.

A more probable cause is small changes in sea surface temperatures. This could be caused, for instance, by tropical storms in the western region of the Pacific. If they are violent enough, or last long enough, they could start the movement of warm water eastwards across the Pacific.

What are the normal conditions in the Pacific Ocean?

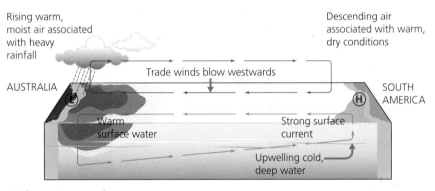

Rising warm, moist air associated with heavy rainfall

Descending air associated with warm, dry conditions

Trade winds blow westwards

AUSTRALIA

SOUTH AMERICA

Warm surface water

Strong surface current

Upwelling cold, deep water

▲ **Figure 1** A normal year

- The surface winds over the Pacific Ocean, known as the trade winds, blow towards the warm water of the western Pacific, off the coasts of Australia and Indonesia.
- Rising air occurs at this location as a result of water heating up the atmosphere. The trade winds across the surface of the Pacific push the warm water westwards from Peru to Australia.
- In the eastern Pacific, off the coast of Peru, the shallow position of the **thermocline** allows winds to pull up water from below. The thermocline is the point at which the temperature changes from warmer surface waters to deeper, colder water. It is this that creates those optimum conditions for fishing, which have already been mentioned, as there is an abundance of phytoplankton within the cold water, supplying the fish with food.
- As a result of the pressure of the trade winds pushing the water westwards, the sea levels in Australasia are about half a metre higher than Peru, with sea temperatures 8 °C warmer.

What happens during El Niño?

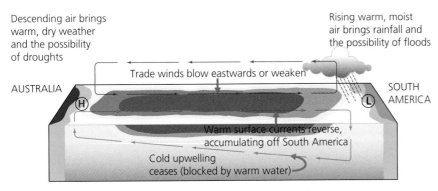

Descending air brings warm, dry weather and the possibility of droughts

Rising warm, moist air brings rainfall and the possibility of floods

Trade winds blow eastwards or weaken

AUSTRALIA

SOUTH AMERICA

H

L

Warm surface currents reverse, accumulating off South America

Cold upwelling ceases (blocked by warm water)

▲ **Figure 2** El Niño

- During El Niño, the trade winds weaken, stop or even reverse in the western Pacific.
- The piled up warmer water around Australasia makes its way back eastwards across the Pacific, leading to a 30 cm rise in sea level around Peru. This prevents the usual cold upwelling.
- As a result, there is more warm water over the coast of Peru leading to rising air and low pressure. The water becomes 6–8 °C warmer in the eastern Pacific.
- Peru would therefore experience more rainfall than normal.
- In Australasia, however, the water becomes cooler and there is less air rising resulting in high pressure and stable, dry conditions.

What happens during La Niña?

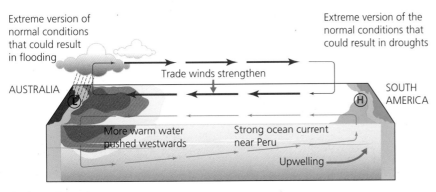

Extreme version of normal conditions that could result in flooding

Extreme version of the normal conditions that could result in droughts

Trade winds strengthen

AUSTRALIA

SOUTH AMERICA

L

H

More warm water pushed westwards

Strong ocean current near Peru

Upwelling

▲ **Figure 3** La Niña

A La Niña event may, but does not always, follow an El Niño event. La Niña refers to unusually cold sea surface temperatures (3–5 °C colder) found in the eastern tropical Pacific. Broadly speaking, the impacts of La Niña are the opposite of El Niño, where Australia would experience **droughts** during El Niño, there could be increased risk of flooding during La Niña. Likewise, Peru could experience droughts during La Niña. La Niña could also be described as a more exaggerated version of a normal year in the Pacific Ocean.

El Niño and La Niña are among the most powerful phenomena on Earth, affecting climate across more than half of the planet. Their consequences are, in fact, global.

How do we know if it is an El Niño year?

Many techniques have been used to identify and predict the occurrence of El Niño.

- Better satellite coverage looking for oceanic patterns.
- Design of buoys has improved. They can now measure sea surface temperatures, surface winds, air temperature and humidity.
- Buoys can be used in mid-ocean or in shallow water and can remain active for one year.
- Buoys transmit to weather forecasting systems, sometimes every hour.
- Sea levels around the world can be measured and recorded.
- Biological recordings. For example, during El Niño, phytoplankton does not grow as there is no upwelling of cold water in the eastern Pacific.

Activities

1. Spot the difference! What are the key differences between the three weather patterns? Use the following table design to help to structure your notes.

	Normal Year	El Niño	La Niña
High pressure			
Low pressure			
Rainfall			
Flooding			
Droughts			
Trade winds			

→ Take it further

2. Represent the information about a normal year, El Niño and La Niña in a flow diagram.

▲ **Figure 4** Satellite image of Typhoon Haiyan approaching the Philippines

Tropical storms are found:

- over tropical and sub-tropical waters between 5° and 30° north and south of the Equator
- where the temperature of the surface layer of ocean water is in excess of 26.5°C and at a depth of at least 50–60 m
- at least 500 km away from the Equator where the **Coriolis effect**, or force, is strong enough to make the weather system spin.

Tip

There are many specific facts on this page. Using these numbers makes your answers more precise and accurate. In reference to the formation of a tropical storm, rather than saying 'the water needs to be warm and the sea fairly deep', say 'sea temperatures need to be approximately 26°C and the ocean depth 50–60 m.

Tropical storms: what, where and when?

What is a tropical storm?

A **tropical storm** begins as a low-pressure system originating in the tropics, known as a tropical depression, and can develop into a tropical cyclone (also known as a hurricane or typhoon). It is a circular storm originating over warm water and is characterised by high winds and heavy rain. A tropical storm has maximum wind speeds ranging from 63 km/h to 118 km/h. When wind speeds are in excess of 119 km/h, the storm becomes a tropical cyclone.

Tropical cyclones are known by different terms depending on where they are in the world:

- In the north Atlantic Ocean and east Pacific they are known as hurricanes. An example is Hurricane Katrina in 2005, which caused the death of 1836 people and led to 80 per cent of the city of New Orleans being under water.
- In the northwest Pacific, they are known as typhoons. In November 2013, Typhoon Haiyan (see Figure 4) hit the Philippines as well as southern China and Vietnam. It was one of the strongest tropical cyclones ever recorded, affecting 11 million people and causing US $2.86 billion of economic damage.
- The term 'tropical cyclone' is most frequently used in the northern Indian Ocean, around countries like Bangladesh. In May 2008, Cyclone Nargis made landfall, causing the worst natural disaster in the history of Myanmar. More than 138,000 people lost their lives, many of whom lived on the densely populated Irrawaddy Delta.

Where in the world do tropical storms occur?

Tropical storms are found in very specific parts of the world, from the Gulf Coast of North America to the northwest of Australia, and from the Indian Ocean island of Mauritius to Bangladesh (see Figure 5).

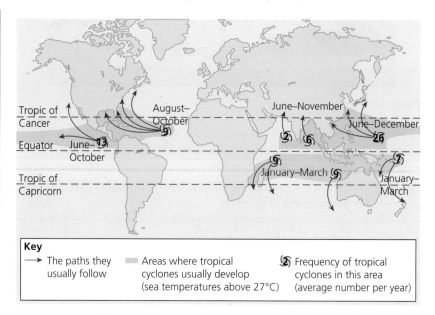

▲ **Figure 5** The global distribution of tropical storms

How does the Coriolis effect help in the formation of tropical storms?

Notice how the clouds form a swirling, circular pattern in Figure 4. This is the result of the Coriolis effect, which acts on winds because the Earth is spinning. Pilots flying long distances have to alter their flight path to allow for the Coriolis effect. The Earth spins faster at the Equator because it is wider than it is at the poles. In the northern hemisphere, winds are deflected to the right and in the southern hemisphere winds are deflected to the left (see Figure 6).

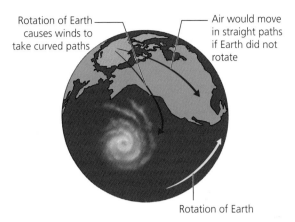

Rotation of Earth causes winds to take curved paths

Air would move in straight paths if Earth did not rotate

Rotation of Earth

▲ **Figure 6** Model of the Coriolis effect

What causes a tropical storm?

The conditions need to be perfect for a tropical storm to form. There needs to be a movement in the air near the surface of the water. In the troposphere, the temperatures need to cool quickly enough for tall clouds to form through condensation. The wind speeds need to change slowly with height. If the speeds are greater in the upper atmosphere, the storm could be sliced in two. Fuelled by the warm ocean, water vapour is evaporated. As warm, moist air rises it expands, cools and condenses to form the clouds. It maintains its strength as long as it remains over warm water.

Wind speeds increase towards the centre of the storm, around the eyewall (see Figure 7). This is typically 15–30 km from the centre of the storm. Deep clouds rise from the Earth's surface up to a height of 15,000 m. This, combined with the heaviest rainfall, makes the eyewall the most destructive and dangerous part of the storm.

When the vertical winds reach the top of the troposphere at 16 km the air flows outwards, deflected by the Coriolis effect.

Inside the eye of the storm is a different story. Wind speeds decrease rapidly and the air is calm. There is a central area of clear skies, warm temperatures and low pressure (typically 960 millibars).

You can recreate the Coriolis effect on a merry-go-round on a children's playground. While standing at the edge of a spinning merry-go-round, try throwing a ball towards the centre and see how it deflects to the left or right.

Tip

Practise being able to reproduce models and diagrams from memory. Study a diagram for one minute, then look away and draw everything you can remember. Study the diagram again and add details that you did not remember. Keep practising until you can reproduce a diagram, map or model confidently without looking.

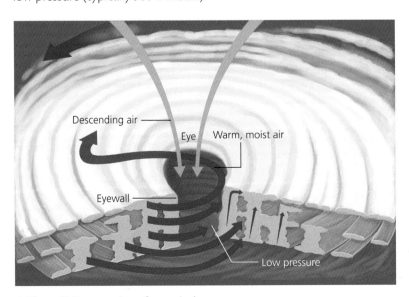

Descending air

Eye   Warm, moist air

Eyewall

Low pressure

▲ **Figure 7** Cross section of a tropical storm

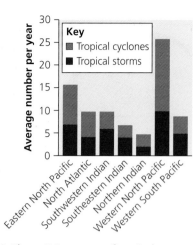

▲ **Figure 8** Frequency of tropical storms and cyclones

How frequently do tropical storms occur?

Tropical oceans generate approximately 80 storms per year. The greatest number is in the Pacific Ocean, followed by the Indian Ocean and the Atlantic ranking third (see Figure 8). The most powerful storms occur in the western Pacific. Tropical storms occur every year during the late summer months from June to November in the northern hemisphere and from November to April in the southern hemisphere.

Has their frequency changed over time?

The number of storms in the Atlantic has increased since 1995, but there is no obvious global trend. There is, however, some evidence to suggest that they are becoming more intense. It has been calculated that the energy released by the average hurricane has increased by 70 per cent in the past 30 years.

During El Niño, winds high over the Atlantic tend to be stronger than normal. This change in the vertical differences of wind speeds decreases hurricane activity as the storm is likely to be torn apart. Elsewhere, more tropical storms occur in the eastern part of the South Pacific during El Niño and less during La Niña.

Scientists are in disagreement about whether climate change has made tropical storms more frequent. Chapter 26 has more information on the impacts of climate change.

Activities

1. Annotate a blank map of the world with:
   a. The locations in which tropical cyclones occur.
   b. The names of tropical cyclones in different parts of the world.
   c. The months in which they occur.
2. Why might tropical storms be more frequent in particular months?
3. Using Figure 7 to help you, work in pairs to create a model of a tropical storm. Consider using materials such as card, sticky notes and cotton wool. Make sure your model has clear labels.
4. When does a tropical storm become a tropical cyclone? Choose your answer from the list below.
   a. When the water depth is less than 50 m.
   b. When the sustained wind speeds reach 119 km/h.
   c. When it is 50 km away from the Equator.
   d. When it reaches land.
5. Explain in the form of a recipe how a tropical storm develops. What are the key ingredients and processes?
6. Has the frequency of tropical storms changed over time?

➡ Take it further

7. To what extent are the data on tropical storm frequency from 1995 reliable?
8. Why are tropical storms often given names? Find out if there is a tropical storm (or hurricane; cyclone or typhoon) in *your* name. When was it? Did it cause a lot of damage?

Droughts: what, where and when?

What is a 'drought'?

Defining a drought is not easy as it can vary from place to place. They develop slowly and it can take weeks, months or even years for the full effects to appear. In some places a drought might be declared after as few as 15 days! In general, a drought occurs when a region experiences below average precipitation. It is a period of time with abnormally dry weather leading to a shortage of water (see Figure 9), which can have a negative effect on vegetation, animals and people over a large area.

Where in the world do droughts occur?

Recent severe droughts have occurred around the world in countries including Australia, Brazil, China, India, parts of the USA and Mexico, as well as the Sahel region of Africa (see Figure 10). Large parts of these countries and regions already have a dry climate and receive low amounts of rainfall per year, so a period of time with less rainfall than usual can have a significant impact on the people and the environment. Less typical places, such as the tropical Amazon basin, can also experience drought if they receive significantly less rainfall than usual over a long period of time. Figure 11 summarises some of the key drought events of the 2000s.

▲ **Figure 9** Dry lake bed in São Paulo, 17 October 2014

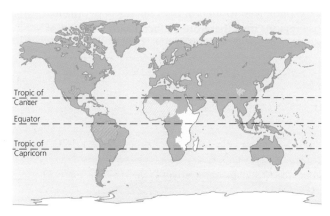

▲ **Figure 10** Location of key drought events in the 2000s

✛ Geographical skills

You will often be required to deconstruct, interpret, analyse and evaluate visual images such as photographs. Look at Figure 9. What question could you ask to the man in the photo that would help you to interpret the situation?

When?	Where?	What?
2002–2005	Amazon Basin, South America	<ul><li>Parts of the basin experienced the worst drought in 100 years.</li><li>Towns lacked food, medicine and fuel as there was no access for boats.</li><li>The drought affected 1.9 million km² of rainforest.</li><li>5 gigatons of carbon was released into the atmosphere as a result of dead trees fuelling forest fires. Usually, the Amazon actually absorbs 1.5 gigatons of carbon in a typical year.</li></ul>
2006	Sichuan Province, China	<ul><li>37.5 million people were affected.</li><li>Nearly 8 million people faced water shortages.</li><li>129 million livestock died.</li></ul>
2010–2013	Texas, USA	<ul><li>2011 was the driest year in the state's history.</li><li>By 2013, 95% of the state was dealing with drought.</li><li>$5.2 billion in agricultural losses.</li></ul>
2011	East Africa including Somalia, Ethiopia, Kenya, Eritrea, Djibouti and South Sudan	<ul><li>Caused by falling rains – the area received 30% less rain than the average.</li><li>50,000 to 100,000 deaths.</li><li>12 million people in need of food aid.</li><li>Crop failures and livestock deaths.</li><li>Increases in malaria and measles.</li></ul>
2012	Western Sahel including Niger, Mali, Mauritania and Burkina Faso	<ul><li>10 million people at risk of famine after a month-long heatwave.</li><li>Over 50% of the crop yield was lost.</li></ul>

▲ **Figure 11** A summary of key drought events in the 2000s

What causes a drought?

The physical causes:

- Most droughts occur when the regular weather patterns have been disturbed. There might be an above average presence of dry, high-pressure systems.
- El Niño brings descending air and high pressure over Indonesia and Australia, leading to drought (see pages 226–227).
- As global temperatures increase, more water is needed to grow crops and more water is lost through evaporation.
- The **intertropical convergence zone** (ITCZ) has been linked the occurrence of drought, particularly in Africa.

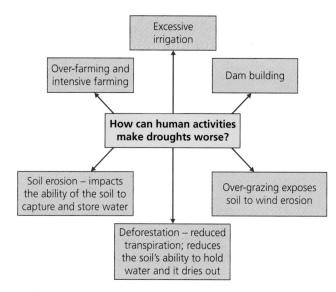

▲ **Figure 12** How can human activities make droughts worse?

What is the intertropical convergence zone (ITCZ)?

The ITCZ is a low-pressure belt which encircles the globe around the Equator. It is where the trade winds from the northeast and southeast meet. The Earth is tilted on its orbit around the Sun, causing the ITCZ to migrate between the Tropics of Cancer and Capricorn with the seasons (see Figure 13). Around 20 June each year, the Sun is overhead at the Tropic of Cancer and around 20 December each year, the Sun is overhead at the Tropic of Capricorn.

Winds and pressure are shifted annually from north to south. The point where the two trade winds meet at the ITCZ results in heavy precipitation and thunderstorms as hot, dry air and warm, moist air combines. Consequently, Africa has parts of the continent that are in a cycle of dry and wet seasons.

In some years, the ITCZ might not move as far northwards or southwards to reach some of the driest areas, and so not relieve them of the dry conditions they have experienced for half of the year. Local people in those regions may therefore be faced with a period of drought.

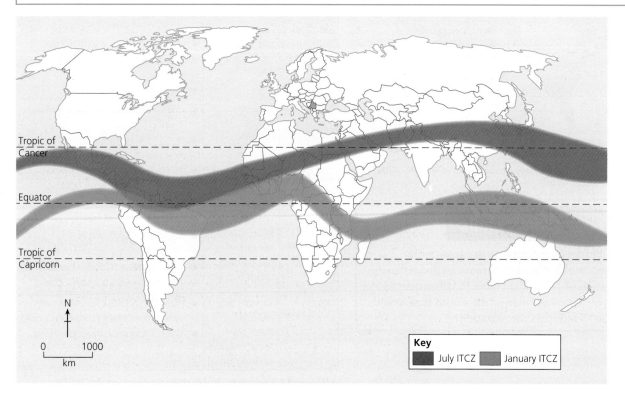

▲ **Figure 13** The location of equatorial and tropical low-pressure systems (ITCZ)

How frequent are droughts?

Many regions of the world, such as California in the USA, experience drought every year. A report by NASA in 2013 predicted that warmer worldwide temperatures will lead to decreased rainfall and more droughts in some parts of the world.

At a national scale, the Met Office has conducted a study on how climate change could affect the frequency of drought in the UK. The worst case scenario predicts that extreme drought could happen once every decade, making them ten times more frequent than they are today.

'Severe droughts such as the one seen in 1976 have a big impact – causing water shortages, health risks, fire hazards, crop failure and subsidence. Understanding how the frequency of these events will change is therefore very important to planning for the future.'

Eleanor Burke, Climate Extremes Scientist, Met Office.

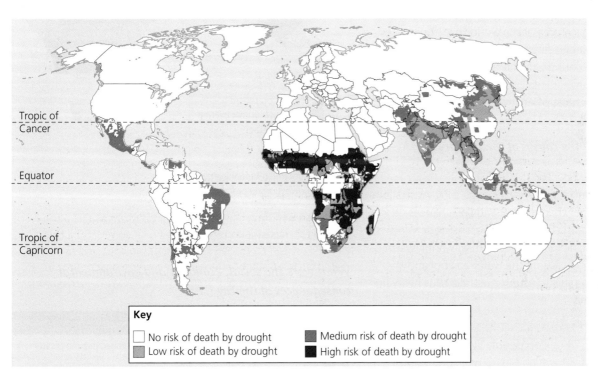

Key

☐ No risk of death by drought
☐ Low risk of death by drought
▨ Medium risk of death by drought
■ High risk of death by drought

▲ **Figure 14** Regions of the world at risk of death from drought

Activities

1. Describe the physical processes that are responsible for drought.
2. Referring to Figure 14, describe the distribution of the risk of death by drought.
3. Working in groups, use a piece of string and sticky notes to create a giant timeline of droughts in the 2000s across your table.
   a. Use the information from Figure 11 (page 223) to add key facts from each drought event.
   b. Research three to five more drought events that have occurred since 2000 and add them to your timeline.

4. Compare your timeline to Figure 14. Which places experience drought but are not at risk of death? Why is this?

→ Take it further

5. Read the quote from the climate scientist above. What happened in 1976? Think like a geographer! Why is it so important for you to study extreme weather events?

Case study: a drought event caused by El Niño/La Niño

The 'Big Dry' – is El Niño to blame for Australia's drought issues?

Which regions of Australia are affected by drought?

Australia is part of the driest inhabited continent and has lived with drought throughout its history. From 2002 to 2009 it experienced the driest period in 125 years, which became known as the Big Dry.

Australia is drought prone because of its geography and changeable rainfall patterns. Australia is located in a sub-tropical area of the world that experiences dry, sinking air leading to clear skies and little rain. For most of the country, rainfall is low and irregular. In 2006, the annual rainfall was 40–60 per cent below normal over most of Australia south of the Tropic of Capricorn.

What were the causes of the Big Dry?

El Niño

When El Niño is present (see page 219), Australia becomes drier than normal and the chances of rainfall decrease. During El Niño, the trade winds over the Pacific Ocean that normally bring warm water weaken, causing the water to cool and the rainfall to diminish. Eastern Australia thus heats up and gets drier.

Other causes

In Australia, 23 million people live in a similar land area to the USA, which has 320 million people. This may not seem like a high number, but it cannot maintain its current population growth in relation to access to water, making the country overpopulated.

Eastern Australia is home to the Murray–Darling river basin. The Murray River is the longest river in Australia, draining an area the size of France and Spain combined! The river basin covers part of New South Wales, Victoria, Queensland and South Australia. The basin is home to 2 million people and is under a lot of pressure to provide the water needed to support agricultural production in the region. Forty per cent of Australia's agricultural produce comes from this region and it contains 70 per cent of irrigated cropland and pasture.

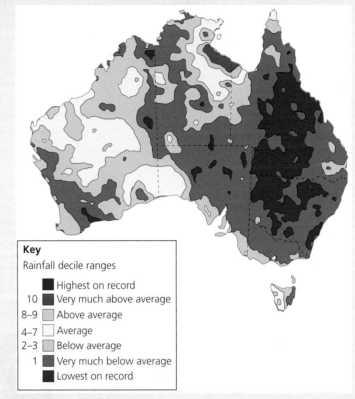

Key

Rainfall decile ranges

	Highest on record
10	Very much above average
8–9	Above average
4–7	Average
2–3	Below average
1	Very much below average
	Lowest on record

▲ **Figure 15** The distribution of rainfall averages across Australia, 2002–03 (El Niño year)

What were the social, economic and environmental consequences of the Big Dry?

	Consequences
SOCIAL	• People in rural areas left due to a lack of water, putting greater pressure on the population of cities. • Rural suicide rates soared.
ECONOMIC	• Farmers had to sell cattle as they could not afford to feed them. • Food prices rose as Australia became more dependent on imports. • Water bills rose 20% in 2008. • Tourism was negatively affected. • Agricultural production was severely affected. • 10,000 people directly employed by the cotton-growing industry were affected. • The number of dairy farms reduced by more than half.
ENVIRONMENTAL	• Loss of vegetation, wildlife and biodiversity as well as soil erosion. As the soil dries out, it becomes looser and it is easier for the wind to blow it away. • Grassland turned to scrubland. • Energy from HEP was reduced leading to more pollution as Australia resorted to the use of fossil fuels. • Water quality reduced as toxic algal outbreaks occured in depleted rivers, dams and lakes.

▲ **Figure 16** Consequences of the Big Dry drought on people, the economy and the environment

How have different stakeholders responded to the drought problems of Australia?

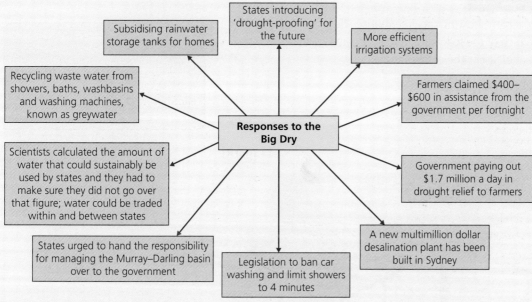

▲ **Figure 17** Responses to the Big Dry

The end of the drought was officially declared by the prime minister on 27 April 2012.

▲ **Figure 18** Desalination plant in Sydney

Activities

1. Using Figure 15 describe the pattern of rainfall in 2002–03.
2. In pairs, take on the role of expert geographers. Create a news bulletin that explains how El Niño causes droughts in Australia. Don't forget to include diagrams, photographs and place-specific details.
3. To what extent is El Niño to blame for the problems of drought in Australia?
4. Read the information about the impacts of drought. Which do you think was the most devastating impact and why?
5. Organise the consequences of the drought into a table with two columns to show short-term (immediate) and long-term consequences.
6. Create a mind map that explains how each of the following stakeholders responded to the drought.
   - Individuals

   - National government
   - Environmentalists
   - Farmers
   - Local government
7. Where else in the world has used desalination plants in response to droughts? Why are they located in these places?

→ Take it further

8. What is the problem with allocating an amount of water that states can use sustainably?
9. The BBC reported a story from Australia with the headline 'Australia Cyclone Yasi roars into Queensland Coast'. Find the article on the internet. Using pages 220–221, suggest why Australia was experiencing cyclones rather than droughts.

Practice questions

1. Study Figure A, a diagram showing the greenhouse effect. Methane is one greenhouse gas. Which of the following human activities produces large quantities of methane? Select the correct answer.

   a) Vehicle exhausts

   b) Burning rainforests

   c) Waste in landfill sites

   d) Making cement   **[1 mark]**

> **Tip**
>
> For multiple choice questions, work through the options eliminating those that are incorrect.

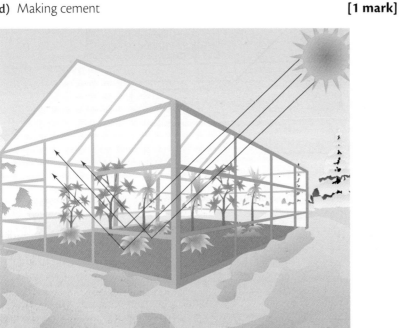

▲ **Figure A** The greenhouse effect

2. What are the Milankovich cycles? Select the correct answer.

   a) Changes in temperature recorded by ice cores

   b) Cycles that relate to the Earth's orbit

   c) Patterns of bird migration

   d) Cycles of nutrients in ponds   **[1 mark]**

3. Look at Figure B. How can volcanic eruptions affect the world's climate?   **[2 marks]**

The eruption of Mount Pinatubo in the Philippines on 15 June 1991 was one of the largest eruptions of the twentieth century.

Satellites recorded the highest concentration of sulfur dioxide since observations began in 1978.

An enormous cloud of ash and gases, including sulfur dioxide, was ejected more than 32 km into the stratosphere.

The aerosols cooled the world's climate for a period of three years by up to 1.3°C.

▲ **Figure B** The eruption of Mount Pinatubo, Philippines, 1991

4. **a)** State one cause of sea level rise. **[1 mark]**

    b) Assess the environmental impacts of sea level rise. **[4 marks]**

5. Explain why flooding may have significant economic impacts in the future. **[6 marks]**

6. Define the 'global circulation system'. **[2 marks]**

7. Why do we find deserts at 30° north and south of the Equator? **[3 marks]**

8. Describe the climate where Hadley cells meet at the Equator. **[3 marks]**

9. Suggest a cause of the El Niño phenomenon. **[1 mark]**

10. Which of the two statements below is true for an El Niño event?

    a) The trade winds blowing westwards over the Pacific Ocean weaken or reverse.

    b) There is a risk of increased flooding in Australia.

    c) There is more warm water around Peru, suppressing the upwelling of cold water.

    d) Rising warm and moist air over Australia and Indonesia brings reliable rainfall. **[1 mark]**

11. Describe the global distribution of tropical storms. **[3 marks]**

12. State two conditions that are needed for a tropical storm to form. **[2 marks]**

13. To what extent are tropical storms becoming more frequent? **[4 marks]**

14. Define the term 'drought'. **[1 mark]**

15. Explain how the inter-tropical convergence zone affects the distribution of droughts. **[4 marks]**

16. Extreme weather conditions vary in contrasting countries. Discuss the differences in extreme weather conditions in contrasting countries. You should develop your ideas fully. **[6 marks]**

17. Case study for a drought caused by El Nino/La Nina. Evaluate how successful attempts were to reduce the impacts of the event. **[6 marks]**

> **Tip**
>
> Look at question 5. Make sure you focus clearly on the demands of the question, i.e. the economic impacts.

> **Tip**
>
> Look at question 16. You need to include well-developed ideas about the weather conditions and the differences in weather conditions in contrasting (that means varying or different) countries. Extremes are likely to include temperature, wind and precipitation, and you should discuss at least two contrasting countries.

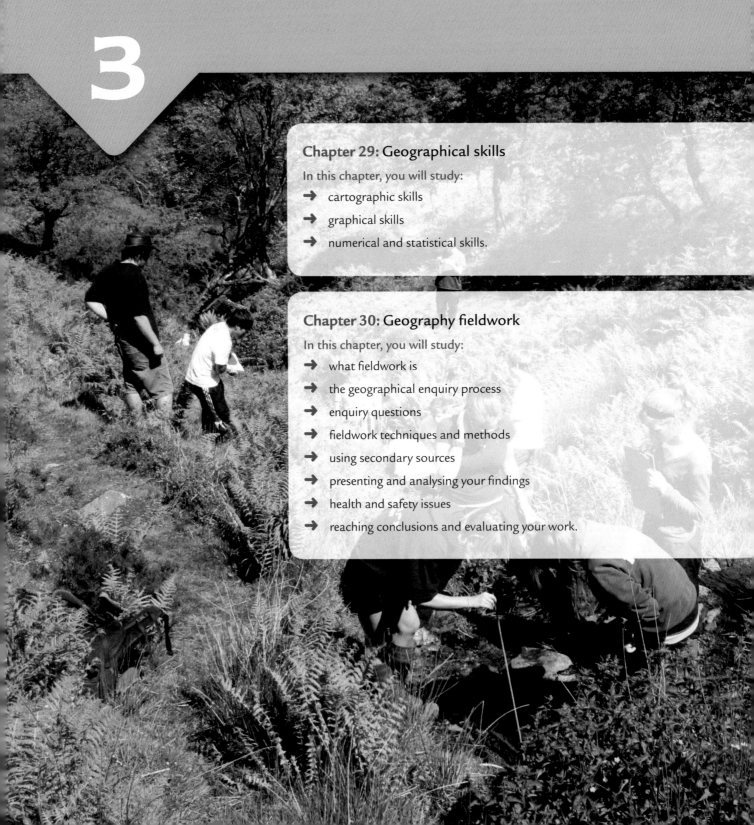

Geographical Skills and Fieldwork

PART **3**

Chapter 29: Geographical skills

In this chapter, you will study:

→ cartographic skills

→ graphical skills

→ numerical and statistical skills.

Chapter 30: Geography fieldwork

In this chapter, you will study:

→ what fieldwork is

→ the geographical enquiry process

→ enquiry questions

→ fieldwork techniques and methods

→ using secondary sources

→ presenting and analysing your findings

→ health and safety issues

→ reaching conclusions and evaluating your work.

CHAPTER

29

Geographical skills

Cartographic skills

With respect to cartographic skills, you should be able to:

- select, adapt and construct maps, using appropriate scales and annotations, to present information
- interpret cross-sections and transects
- use and understand coordinates, scale and distance
- extract, interpret, analyse and evaluate information
- use and understand gradient, contour and spot height (on OS and other isoline maps)
- describe, interpret and analyse geo-spatial data presented in a GIS framework.

For most of the maps in this section, you need to extract, interpret, analyse and evaluate information, which means studying the map to answer specific questions, for example describing distributions and patterns of human and physical features. It is useful for you to become familiar with a wide range of maps from a variety of places throughout your GCSE Geography course.

Atlas maps

Atlases, such as the Philip's Modern School Atlas, contain a variety of reference maps including:

- political maps showing national boundaries and capital cities
- physical maps which have hill-shading to show the landscape with mountains, rivers and lakes marked, as well as towns, roads and railways.

You will need to be able to use atlas maps to extract, interpret, analyse and evaluate information. For example, in Chapter 1, page 4, you are asked to describe the location of glaciated upland areas in Figure 1.

Ordnance Survey (OS) maps

You need to be able to interpret maps including Ordnance Survey maps at 1: 50,000 and 1: 25,000 scales. The scale of a map refers to how a specified area relates to real life distances, for example on 1: 50,000 scale maps, 1 cm on the map is 50,000 cm in real life (500 m). On 1: 25,000 scale maps, 1 cm on the map is 25,000 cm in real life (250 m). You can find examples of OS maps in this textbook:

- **Page 31** – Figure 14: OS map of Sheringham, scale 1:25,000

- **Page 31** – Figure 15: OS map of Blakeney National Reserve, scale 1:25,000
- **Page 55** – Figure 13: OS map of Salford Quays, scale 1:25,000

You can also find OS maps at www.ordnancesurvey. co.uk or by going to www.bing.com/maps and selecting 'Ordnance Survey' from the dropdown menu.

You will need to be able to use OS maps in a variety of ways including:

- using the maps to extract, interpret, analyse and evaluate information, for example describing distributions and patterns of human and physical features
- using OS map grid coordinates for referring to specific features (using four and six figure grid references)
- using OS map scales to measure distance
- using OS maps to draw sketch maps
- studying gradient, contour and spot height and using these to draw cross-sections.

Alongside the OS map extracts in this book, you will find a variety of activities to use with the extract, including using maps with photographs, providing grid references or using them to identify features, and calculating distances.

Base maps

A base map is the background setting for a map showing basic information, onto which detail can then be added. For example, you may want to use a base map of a town centre which just includes the main roads, and then add your own information using data to indicate areas where there has been a lot of criminal activity. This could either be done physically, or using base maps to layer information on top using a Geographical Information System (GIS).

Choropleth maps

A choropleth map is shaded according to a key to show different values, for example Figure 1 shows the percentage of people employed in the service industry across the UK in 2013. The colours are darker as the percentage increases.

You will need to interpret these, and use them to obtain data, for example describing patterns or extracting information about a specific area.

Strengths: It is very clear to see spatial patterns.

Weaknesses:

● No variations within individual areas.
● Suggests figures change abruptly at the edge of each boundary line, whereas in real life this is likely to be gradual.
● If there are a large number of classes, it is difficult to achieve a number of shades within one overall colour if only one colour is used.

Isoline maps

An isoline map is a way of portraying data. An isoline is a line which is drawn to link different places that are of equal value.

● Contours are isolines that join points of the same height above ground. You can see examples of contour lines on the OS map of Sheringham in Figure 14 on page 31.
● Another example of isolines are lines which join places of equal pressure on a weather map (see Figure 2).

Strengths: Useful to interpret general trends in distribution.

Weaknesses: To join up the lines between individual values, you may have to guess where the isolines should be positioned, so these can be subjective depending on how many individual values you have.

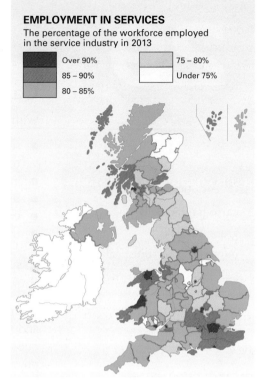

EMPLOYMENT IN SERVICES
The percentage of the workforce employed in the service industry in 2013

Over 90%	75 – 80%
85 – 90%	Under 75%
80 – 85%	

▲ **Figure 1** Employment in services, 2013

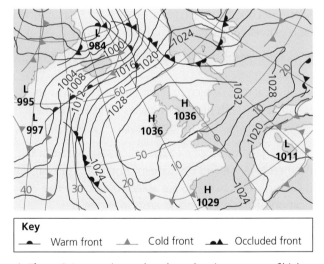

Key
— Warm front   — Cold front   — Occluded front

▲ **Figure 2** A synoptic weather chart showing an area of high pressure over the UK recording 1036 millibars

Flow line maps

A flow line map is another way of portraying data. Flow lines show movement between places, for example, the value of exports from the UK to other countries. The thickness of the line reflects the value given to it, for example the number of migrants moving from one country to another, or the value of imports to the UK from other countries (see Figure 2a, page 39).

Strengths: Shows direction and size of movement in a visual way.

Weaknesses: Can lack precise information unless specific values are given as well.

Desire-line maps

A desire line is drawn to show direction of movement, for example, the number of people travelling from various countries to one tourist destination. The line is drawn from the origin straight to the destination in a straight line, rather than following the actual path of movement as is the case with flow lines.

Strengths: Shows direction in a visual way.

Weaknesses: Lots of desire lines may overwhelm the map and make it difficult to interpret.

Sphere of influence maps

A sphere of influence is often referred to when describing settlements. For example, a town may attract people from a wider area because of the facilities they offer, such as a supermarket. The sphere of influence is the area from which people come to the town. This can be shown on a map as a circle or oval to show how far people come from the surrounding area to use the facilities.

Strengths: Highly visual.

Weaknesses: Does not show precise data.

Thematic maps

These are maps that compare nation with nation, or area with area, on key social and economic topics such as population, health, standards of living, tourism and the environment. Figure 4 below is a thematic map showing the Human Development Index patterns across the world.

Route maps

A route map basically contains information that shows the user how to get from one place to another between two locations, for example, a road map.

Sketch maps

A sketch map is a simple representation of the main features in a given map. You may be asked to draw or complete a sketch map in your exam. You can practice drawing sketch maps using the OS map extracts in this book.

- Draw a frame in which to produce your sketch.
- Draw the outlines of the location as if you are looking down on the location.
- Add the main features to your map, for example rivers or roads.

Strengths: Good visual memory aid, especially if annotated.

Weaknesses: Not accurate.

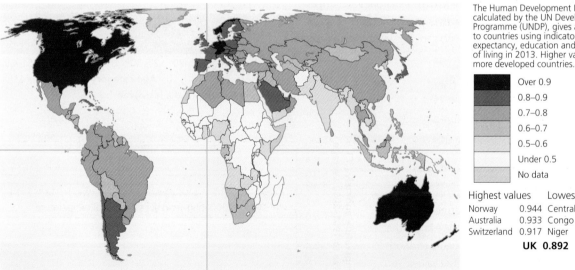

The Human Development Index (HDI), calculated by the UN Development Programme (UNDP), gives a value to countries using indicators of life expectancy, education and standards of living in 2013. Higher values show more developed countries.

■	Over 0.9
■	0.8–0.9
■	0.7–0.8
■	0.6–0.7
■	0.5–0.6
□	Under 0.5
■	No data

Highest values		Lowest values	
Norway	0.944	Central Africa	0.341
Australia	0.933	Congo (DR)	0.338
Switzerland	0.917	Niger	0.337

UK 0.892

▲ **Figure 4** Human Development Index patterns worldwide

Graphical skills

With respect to graphical skills, you should be able to:

● select, adapt and construct appropriate graphs and charts, using appropriate scales and annotations to present information
● effectively present and communicate data through graphs and charts
● extract, interpret, analyse and evaluate information.

Bar graphs

There are various activities throughout this book where you are asked to draw bar graphs using figures given in a table. In a bar graph, each bar is the same width but of varying length depending on the figure it is showing. The length of the bar is proportional to the values that they represent. They can be shown as horizontal, vertical and divided.

● **Horizontal** – a bar graph in which the length of each bar goes across from left to right, for example Figure 6, page 43.
● **Vertical** – a bar graph in which the length of each bar goes up from the bottom, for example Figure 9, page 45.
● **Divided** – a horizontal or vertical bar graph which shows percentages, for example Figure 5, page 58.

Strengths:

● Good visual representation of data.
● Easy to construct and interpret.

Weaknesses:

● Can only use with discrete data.
● Not much space to label categories.

Histograms

A histogram is a type of bar graph where the categories are ranges of numbers, for example ranges of ages in years. There are no gaps between the bars because there are no gaps between the age ranges.

Strengths:

● Good visual representation of data.
● Easy to construct and interpret.

Weaknesses:

● Not much space to label categories.

Line graphs

Line graphs are used to show points that can be joined in a line, for example temperatures over a given number of years (see Figure 6). We know that temperatures don't jump from one figure to another, but rise or fall through the temperature values. You may be asked to interpret a line graph by describing its pattern, or by finding a specific value, for example, giving the temperature reached in a specific year.

Strengths:

● Easy to compare more than one set of data.
● Lines drawn can help suggest possible data between specific values

Weaknesses:

● Can only use with continuous data.

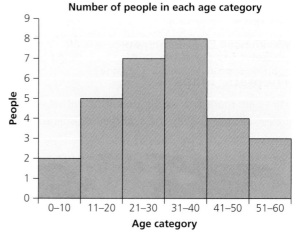

▲ **Figure 5** Example of a histogram

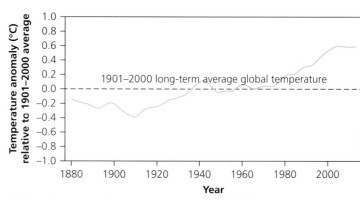

▲ **Figure 6** Average global temperatures, 1880–2013

Positive correlation

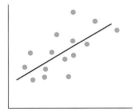

Negative correlation

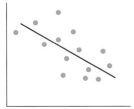

No correlation

▲ **Figure 7** Scatter graphs: (top) positive correlation; (middle) negative correlation; (bottom) no correlation

Scatter graphs

A scatter graph is used to plot two sets of data and then analyse them to see whether there is a relationship between the two. After all the data has been plotted on the graph, a line of 'best fit' is drawn (if possible). This will show either a positive correlation (bottom left to top right), a negative correlation (top left to bottom right) or no correlation (there is no pattern that can be seen) (see Figure 7).

Strengths:

- Shows you a correlation between two sets of data.
- Easy to construct.
- Anomalies easy to spot.

Weaknesses:

- Too few data points can show unreliable correlation.
- Too many data points can make the graph unreadable.
- Can only show relationship between two variables.

Dispersion graphs

A dispersion graph is used to plot data to see if there is a pattern in the distribution of the data. Each value is plotted as an individual point against the vertical axis. You can plot two sets of data on the same graph to see if there is a comparison (see Figure 8). You can use dispersion graphs to plot the median, upper and lower inter-quartile values and the inter-quartile range (see page 240).

Strengths:

- Easy to see patterns and show the spread from the mean.
- Good for making comparisons between sets of data.
- Anomalies can be shown.

Weaknesses:

- Need to use data that can be placed along a number line.

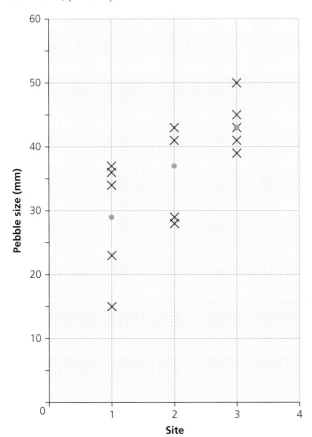

▲ **Figure 8** Pebble sizes at three sites on Walton beach

Pie charts

A pie chart is a circle that is cut up into segments. It is easy to compare different values, for example the percentage of the UK's energy, as shown in Figure 8 below.

To use data to draw a pie chart:

- Remember that you will need to multiply each percentage figure by 3.6 to convert it to degrees.
- Check that your total adds up to 360 degrees.
- If it doesn't add up, round the largest figure up or down.
- Using a protractor and your figures, draw your bar chart.
- Shade in the different areas in different colours and add labels or a key.
- Remember to add a title.

Strengths:

- Good when showing percentages.
- Good visual way of representing data.
- Easy to construct and interpret.

Weaknesses:

- Too many segments make the chart difficult to read and interpret.
- No specific numerical data unless labelled.

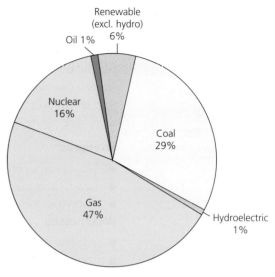

▲ **Figure 9** Energy sources in the UK, 2010

Climate graphs

A climate graph (see Figure 10) shows the average temperature and rainfall for a place during a year. It is measured using months of the year on the x axis and both y axes are used to plot the rainfall in bars and the temperature as a line.

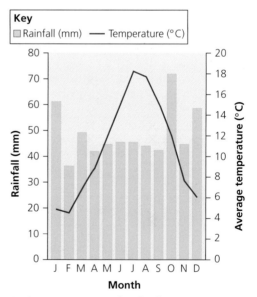

▲ **Figure 10** An example of a climate graph

Proportional symbols

Proportional symbols are symbols that are drawn in proportion to the size of what is being represented. Examples of this can be seen in the maps in Figure 3, page 180, which show circles that appear relative to the population of the cities that they represent.

Strengths: Good visual representation of data.

Weaknesses: Scale needs to be accurate.

Pictograms

A pictograph is like a bar graph, but instead of using an axis with numbers it uses pictures to represent a particular number of items. For example, you could use a pictograph to indicate the number of cars that were sold by a company in different years (see Figure 11).

Strengths:

● Good visual representation of data.
● Easy to construct and interpret.

Weaknesses: Doesn't provide specific numerical data.

Year	Number of cars	= 1000 cars
2011	🚗🚗🚗	
2012	🚗🚗🚗	
2013	🚗🚗🚗🚗	
2014	🚗🚗🚗🚗🚗	
2015	🚗🚗	

▲ **Figure 11** Cars sold, 2011–2015

Cross-sections

A cross section shows the variation in relief along a chosen line. It shows distance along the x-axis and height on the y-axis. Cross-sections can be drawn using contour lines on OS maps. They can also be drawn from data gathered from actual sites using measurements obtained during fieldwork investigations. Figure 12 is a cross-section of a river bed.

Strengths: Shows a view of a segment.

Weaknesses: Only one moment in time so may not be representative.

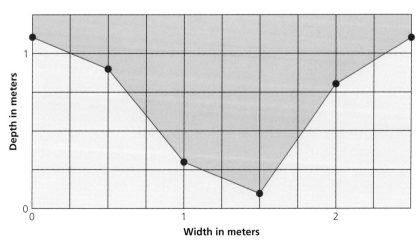

▲ **Figure 12** Cross-section of a river bed

Population pyramids

A population pyramid is a type of graph which shows the number of people in a range of cohorts (age groups). It shows the population structure of a country and allows for long-term planning as the relative sizes of each cohort will reduce over time, unless there are significant changes in birth and death rate. There is more information about this type of diagram on page 57.

Strengths:

- Shows how population is composed.
- General shape can indicate type of population structure.

Weaknesses:

- Can only use for population structure.
- Figures broken into age categories so some detail may be lost within them.

Radial graphs and rose charts

You may be given radial graphs to interpret in your exam.

Radial graphs are used:

- when one variable is do to with time, for example showing the flow of traffic over a period of time (see Figure 13). In this case, the times are written around the outside the circle (24 hour clock).
- when one variable is to do with directions, for example the point of a compass (see Figure 14). The compass directions are written around the outside of the circle.

A rose chart is a type of radial diagram that is specifically used to show both the direction and frequency of wind.

Strengths:

- Show several different sets of data at once.
- Good visual representation of data.

Weaknesses:

- Can only be used with specific types of data.
- Hard to spot anomalies.

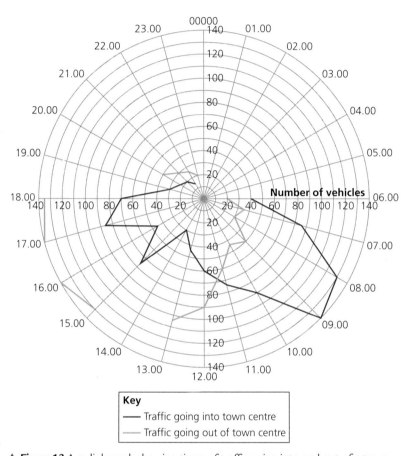

Key
— Traffic going into town centre
— Traffic going out of town centre

▲ **Figure 13** A radial graph showing times of traffic going into and out of a town centre

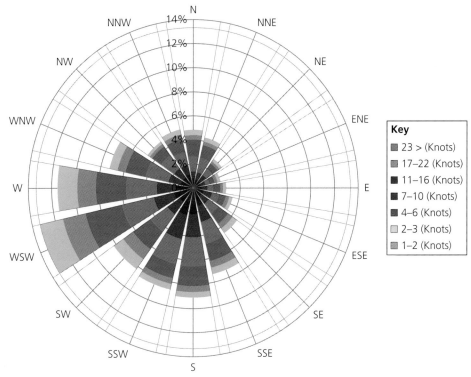

▲ **Figure 14** A wind-rose diagram

Numerical and statistical skills

Number, area and scale

Numerical skills are discussed in other areas of this textbook, such as designing fieldwork data sheets, collecting data and drawing informed conclusions from numerical data.

Area is measured in square units – the length of an area times the width of an area. For example, on a map where the scale is 1 cm = 0.5 km, you may be asked to calculate the area that is two grid squares in length and four grid squares in width.

2 cm x 4 cm = 8 cm square

= 4 km square

Scale is associated with maps. The scale of a map refers to how a specified area relates to real life distances, for example on 1: 50,000 scale maps, 1 cm on the map is 50,000 cm in real life (500 m). On 1: 25,000 scale maps, 1 cm on the map is 25,000 cm in real life (250 m).

Proportion, ratio, magnitude and frequency

A ratio is a comparison between two different things. In geography the most frequent ratio you will experience is the scale on maps, for example, 1:50,000. This means that for every 1 cm on the map there are 50,000 cm on the ground. You could come across questions about ratios on the examination paper.

Proportions can be built from ratios, for example a half is a proportion of 5:10. For example, half of the forest could be deciduous trees and half coniferous trees.

In geography, magnitude is the relative size of something. The term is used most frequently when assessing the impact of an earthquake. It is a measurement of the energy released by the earth. However, the term could also be used in relation to settlements. One settlement could have double the population numbers of another. One area could have triple the amount of average rainfall of another area.

Frequency is how often something occurs. Therefore you could be asked about the frequency of volcanic eruptions or earthquakes in an area.

Central tendency, spread and cumulative frequency

- The **median** is the middle value of a set of data. The numbers should be arranged in rank order.
- The **mean** is calculated by adding up all of the values in the data set and dividing the total by the number of values in the data set.
- The **mode** is the value that occurs most frequently in a set of data. If the set of data is very large, it may be a good idea to group the data into classes before working out the mode. The class with the highest frequency, with the most values in it, is the **modal class**. The modal class does not have to contain the mode of the set of data.
- The **range** is the difference between the highest and lowest value in the data set. For example, when looking at temperatures for a settlement for the year, the range of temperature would be the difference between the highest and lowest temperature.
- The **inter-quartile range** (IQR) shows the spread of a set of data, but is more accurate than using the range because it doesn't include the extremities. The IQR indicates the spread of the middle 50 per cent of the data set, as it omits the top and bottom 25 per cent. It gives a better idea of how the data is spread around the median value.

Percentages and percentiles

There could be questions on the examination paper which ask you to calculate a percentage increase or decrease between two numbers. The way to work this out is to:

- work out the difference between the two numbers
- divide the increase (difference) by the first number
- multiply the answer by 100.

If your answer is a positive number, there has been a percentage increase between the numbers. If the answer is a negative number, then there has been a percentage decrease between the two numbers.

CHAPTER 30

Fieldwork

What is fieldwork?

> **Fieldwork:** the experience of understanding and applying specific geographical knowledge, understanding and skills to a particular and real out-of-classroom context.

Fieldwork is an essential part of your GCSE studies. It gives you an opportunity to compare what you have learnt in your lessons to what geography is like in the real world. It will also help you to remember the geographical content you need to learn for your exams, as it is easier to visualise coastal and river landscapes and processes if you have walked alongside them.

As you read through this textbook, you will have noticed that there are fieldwork ideas alongside the main content of the chapters. This may give you some ideas about what types of question you might want to investigate as part of your fieldwork.

You will be doing fieldwork on at least two separate occasions in contrasting locations. One will be in a physical geography context and the other will be in a human geography context. In Paper 3, you will be examined on your physical geography fieldwork and your human geography fieldwork. You will be asked questions based on fieldwork in an unfamiliar context (for example, looking at the way a student has presented their fieldwork results), as well as questions about your own fieldwork experience (for example, evaluating the techniques you used to collect your fieldwork data).

> In order to answer the fieldwork questions in your exams, you will need to:
>
> - understand the geographical enquiry process
> - decide on an enquiry question or hypothesis
> - collect data on your field trip using a range of fieldwork techniques and methods
> - write up your findings by:
>   - presenting the data you have collected in various ways, such as drawing maps, graphs and diagrams
>   - analysing the data you have collected using your geographical knowledge
>   - drawing conclusions and summaries
>   - reflecting on your fieldwork investigation, including looking at the limitations of data-gathering methods and any conclusions you have drawn.

▲ **Figure 1** Fieldwork is an essential part of your studies

What is the geographical enquiry process?

Figure 2 shows the process of geographical enquiry.

How does this relate to your fieldwork?

- **Step 1 Ask questions:** identify an issue and decide on an enquiry question; for example, you may decide to compare the quality of life in an inner suburb of your local town with an outer suburb.
- **Step 2 Gather information:** you will need **primary data** from your field trip and **secondary data** collected by other people, for example from sources on the internet.
- **Step 3 Select the best information:** analyse your findings by looking at the data you have collected and explaining what the information means.
- **Step 4 Produce your work:** write up your report in a suitable format including appropriate graphical techniques.
- **Step 5 Evaluate:** evaluate your findings, identifying any issues, for example problems with data collection or limitations of data collected.

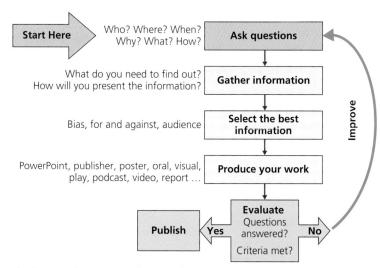

▲ **Figure 2** The process of geographical enquiry

How do you decide on an enquiry question?

Each piece of fieldwork will be based on an enquiry question which will help you decide what data to collect and how to focus your fieldwork visit.

What issues are suitable for physical geography fieldwork?

Physical fieldwork involves the study of physical features and the processes that have led to their formation. For example, you might choose to study wave energy and its impact on longshore drift by looking at the arrangement of pebbles on a beach and their height either side of groynes. Some common areas to explore are listed below.

- **Hydrology:** rivers and fluvial environments; explorations of flood management and changes to drainage basins, including the perception of flood risk to residents
- **Coasts:** processes acting to change the coastline and the management of these processes which may involve hard or soft engineering methods
- **Upland glacial landscapes:** mountain landscapes which show evidence of past glacial activity and how they are currently being used
- **Ecosystems:** these could include coastal areas such as sand dunes or salt marshes, or woodlands or other habitats associated with particular environments; some of these may act as an additional amenity for people or be affected by changes in land use

▲ **Figure 3** Local issues can make good fieldwork topics

What issues are suitable for human geography fieldwork?

Human fieldwork involves the study of urban environments or processes which involve human interaction. As humans are not as 'reliable' as physical processes, there needs to be an element of flexibility in the planning. While tide times are predicted months in advance, it is impossible to guarantee that people with a full range of ages and genders will be standing around waiting to be questioned in a location you have selected.

Human fieldwork options will vary depending on the location of your school. Common areas to explore are listed below.

- **Urban areas:** looking at urban land use and structure, social inequality or changes that have taken place in recent times; this can include processes such as gentrification, urban redevelopment and rebranding
- **Tourism:** impact of large numbers of visitors on the nature of a place; while a large volume of tourists may change the character of a place, they may also provide economic stability for local residents
- **Industrial change:** how has employment changed in an area over time; the relative balance of primary, secondary and tertiary opportunities
- **Environmental impacts:** the impacts of human activities on land, air or water quality

What fieldwork techniques and methods can be used?

Ways of collecting primary data include:

- measurements that you make using a variety of equipment
- images, such as photos you take or sketches you draw
- maps or diagrams you complete while you are outside
- responses to questions you ask people through questionnaires or interviews.

There are two main types of primary data that students may collect on fieldwork: quantitative and qualitative.

> ### Tip
> Refer to data as plural: data are, rather than data is.

Quantitative data refer to numbers. These could be the sizes of pebbles on a beach, number of cars in a car park or footfall past a shoe shop. Numbers can be counted, averaged, graphed and compared over time. They may then be used to refer to expectations: are they are higher or lower than average; how do they compare with other places and different times of day or year.

Qualitative data do not necessarily involve numbers but refer to the wider exploration of a place. They could involve a sense of how safe people feel, which could, for example, be rated out of 10 but is not based on an actual 'value' that everyone would give. It could refer to a feeling that a place provides. Traffic counts or visitor numbers are, by contrast, quantitative data.

▲ **Figure 4** Students carrying out fieldwork in a river landscape

Questionnaires

Questionnaires can be used when you want to consult a group of people to find out what their thoughts and opinions are on a particular subject or issue (see Figure 5). These may be physical sheets of paper or you could create a questionnaire online using a survey tool, such as SurveyMonkey.

- First, work out what information you need to find out. You may have an issue which requires people to have an opinion or perception, or you may be asking them to tell you some specific factual information.
- Each question should aim to collect a specific piece of data, which can then contribute towards the final conclusion.
- Do not have too many questions; even if they are quite brief, people may feel they don't have the time to answer them.
- Start off with a few easy questions to put people at ease. This might include asking them whether they are visitors or residents, for example.
- Have a mixture of open and closed questions. Open questions enable people to offer any answer or opinion. Closed questions may offer a choice of response, such as 'yes' or 'no', which are useful for later analysis.
- Avoid asking leading questions such as, 'What do you think of the horrible effects of noise pollution?', as this prompts people to answer in a particular way.
- You may want to ask some questions which require people to rate or score something, perhaps on a scale from 1 to 5, or 1 to 10. Be aware that if you have an odd number of scores, there may be a tendency for people to give the middle answer and 'sit on the fence'.
- Think carefully about where to stand. Some supermarkets may not like you to stand near the entrance to their store. Also, by standing outside a particular shop, it may add a bias to your questions on which supermarkets respondents most often use.
- Think carefully about the sampling method that is used to identify the people who will complete the questionnaires. A questionnaire is designed to provide a sample from the total population so the people you approach need to be representative of the population as a whole.

▲ **Figure 5** Questionnaires are a useful way of collecting primary data

Using mobile devices

Tablets and smartphones are increasingly being used during fieldwork. This could include:

- apps to record sounds or interviews with people
- apps to collect data at particular points, which are then added to mapping tools
- apps to transform or label images (e.g. Skitch)
- video apps to record and then slow down a physical process (e.g. a wave breaking, so that it can be analysed as to whether it is a destructive or constructive wave).

How can you use secondary sources?

Secondary sources can provide support and offer further insights to help develop your enquiry. These are increasingly digital in nature. The Office for National Statistics (ONS) releases census data and a range of other information from time to time. Other downloads and data are produced by organisations such as Natural England and the British Geological Survey.

Using geographical information systems

Geographical data may have a location, which means that they can be mapped. By mapping the data, patterns often emerge. Maps can be obtained from the trace of a base map or by finding an existing map. You may need to use interactive maps which have been produced for a specific purpose. The Environment Agency, for example, produces flood risk data for specific addresses. This information could be used alongside some practical fieldwork involving questionnaire surveys of householders in areas which have (and haven't) experienced recent flooding (see Figure 6).

▲ **Figure 6** An interactive map from the website of the Environment Agency, https://flood-warning-information.service.gov.uk/

Students and teachers also have access to a free version of Google Earth Pro, which allows for the production of high-quality images showing cross sections across a path which the user has created. Figure 7 shows a cross section across Llyn Idwal in Snowdonia. The line is drawn as a path and the elevation profile along the path is then added and displayed. Students may be able to explore cross and long profiles of river valleys, or the changes that glaciation makes to upland landscapes before they go out and experience these places.

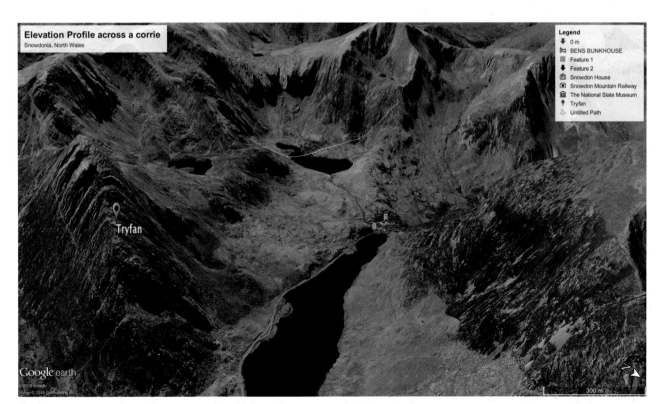

▲ **Figure 7** Use Google Earth Pro to produce high-quality cross-sections

How can you present your findings?

You will be studying and using a range of geographical skills during your GCSE course. Some of the presentation and interpretation of data skills can be best covered as part of your fieldwork enquiry. You can be tested on these skills in all of your exams.

Figure 8 shows some of the ways that you could present your data.

How do you analyse your findings?

You will need to analyse the primary data that you gather during your fieldwork trip, along with any secondary data you may gather from other resources, such as through websites.

You may analyse the data in various ways.

- Look at relationships between different sets of data that you collect.
- Make predictions from trends that can be seen in your data.
- Look at the trend lines on scatter graphs.
- Draw lines of best fit.
- Look at a map that you have created using the data and analyse any relationships that you see on that map between different types of data.

When analysing maps, use the acronym GAS to explore and critique what they are showing.

- Look at the **general** pattern that you can see (**G**).
- Look for **anomalies**; areas which don't quite fit the expected pattern (**A**).
- Finish by being **specific** about something that the map is telling you about one or more areas (**S**).

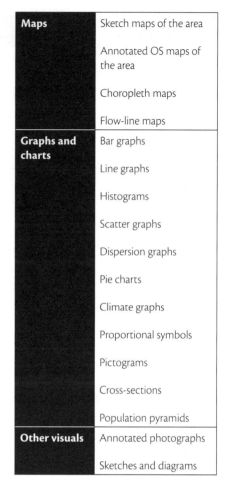

Maps	Sketch maps of the area
	Annotated OS maps of the area
	Choropleth maps
	Flow-line maps
Graphs and charts	Bar graphs
	Line graphs
	Histograms
	Scatter graphs
	Dispersion graphs
	Pie charts
	Climate graphs
	Proportional symbols
	Pictograms
	Cross-sections
	Population pyramids
Other visuals	Annotated photographs
	Sketches and diagrams

▲ **Figure 8** Data presentation methods

Health and safety

Taking students off site can be nerve wrecking but, with appropriate preparation, everything will go smoothly. Your school's fieldwork protocols should be followed to the letter. Risk assessments must be carried out on the chosen area to identify hazards and ways that they can be dealt with effectively. The location may need to be changed, even on the day itself if circumstances change.

You should be properly briefed and have practised techniques in advance if possible, so that you don't waste time learning how to use pieces of fieldwork equipment when you could be more active and actually collecting data.

Here are some brief suggestions for specific locations that might be visited as part of GCSE geography fieldwork.

River work

You must stick to the measurement area at all times, and not push people or otherwise mess about in water. You should take extreme care near river banks, especially where the ground is steep or wet, and wear suitable footwear. Remember that electrical equipment such as iPhones don't like water.

Coastal fieldwork

On the beach, don't climb on groynes or sea defence structures. Be careful not to handle beach litter. Agree on a particular distance that you must stay away from the tide line and keep an eye on the waves. Do not enter the sea under any circumstances. Check tide times carefully and ensure that it is going out before entering low-lying coastlines. These they can be found at www.tidetimes.org.uk.

Town centre

Stay in your designated group and make sure you have contact numbers for your supervisors. Familiarise yourself with the area. Only question people you are comfortable talking to, and who are happy to help. Avoid asking the same people as another group working in the same area, particularly if there are lots of groups operating within a small area. Avoid blocking pavements, and cross the road at designated points.

How do you reach conclusions and evaluate your work?

Conclusions are not just the end of a fieldwork write-up, they are also the beginning of your understanding and also the start for further exploration, which can be suggested even if there is no time to actually carry it out. You may be asked what you would do differently if you were to start the process again and should consider the limitations of the methods used.

- Fieldwork should be summed up using the main themes which were introduced at the start of the process, and the extent to which the main enquiry questions have been answered.
- How robust are the conclusions that have been reached?
- What unexpected results have you come across? How far did this change your conclusion?

You should always evaluate the work you have completed. This means assessing the value of it. In order to do this you should ask yourself the following questions.

1. Were the methods I used appropriate?
2. Did the methods I used help me to answer my question?
3. Was I able to answer my original question given the primary and secondary data I collected?
4. How could I improve my study?

Useful weblinks for fieldwork

- The Royal Geographical Society website has a well-developed fieldwork section, complete with ideas for enquiries, recording sheets and suggestions on places to visit: www.rgs.org/ OurWork/Schools/Fieldwork+and+local+learning/ Fieldwork+and+local+learning.htm
- The Geographical Association has published a very useful book called *Fieldwork through Enquiry*. This book details ten fully worked fieldwork ideas and included ideas for using modern technology and apps to help collect and analyse fieldwork data. It has also collated a number of useful links for helping with statistical analysis of fieldwork

data: http://geography.org.uk/resources/ conductingstatisticaltestsforfieldwork/

- Google Earth Pro can be downloaded from here: www.google.co.uk/earth/download/gep/agree.html
- ArcGIS Online can be accessed via: www.arcgis. com/home/. Click on MAP to get started.
- Details of Digimap for Schools can be seen here: http://digimapforschools.edina.ac.uk/
- Look for fieldwork providers that display the Learning Outside the Classroom Quality Badge: http://lotcqualitybadge.org.uk/

Practice questions

Physical geography fieldwork

1. Figure A shows a data collection technique being used by a group of students carrying out a physical geography fieldwork investigation.

▲ **Figure A** Students carrying out primary data collection

  a) Name this data collection technique. **[1 mark]**
  b) Evaluate how effective this technique would be to compare the ecosystems found in deciduous and coniferous woodlands. **[2 marks]**
  c) Suggest one sampling method you could use to decide which specific locations you would use this technique within your study area. **[2 marks]**

2. Name a primary data collection technique suitable for carrying out a physical geography fieldwork investigation looking at the impact of groynes on the movement of sediment. **[1 mark]**

3. Figure B shows part of a data collection sheet from a physical geography fieldwork investigation. The students were asked to sample sediment sizes at several locations on Cromer Beach. These were the sizes of one sample of ten randomly selected pebbles, measured 20 m south of the pier.

92	86	156	49	215
73	68	90	83	73

▲ **Figure B** Sediment sizes from a sample measured 20 m south of Cromer Pier

  a) Calculate the mean. **[1 mark]**
  b) Calculate the mode. **[1 mark]**

Figure C shows the average sizes of sediment with distance south of the pier.

Distance south of the pier (m)	10	20	30	40	50	60
Average sizes of sediment (mm)	44	98.5	112.5	140	154	103.5

▲ **Figure C** Results of a beach sediment survey

  c) Draw a graph to present the data in the table. **[1 mark]**

4. You will have carried out some physical geography fieldwork as part of your GCSE Geography course. Briefly describe the fieldwork, and explain how your fieldwork conclusions improved your understanding of a geographical question or issue. **[8 marks]**

Human geography fieldwork

5. Name a primary data collection technique suitable for investigating how the quality of the environment changes with distance from the city centre. **[1 mark]**

6. Study Figure D, part of a survey sheet used by a group of students to investigate the environmental quality of an urban area. Complete the three remaining rows with appropriate categories for this type of survey. **[2 marks]**

Negative	1	2	3	4	5	Positive
Shops are closed down and boarded up						Shops are open and well maintained
Buildings are derelict and falling down						Buildings are new and well maintained

▲ **Figure D** Environmental quality survey sheet

7. Is this type of survey designed to collect quantitative or qualitative data? Explain your answer. **[4 marks]**

8. State two types of data that could be used during an investigation into changing land use in a CBD over the last ten years and give reasons for your choices. **[4 marks]**

9. For a human geography fieldwork investigation that you have completed, evaluate **one** technique that you used to collect **quantitative** data. **[2 marks]**

10. Study Figure E, a graph from a data presentation part of a human geography fieldwork investigation. Residents of a town were asked to give a score for their views on the plans for a proposed new supermarket being built. A score of 0 indicated they were very much against, and a score of 5 meant they were very much in favour.

    Suggest what Figure E indicates about variations in views on these plans. **[3 marks]**

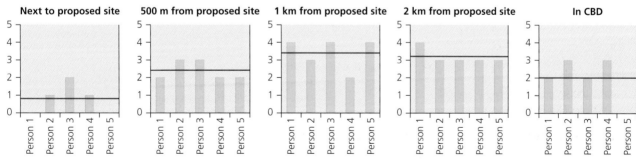

▲ **Figure E** Approval for a proposed new supermarket among local residents

11. You will have carried out some human geography fieldwork as part of your GCSE Geography course. Briefly describe the fieldwork and evaluate the methods that you used and the accuracy of the results that you obtained. **[8 marks]**

blackstorm325

Glossary

Abiotic – the physical, non-living parts of the ecosystem, including temperature, water and light

Abrasion (or corrosion) – the scraping, scouring or rubbing action of materials being carried by moving features such as rivers, glaciers or waves, which erode rocks

Advanced country (AC) – countries that share a number of important economic development characteristics including well-developed financial markets, high degrees of financial intermediation and diversified economic structures with rapidly growing service sectors; ACs are classified by the IMF

Ageing population – population structure that becomes distorted with a high and increasing proportion of people in middle and old age

Aid – a transfer of resources from one country to another, typically from a more economically country to a less economically developed country

Air mass – a large parcel of air in the atmosphere. All parts of the air mass have similar temperature and moisture content at ground level.

Anomalies – data values which don't match the pattern of a sample

Atmospheric air pressure – the force exerted on the Earth's surface by the weight of the air, measured in millibars

Attrition – a reduction in the size of material

Backwash – the movement of water down the surface of a beach and through the beach sediment as a result of gravity after a wave has broken

Bay – an indentation in the coastline between two headlands. They are made of less resistant rock than headlands, and the land has been eroded back by the sea

Bedding planes – within a sedimentary rock, these represent the points where layers of sediment accumulates; they may later form horizontal weaknesses within the rock along which water may penetrate them

Biomass – the total mass of plants and animals in an ecosystem

Biome – large-scale ecosystems that are spread across continents and have plants and animals that are unique to them

Biotic – all of the living elements of the ecosystem including plants, animals and bacteria

Built – see Urban

Carnivore – an animal that eats other animals

Cave – a natural underground chamber or series of passages, especially with an opening to the surface; may also refer to the extended cracks at the base of a cliff

Circumpolar winds – flows of air around the Earth's poles

Climate – the long-term average of the temperature and rainfall experienced at a location

Climate change – changes in long-term temperature and precipitation patterns that can either be natural or linked to human activities

Climate zone – divisions of the Earth's climates into belts, or zones, according to average temperatures and average rainfall. The three major zones are polar, temperate and tropical

Condensation – the process whereby rising water vapour becomes a liquid

Coniferous – trees that are evergreen and have needle-shaped leaves

Continental shelf – the area of seabed around a large land mass where the sea is relatively shallow compared with the open ocean

Conurbation – a large urban agglomeration that results from several cities merging over time, forming a continuous urban area

Convectional rainfall – occurs frequently in the tropics where it is hot; hot air close to the ground rises, cools and condenses to form rain; if the air is hot enough, it rises very quickly and can lead to thunderstorms

Coriolis effect – the result of Earth's rotation on weather patterns and ocean currents, making storms swirl clockwise in the southern hemisphere and anticlockwise in the northern hemisphere

Counter-urbanisation – the movement of people from urban areas into rural areas; these may be people who originally made the move into a city

Deciduous – trees that shed their leaves during winter to retain moisture, also known as broadleaved trees

Deforestation – the cutting down of trees, transforming a forest into cleared land for other uses such as building or growing crops

Demographic transition model – a theoretical model based on the experience in the UK showing changes in population characteristics over time more arid and desert-like, usually because of drought, deforestation, over-cultivation or over-extraction of water

Deposition – the laying down of materials that have been transported and can created new landforms such as beaches

Development – the state of growth or advancement whereby people and places improve over time

Drift – all sediments deposited by glaciers

Dominant (wind) – see Prevailing

Drought – a prolonged period of time with unusually low rainfall; droughts occur when there is not enough rainfall to support people or crops

El Niño – climatic changes affecting the Pacific region and beyond every few years, characterised by the appearance of unusually warm water around northern Peru and Ecuador, typically in late December; the effects of El Niño include the reversal of wind patterns across the Pacific, causing drought in Australasia, and unseasonal heavy rain in South America

Emerging and developing country (EDC) – countries which neither share all the economic development characteristics required to be advanced or are eligible for the Poverty Reduction and Growth Trust; EDCs are classified by the IMF

Emigrants – people who leave one country to settle in another

Energy mix – a measure of the different sources of energy in a given region

Enhanced greenhouse effect – the exaggerated warming of the atmosphere caused by the emission of gases from human activities resulting in the natural greenhouse effect becoming more effective

Erosion – the wearing away and removal of material by a moving force, such as a breaking wave

Ethnicity – relates to a group of people who have a common national or cultural tradition

Eutrophication – the process of excessive nutrients (particularly nitrogen and phosphates) building up in water sources, usually because of leaching and surface runoff

Evapotranspiration – the process by which water is transferred from the land to the atmosphere by evaporation from surfaces, e.g. lakes, and by transpiration from plants

Exports – the selling of goods to another country

Fauna – another term for the animals in an ecosystem

Flora – another term for the plants in an ecosystem

Floodplain – the flat area of land either side of a river channel forming the valley floor, which may be flooded

Fracking – hydraulic fracturing; a controversial practice for extracting gas and oil from shale rocks

Freeze-thaw cycle – the daily fluctuations of temperature either side of freezing point; when repeated they contribute to physical weathering

Front – a boundary separating two masses of air with different densities, usually heavier cold air and lighter warm air

Fuel poverty – a situation that occurs when people's income means that spending money to heat their home would take them below the official poverty line; having higher than average fuel costs

Function – a role performed by something; in the case of a city, this may be administrative or related to a sphere of activity

Gabion – metal cages filled with rocks which can form part of a sea defence structure or be placed along rivers to protect banks from erosion; an example of hard engineering

Geodiversity – the natural range of geological, geomorphical, soil and water features that compose and shape the physical landscape

Geology – the study of rocks and their formation, structure and composition

Geomorphic processes – processes that result in a change in the shape of the Earth; from 'geo' meaning the earth and 'morph' meaning to change shape

Glacial periods – historic cold periods associated with the build-up of snow and ice and the growth of ice sheets and glaciers

Global warming – a trend associated with climate change involving a warming trend (0.85°C since 1880)

Globalisation – the process whereby places become interconnected by trade and culture

Gorges – narrow, steep sided valleys, often formed as a waterfall retreats upstream

Green belt – an area of land around several major urban areas, given protection under the Town and Country Planning Act of 1947, to prevent urban sprawl

Greenhouse effect – natural warming of the atmosphere as heat given off from the Earth is absorbed by liquids and gases, such as carbon dioxide

Gross domestic product (GDP) – the total value of the goods and services produced in a country

Headland – an area of land that extends out into the sea, usually higher than the surrounding land; also called a point

Hemisphere – a half of the earth, usually as divided into northern and southern halves by the Equator

Herbivore – an animal that feeds on plants

High pressure – when there is more air pressing down on the ground, caused by air sinking; air descends as it cools, leading to high pressure at the surface

Holocene epoch – the period of geological time from 12,000 years ago, which continues to the present day

Human Development Index (HDI) – a scale that measures development and gives a score from 0 to 1, with 1 being the highest

Hydraulic action – an erosive process which involves the pressure of water hitting a surface, compressing air in any cavities which exist, and resulting in the removal of rock fragments over time

Hydrolysis – chemical breakdown of a material due to interaction with water

Ice age – a glacial episode characterised by lower than average global temperatures and during which ice covers more of the Earth's surface

Igneous – when referring to rocks, this means rocks formed within the interior of the Earth, and shaped by heat

Immigrants – people who move from one country to settle in another

Impermeable – a surface or substance that doesn't allow water to pass through it

Imports – the purchase of goods from another country

Industrialisation – the process whereby factories, industry and manufacturing increase and dominate

Informal sector – refers to jobs that don't offer regular contracted hours, salary, pensions or other features of more formal employment; may refer to illegal or unlicensed activity

Infrastructure – the basic structures and facilities needed for a society to function, such as buildings, roads and power supplies

Interdependence – the reliance of every form of life on other living things and on the natural resources in its environment, such as air, soil and water

Inter-glacial periods – historic warm periods in-between glacial periods where conditions were much the same as they are today

Internal growth – growth within a city that results from births among the resident population rather than people moving into the city

Intertropical convergence zone – a low-pressure belt that encircles the globe around the Equator; it is where the trade winds from the northeast and southeast meet; the Earth is tilted on its orbit around the Sun, causing the ITCZ to migrate between the Tropics of Cancer and Capricorn with the seasons

Jet stream – A jet stream is a narrow band of very strong wind currents that circle the globe several kilometres above the Earth

Joints – vertical cracks within a rock, such as limestone, which result from the natural shrinking of the rock over time as it was formed; these may form weaknesses allowing water to penetrate the rock

Katabatic winds – movements of cold dense air that flow downhill and along valley floors; in Antarctica, most winds blow towards the coast from the centre

Latitude – the imaginary lines that surround the Earth ranging from 0° at the Equator to 90° at the poles

Life expectancy – the average number of years a person might be expected to live

Litter – the total amount of organic matter, including humus (decomposed material) and leaf litter

Longshore (littoral) drift – the movement of sediments along a stretch of coastline as a result of wave action

Low pressure – caused when the air is rising, so less air is pressing down on the ground; air rises as it warms, leading to low pressure at the surface

Low-income developing country (LIDC) – countries that are eligible for the Poverty Reduction and Growth Trust from the IMF; LIDCs are classified by the IMF

Mass movement – the downhill movement of weathered material under the force of gravity; the speedy can vary considerably

Mechanisation – the process whereby machinery is introduced to complete work normally done by hand, for example washing machines, tractors, industrial robotics, engines, automated tools, etc.

Megacity – usually defined as a city that has a population of over 10 million, although the exact number varies

Metamorphic – rocks that have been changed as a result of heat and pressure being applied to them over long periods of time

Migration – the movement of people from one place to another; may be voluntary or forced, permanent or temporary, domestic or international

Monsoon – heavy rainfall that arrives as a result of a seasonal wind, notably in southern Asia and India between May and September

Multiplier effect – the chain of consequences in which investment leads to wealth, which leads to more investment, leading to more wealth; a spiral of improvement

Natural arch – an arch-shaped structure formed as a result of natural processes within a rock feature such as a cliff

Natural increase/decrease – the difference between the birth rate and death rate, usually expressed as a percentage

North Atlantic Drift – a powerful ocean current responsible for maintaining warm conditions throughout the UK

Nutrient cycling – a set of processes whereby organisms extract minerals necessary for growth from soil or water, before passing them on through the food chain, and ultimately back to the soil and water

Omnivore – an animal that eats both plants and animals

Oxidation – a chemical reaction between a substance and the air; it can change its appearance or weaken it

Population density – the number of people in an area, usually expressed as people per square kilometre

Population pyramid – a diagram, essentially a bar graph, that shows the structure of a population by sex and age category that may resemble a pyramid shape

Population structure – the composition of a population

Precipitation – the collective term for moisture that falls from the atmosphere; this could be in the form of rain, sleet, snow or hail

Prevailing wind – the most frequent, or common, wind direction

Primary data – data collected by students personally during fieldwork as a result of measurement and observations

Primary industries – an economic activity that involves collecting raw materials, such as fishing, farming or mining

Pull factor – a positive factor that attracts people into an urban/rural area

Push factor – a negative factor that results in the movement of people away from an urban/rural area

Qualitative data – data involving the quality or nature of something rather than its quantity; can be used to refer to observations or opinions of people rather than something that can be given a numerical value

Quantitative data – data involving numerical values

Quaternary industry – work in the 'knowledge economy' that involves providing information and the development of new ideas

Quaternary geological period – the most recent geological period covering the last 2.6 million years, during which time there were several cold and warm periods

Rain shadow – an area or region behind a hill that has little rainfall because it is sheltered from rain-bearing winds

Re-urbanisation – the use of initiatives to counter problems of innercity decline

Renewable energy – energy harvested from resources which are naturally replenished on a short timescale

Rip-rap barriers – a type of sea defence involving a wall or pile of boulders, often igneous, along the sea front; an example of hard engineering

Rock slide – the movement of loose rocks down a slope as an avalanche of material, and the resulting mass of stony material that is produced

Rotational slumping – a process that involves the base of a slope failing, resulting in the rest of the landform falling down and moving in a curve along a plane as it does, so that the base of the feature extends outwards

Rural – areas which are not urban; characteristic of the countryside rather than towns and cities

Rural urban migration – the movement of people from the countryside into towns and cities; occurs as a result of push and pull factors relevant to both locations

Sea walls – curved concrete structures placed along a sea front, often in urban areas such as the fron of a promenade, designed to reflect back wave energy; an example of hard engineering

Secondary data – data collected from sources other than the student; may include published material, reports from public bodies and the work of other people

Secondary industries – manufacturing industries; the number of people employed in this sector increases as a country develops

Sediment – naturally occurring material that is broken down by processes of weathering and erosion

Sedimentary – rocks that have been produced from layers of sediment, usually at the bottom of the sea

Services – a function, or 'job', that an ecosystem provides

Social inequality – the extent to which people have unequal opportunities and rewards as a result of the position they occupy within the society; different groups, characterised by age, gender, 'class' and ethnicity, may have different levels of access to employment, education and healthcare

Soil – the top layer of the earth in which plants grow; it contains organic and inorganic material

Solution (or corrosion) – a type of erosion that involves rock being chemically changed such that it is taken into solution and removed; e.g. the action of acidic water on limestone

Stack – a coastal feature that results from erosion; a section of headland that has become separated from the mainland and stands as a pillar of rock

Stump – a coastal feature that results from the collapse of a stack to form a protrusion of rock close to the sea surface

Sub-aerial processes – processes that aid weathering and the mass movement of material; they include the action of the weather

Subsistence – only producing enough goods to meet your own basic needs, with no extra to trade

Suburbanisation – a change in the nature of rural areas such that they start to resemble the suburbs

Sustainable (sustainability, sustainable development) – this approach places emphasis on improving the current quality of life but still maintaining resources for the future; it is a balance of providing social, economic and environmental benefit long term

Swash – the movement of water up a beach following the breaking of a wave on the coastline

Symbiotic – organisms that live together; one or both of the organisms may benefit from this arrangement

Temperate – a region or climate with typically mild temperatures

Tertiary industries – service industries and jobs such as teaching; very few people are employed in this sector in a developing country

Thermocline – the point at which the temperature changes from warmer surface waters to deeper, colder water

Tides – changes in sea level as a result of the Moon; regular movements which occur every day

Tors – natural piles of stones found on the tops of low hills

Trade – the buying and selling of goods and services between countries

Trade deficit – the amount by which a country's imports exceed the value of its exports

Trade winds – the prevailing pattern of easterly surface winds found in the tropics, within the lower section of the Earth's atmosphere

Transpiration – the process by which plants lose water vapour through their leaves

Transportation – the movement of eroded material

Tropical storm (hurricane, cyclone, typhoon) – an area of low pressure with winds moving in a spiral around the calm central point called the 'eye' of the storm. Winds are powerful and rainfall is heavy.

Troposphere – an area of the atmosphere, from the Earth's surface to a height of 10–15 km, in which the weather takes place

Tundra – a vast, flat, treeless Arctic region of Europe, Asia, and North America in which the soil is permanently frozen

Urban (built) – refers to areas that have been built by people; towns and cities

Urban belt – an area of land which has become more urban in character

Urban forestry – the management of tree populations in urban environments

Urbanisation – the process of towns and cities developing and becoming bigger as their population increases

V-shaped valley – a valley formed near a river's source via vertical erosion

Volcanic winter – cooling trend caused by volcanic particles in the atmosphere blocking out some of the Sun's radiation

Waterfalls – a steep fall of river water where its course crosses between different rock types, resulting in different rates of erosion

Wave-cut platform/notch – a flat area along the base of a cliff produced by the retreat of the cliff as a result of erosive processes

Waves – elliptical or circular movement of the sea surface that are translated into a movement of water up the beach as they approach the coastline

Weather – the day-to-day changes in temperature and precipitation

Weathering – the breakdown of material in situ by physical, chemical and biological processes; if movement is involved, this becomes erosion

Wind – the movement of air on a large scale over the Earth's surface

World city – a city considered to be an important node in the global economic system, and one which has iconic status and buildings, e.g. London and New York; also known as a global or alpha city

Xerophytic – a type of plant that can survive on very little water

Index

Key for Ordnance Survey 1:50,000 maps

Communications

ROADS AND PATHS / VOIES DE COMMUNICATION / STRASSEN UND WEGE

Not necessarily rights of way

Service area — S — Junction number 1

Elevated / En Viaduc / Erhöht

M 1

Motorway (dual carriageway)
Autoroute (chaussées séparées) avec aire de service et échangeur numérote
Autobahn (zweibahnig) mit Servicestation und Anschlusstelle sowie Nummer der Anschlusstelle

Dual carriageway / Chaussées séparées / Zweibahnige Strasse

Motorway under construction
Autoroute en construction
Autobahn im Bau

A 470 — Primary Route
Itinéraire principal
Fernstrasse

Primary route under construction
Itinéraire principal en construction
Fernstrasse im Bau

Main road
Route principale
Hauptstrasse

Main road under construction
Route principale en construction
Hauptstrasse im Bau

Secondary road
Route secondaire
Nebenstrasse

Narrow road with passing places
Route étroite avec voies de dépassement
Enge Strasse mit Ausweichstelle

Road generally more than 4m wide
Route généralement de plus de 4m de largeur
Strasse, im allg.über 4m breit

Road generally less than 4m wide
Route généralement de moins de 4m de largeur
Strasse, im allg.unter 4m breit

Other road, drive or track
Autre route, allée ou sentier
Sonstige Strasse, Zufahrt oder Feldweg

Path / Sentier / Fussweg

Gradient: steeper than 20% (1 in 5)   14% to 20% (1 in 7 to 1 in 5)
Pente: Supérieure à 20% (1 pour 5)   14% à 20% (1 pour 7 à 1 pour 5)
Steigung über 20%   14% bis 20%

Gates / Barrières / Schranken

Road tunnel
Tunnel routier
Strassentunnel

Sans clôture — Footbridge
A 493 — Passerelle
Fussgängerbrücke

Nicht eingezäunt
B 4518

A 855   B 885

Bridge / Pont / Brücke

Ferry (passenger) / Bac pour piétons / Personenenfähre
Ferry (vehicle) / Bac pour véhicules / Autofähre

Ferry P   Ferry V

PRIMARY ROUTES

These form a network of recommended through routes which complement the motorway system

PUBLIC RIGHTS OF WAY / DROIT DE PASSAGE PUBLIC / ÖFFENTLICHE WEGERECHTE

.... Footpath
------------ Road used as a public path
-·-·-·-·-· Bridleway
-+-+-+-+- Byway open to all traffic

Public rights of way shown on this map have been taken from local authority definitive maps and later amendments. The map includes changes notified to Ordnance Survey by 1st August 1997.
The symbols show the defined route so far as the scale of mapping will allow.
Rights of way are not shown on maps of Scotland

Rights of way are liable to change and may not be clearly defined on the ground. Please check with the relevant local authority for the latest information

The representation on this map of any other road, track or path is no evidence of the existence of a right of way

OTHER PUBLIC ACCESS / AUTRES ACCES PUBLICS / ANDERE ÖFFENTLICHE WEGE

• • • Other route with public access {not normally shown in urban areas

The exact nature of the rights on these routes and the existence of any restrictions may be checked with the local highway authority. Alignments are based on the best information available. These routes are not shown on maps of Scotland

● ● ● National/Regional Cycle Network
— — Surfaced cycle route

4 National Cycle Network number
8 Regional Cycle Network number

Danger Area — Firing and Test Ranges in the area. Danger! Observe warning notices.
Champs de tir et d'essai. Danger! Se conformer aux avertissements.
Schiess und Erprobungsgelände. Gefahr! Warnschilder beachten.

♦ National Trail, European Long Distance Path, Long Distance Route, selected Recreational Routes

RAILWAYS / CHEMINS DE FER / EISENBAHNEN

——— Track multiple or single
— — — Track under construction
Light rapid transit system, narrow gauge or tramway
Bridges, Footbridge
Tunnel

● Station, (a) principal
—○— Siding
—⊙— Light rapid transit system station
—LC— Level crossing
Viaduct

General Information

LAND FEATURES

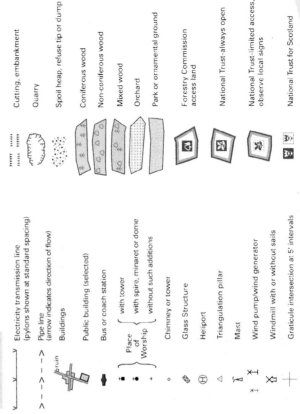

Electricity transmission line (pylons shown at standard spacing)
Pipe line (arrow indicates direction of flow)
Buildings
Public building (selected)
Bus or coach station

Place of Worship { with tower
with spire, minaret or dome
without such additions

Chimney or tower
Glass Structure
Heliport
Triangulation pillar
Mast
Wind pump/wind generator
Windmill with or without sails
Graticule intersection at 5' intervals

Cutting, embankment
Quarry
Spoil heap, refuse tip or dump
Coniferous wood
Non-coniferous wood
Mixed wood
Orchard
Park or ornamental ground
Forestry Commission access land
National Trust-always open
National Trust-limited access, observe local signs
National Trust for Scotland

Tourist I...

BOUNDARIES
Administrative boundaries as at January 2002

+—+—+— National
—·—·—·— County, Unitary Authority, Metropolitan District or London Borough
+ + + + District
National Park

WATER FEATURES

Marsh or salting

Aqueduct · Towpath · Lock · Weir · Footbridge · Bridge · Canal · Normal tidal limit · Ford

Lake · Canal (dry)

Contour values in lakes are in metres

High water mark
Low water mark
Cliff
Slopes
Flat rock
Lighthouse (in use)
Lighthouse (disused) ▲ Beacon
Sand
Dunes
Mud
Shingle

CONVERSION
METRES – FEET
1 metre = 3.2808 feet

3000
2500
2000
1500
1000
500

1000
900
800
700
600
500
400
300
200
100

Metres 0   0 Feet
15.24 metres = 50 feet

ABBREVIATIONS

CH Clubhouse
MS Milestone
PC Public convenience (in rural area)
TH Town Hall, Guildhall or equivalent

CG Coastguard
P Post office
MP Milepost
PH Public house

ARCHAEOLOGICAL AND HISTORICAL INFORMATION

+ Site of monument
· o Stone monument
⚔ Battlefield (with date)
☆ ··· Visible earthwork
VILLA Roman
Castle Non-Roman

Information provided by English Heritage for England and the Royal Commissions on the Ancient and Historical Monuments for Scotland and Wales

HEIGHTS

—50— Contours are at 10 metres vertical interval

·144 Heights are to the nearest metre above mean sea level

Heights shown close to a triangulation pillar refer to the ground at the base of the pillar and not necessarily to the summit

ROCK FEATURES

Outcrop
Cliff
600
600
Scree

TOURIST INFORMATION

□ PC Public convenience
Toilettes (à la campagne...
Öffentliche Toilette (in ländli...

Selected places of tourist interest
Endroits d'un intérêt touristique particulier
Ausgewählter Platz von touristischem Interesse

📞 📞 Telephone, public / motoring organisation
Téléphone, public / associations automobiles
Telefon, öffentlich / automobilklub

🌟 Viewpoint
Point de vue
Aussichtspunkt

V Visitor centre
Centre pour visiteurs
Besucherzentrum

👣 Walks / Trails
Promenades
Wanderwege

▲ Youth hostel
Auberge de jeunesse
Jugendherberge

Technical Information

NORTH POINTS

Difference of true north from grid north at sheet corners

NW corner   NE corner
1° 03' (19 mils) E   0° 33' (10 mils) E

SW corner   SE corner
1° 02' (18 mils) E   0° 32' (10 mils) E

To plot the average direction of magnetic north join the point circled on the south edge of the sheet to the point on the protractor scale on the north edge at the angle estimated for the current year

True North
Grid North
Magnetic North
Diagrammatic only

Magnetic north varies with place and time. The direction for the centre of the sheet is estimated at 3° 19' (59 mils) **west** of grid north for July 2004.
Annual change is about13' (4 mils) **east**

Magnetic data supplied by the British Geological Survey

Base map constructed on Transverse Mercator Projection, Airy Spheroid, OSGB (1936) Datum. Vertical datum mean sea level (Newlyn)

INCIDENCE OF ADJOINING SHEETS

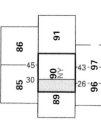

85   86
89   90 NY   91
96   97

45   43
30   26

The red figures give the grid values of the adjoining sheet edges. The blue letters identify the 100 000 metre square

HOW TO GIVE A NATIONAL GRID REFERENCE TO NEAREST 100 METRES

SAMPLE POINT: **Goodcroft**

1. Read letters identifying 100 000 metre square in which the point lies .....NY

2. FIRST QUOTE EASTINGS
Locate first VERTICAL grid line to LEFT of point and read LARGE figures labelling the line either in the top or bottom margin or on the line itself 53
Estimate tenths from grid line to point 4

3. AND THEN QUOTE NORTHINGS
Locate first HORIZONTAL grid line BELOW point and read LARGE figures labelling the line either in the left or right margin or on the line itself 16
Estimate tenths from grid line to point 1

SAMPLE REFERENCE   NY 534 161

For local referencing grid letters may be omitted

IGNORE the SMALLER figures of the grid number at the corner of the map. These are for finding the full coordinates. Use ONLY the LARGER figure of the grid number. EXAMPLE: 3 1 7000m

TOURIST INFORMATION

△ Camp site
Terrain de camping
Campingplatz

🚐 Caravan site
Terrain pour caravanes
Wohnwagenplatz

❋ Garden
Jardin
Garten

⌐ Golf course or links
Terrain de golf
Golfplatz

ℹ️ Information centre, all year / seasonal
Office de tourisme, ouvert toute l'année / en saison
Informationsbüro, ganzjährig / saisonal

Nature reserve
Réserve naturelle
Naturschutzgebiet

P&R / P&R Parking / Park and ride, all year / seasonal
Parking / Parking et navette, ouvert toute l'année / en saison
Parkplatz / Park & Ride, ganzjährig / saisonal

⊠ Picnic site
Emplacement de pique-nique
Picknickplatz

Key for Ordinance Survey 1:25,000 maps

Communications

ROADS AND PATHS

Not necessarily rights of way

M1 or A 6(M)   Motorway

A 35   Dual carriageway   Service area

A 30   Main road

B 3074   Secondary road

Narrow road with passing places

Road under construction

Road generally more than 4 m wide

Road generally less than 4 m wide

Other road, drive or track, fenced and unfenced

Gradient: steeper than 20% (1 in 5); 14%(1 in 7) to 20% (1 in 5)

Ferry; Ferry P - passenger only

Path

RAILWAYS

Multiple track
Single track   } standard gauge

Narrow gauge or
Light rapid transit system (LRTS) and station

Road over; road under; level crossing

Cutting; tunnel; embankment

Station, open to passengers; siding

PUBLIC RIGHTS OF WAY

(Rights of way are not shown on maps of Scotland)

Footpath

Bridleway

Byway open to all traffic

Restricted byway (from 2nd May 2006) roads used as public paths were redesignated as restricted byways. They provide a right of way for walkers, horse riders, cyclists and other non-mechanically propelled vehicles)

Public rights of way shown on this map have been taken from local authority definitive maps and later amendments.
Rights of way are liable to change and may not be clearly defined on the ground.
Please check with the relevant local authority for the latest information.

The representation on this map of any other road, track or path is no evidence of the existence of a right of way.

OTHER PUBLIC ACCESS

• • • •   Other routes with public access (not normally shown in urban areas)
The exact nature of the rights on these routes and the existence of any restrictions may be checked with the local highway authority. Alignments are based on the best information available.

National Trail / Long Distance Route ; Recreational Route

Permissive footpath   } Footpaths and bridleways along which landowners have permitted public use but which are not rights of way.

Permissive bridleway

Traffic-free cycle route

National cycle network
route number - traffic free

National cycle network
route number - on road   The agreement may be withdrawn

Scotland

In Scotland, everyone has access rights in law over most land and inland water, provided access is exercised responsibly. This includes walking, cycling, horse-riding and water access, for recreational and educational purposes, and for crossing land or water.
Access rights do not apply to motorised activities, hunting, shooting or fishing, nor if your dog is not under proper control. The Scottish Outdoor Access Code is the reference point for responsible behaviour, and can be obtained at www.outdooraccess-scotland.com or by phoning your local Scottish Natural Heritage office.   `Land Reform (Scotland) Act 2003`

National Trust for Scotland, always open / limited opening - observe local signs

Forestry Commission Land / Woodland Trust Land

England & Scotland

DANGER AREA   Firing and test ranges in the area. Danger! Observe warning notices. Champs de tir et d'essai. Danger! Se conformer aux avertissements. Schiess-und Erprobungsgebiete. Gefahr! Warnschilder beachten.
Visit www.access.mod.uk for information

ACCESS LAND

England

Portrayal of access land on this map is intended as a guide to land which is normally available for access on foot, for example access land created under the Countryside and Rights of Way Act 2000, and land managed by the National Trust, Forestry Commission and Woodland Trust. Access for other activities may also exist.
Some restrictions will apply; some land will be excluded from open access rights. The depiction of rights of access does not imply or express any warranty as to its accuracy or completeness. Observe local signs and follow the Countryside Code.
Visit www.countrysideaccess.gov.uk for up-to-date information

Access land boundary and tint

Access land in woodland area

Access land information point

MANAGED ACCESS   Access permitted within managed controls for example, local byelaws
Visit www.access.mod.uk for information

General Information

VEGETATION

Limits of vegetation are defined by positioning of symbols

Coniferous trees

Non-coniferous trees

Coppice

Scrub

Bracken, heath or rough grassland

Marsh, reeds or saltings

Orchard

GENERAL FEATURES

Place of worship

Current or former
place of worship   with tower
with spire, minaret or dome
Building; important building

Glasshouse

Youth hostel

Bunkhouse/camping barn/other hostel

Bus or coach station

Lighthouse; disused lighthouse; beacon

Triangulation pillar; mast

Windmill, with or without sails

Wind pump; wind turbine

Electricity transmission line

pylon   pole

Slopes

Gravel pit

Other pit or quarry

BP;BS   Boundary post/stone
CG   Cattle grid
CH   Clubhouse
FB   Footbridge
HP; MS   Milepost ; milestone
Mon   Monument
PO   Post office
Pol Sta   Police station
Sch   School
TH   Town hall
NTL   Normal tidal limit
W; Spr   Well; spring

Sand pit

Landfill site or slag/spoil heap

Loose rock   Boulders   Outcrop   Scree

Water   Mud   Sand; sand & shingle

BOUNDARIES

National

County (England)

Unitary Authority (UA), Metropolitan District (Met Dist), London Borough (LB) or District (Scotland & Wales are solely Unitary Authorities)

Civil Parish (CP) (England) or Community (C) (Wales)

National Park boundary

HEIGHTS AND NATURAL FEATURES

52   Ground survey height   Surface heights are to the nearest metre above mean sea level. Where two heights are shown, the first height is to the base of the triangulation pillar and the second (in brackets) to the highest natural point of the hill

284   Air survey height

Contours may be at 5 or 10 metres vertical interval

Vertical face/cliff

ARCHAEOLOGICAL AND HISTORICAL INFORMATION

+   Site of antiquity   VILLA   Roman
×   Site of battle (with date)   Castle   Non-Roman
    Visible earthwork

Information provided by English Heritage for England and the Royal Commissions on the Ancient and Historical Monuments for Scotland and Wales

Selected Tourist and Leisure Information

RENSEIGNEMENTS TOURISME ET LOISIRS SÉLECTIONNÉS   AUSGEWÄHLTE INFORMATIONEN ZU TOURISTIK UND FREIZEITGESTALTUNG

P   Parking / Park & Ride, all year/seasonal
Parking / Parking et navette, ouvert toute l'année/en saison
P&R   Parkplatz / Park & Ride, ganzjährig/saisonal

i   Information centre, all year/seasonal
Office de tourisme, ouvert toute l'année/en saison
Informationsbüro, ganzjährig/saisonal

V   Visitor centre
Centre pour visiteurs
Besucherzentrum

Forestry Commission visitor centre
Commission Forestière Centre de visiteurs
Staatsforst Besucherzentrum

PC   Public convenience
Toilettes
Öffentliche Toilette

Telephone, public/roadside assistance/emergency
Téléphone, public/borne d'appel d'urgence/urgence
Telefon, öffentlich/Notrufsäule/Notruf

Camp site/caravan site
Terrain de camping/Terrain pour caravanes
Campingplatz/Wohnwagenplatz

Recreation/leisure/sports centre
Centre de détente/loisirs/sports
Erholungs-/Freizeit-/Sportzentrum

Golf course or links
Terrain de golf
Golfplatz

Theme/pleasure park
Parc à thèmes/Parc d'agrément
Vergnügungs-/Freizeitpark

Preserved railway
Chemin de fer touristique
Museumseisenbahn

Walks/trails
Promenades
Wanderwege

Cycle trail
Piste cyclable
Radfahrweg

Mountain bike trail
Chemin pour VTT
Mountainbike-Strecke

Horse riding
Équitation
Reitstall

Public house/s
Pub/s
Gaststätte/n

Viewpoint
Point de vue
Aussichtspunkt

Picnic site
Emplacement de pique-nique
Picknickplatz

Country park
Parc naturel
Landschaftspark

Garden/arboretum
Jardin/Arboretum
Garten/Baumgarten

Nature reserve
Réserve naturelle
Naturschutzgebiet

Fishing
Pêche
Angeln

Water activities
Jeux aquatiques
Wassersport

Slipway
Cale
Helling

Other tourist feature
Autre site intéressant
Sonstige Sehenswürdigkeit

Cathedral/Abbey
Cathédrale/Abbaye
Kathedrale/Abtei

Museum
Musée
Museum

Castle/fort
Château/Fortification
Burg/Festung

Building of historic interest
Bâtiment d'intérêt historique
Historisches Gebäude

National Trust

English Heritage

Historic Scotland